QUANTUM THEATRE
SLAPSTICK TO SHAKESPEARE

IRA SEIDENSTEIN

QUANTUM THEATRE: SLAPSTICK TO SHAKESPEARE

COPYRIGHT

Quantum Theatre: Slapstick to Shakespeare. Copyright © 2020 by Ira Seidenstein

All Rights Reserved. Except as permitted under current legislation no part of this work may be photocopied, stored in retrieval system, published, performed in public, adapted, broadcast, transmitted, recorded or reproduced in any form by any means, without the prior permission of the copyright owner, except for short quotes for the purpose of academic publications and reviews. For information, contact Ira Seidenstein, PhD iraseid@gmail.com

ISBN: 978-0-6484216-2-7 (Paperback)
ISBN: 978-0-6484216-3-4 (Ebook)

Cover Photograph
Fred Copperwaite as Semyon Podsekalnikov
Ellen Osborn as Father Elpidi
The Suicide by Nicolai Erdman
Director Ira Seidenstein
Producer Fred Copperwaite

ACKNOWLEDGEMENTS

Thank You to the people who helped with editing and proof reading *Quantum Theatre: Slapstick to Shakespeare*: Tammy Brennan, librettist, theatre maker; Flloyd Kennedy, PhD creator of Being In Voice; Ellen Osborn; Tom Osborn, PhD; Caspar Schjelbred, MA, creator of Impro Supreme.

The sentiments stated in my first book *Clown Secret* remain true for *Quantum Theatre: Slapstick to Shakespeare*: Thank You to a galore of participants in my classes, to my colleagues, to my friends, to people who I shared living with, to people I shared life with, to my family. Each person who I helped also helped me. It has been an international voyage so Thank You goes to people in an array of countries and cultures. There is something special in this book for each Reader. You'll have to find it for yourself. This book from the beginning pages to the last pages is a risk.

FOREWORD

TRAINING TO LIVE

I dearly wish all aspiring actors, performers, directors and teachers would read this book. Own it. Have it on their bookshelf, available when they need it. For their own good – and by that I mean also for the common good; for their colleagues; for their audiences; for their students. In short: for all of us. It's so easy to forget that we're all in it together. This life here. Which we sometimes think we know, from all the parts we play in it.

What's the book about then? If I knew, I'd tell it to you straight. I'd tell you what I think I know about the subject matter, if this something could be told directly in a meaningful way. I'm not so sure it can. However, I do know that it's possible to give valuable hints and clues – and this book is absolutely packed with them.

It's not just another book on acting. It's a testament to life in theatre and theatre in life. Neither of them separately and certainly not just one or the other, i.e. life or theatre – two impossible and unmanoeuvrable abstractions that nobody really cares about anyway. It's always something else. I'll say it again: life in theatre *and* theatre in life.

Familiarity is one of the inevitable traps and everywhere to be found. We fall into thinking we know something, and of course we do know things, but what good does our knowledge do us? How do we know what we know? What can it do in the world? Is it of universal use – or strictly unique to ourselves? Learning to know and how to know are, in my view, central to Ira Seidenstein's *Quantum Theatre: Slapstick to Shakespeare*.

I used to be very familiar with this type of questions when I studied history of science at the university fifteen years ago. Handled with diligence, they could lead to glorious moments of intellectual enlightenment, often, however, followed by existential hangovers. I thought therefore I was. But what if I didn't think for a second? What if I just felt? Uh-oh, the abyss of existence opened beneath me. Back to pondering. Don't let's feel anything, it's safer. Or how about a glass of wine? Ah, that feels better. Full-bodied. Nice. Goodnight.

It was not long after finishing my official studies that I met Ira Seidenstein and very soon began to practise his method regularly. It was a perfect fit with its clarity and logic; a hands-on tool for practical knowledge – and with no directly related hangovers, just sore muscles and a bruised ego from time to time. Today, I'm still very much concerned with the above-mentioned questions, only on a much more pragmatic and personal level. It's healthier thinking, in the sense that it's more complete. There is more feeling involved. Are you ready for the joke? I specialised in the history of psychology and the study of the emotions. One could say I had it coming. At any rate, I finally got what I'd asked for, but not from where I'd thought I'd get it.

And now? On the best of days, the wonder show of the world goes on with no end in sight. No futile hope for a final destination. No reckoning of a superior vantage point from where life or theatre can be known and comprehended once and for all. Knowing or knowledge as end product is not what it's all about. Which is not say that it isn't of immense value. It is. I know it. And I love it, particularly what remains of it: records of knowledge. Ancient scrolls of wisdom. Books! The distillation of human experience, paired with deep insight and organised so that those who come afterwards have a fair chance of benefitting from it. We're back where we started. What's this book about? What can you get from it?

Like you've probably guessed, and although Ira will certainly tell things to you straight, what you'll get from this book is not straight academic knowledge. Rather, you'll get an opening, multiple invitations and a host of suggestions of how to move on from wherever you're at, be it on or off stage. Now this doesn't mean that you always have to move forward. One particularly valuable aspect of Ira's teaching is how he connects the dots and acknowledges those that came before. Study them, their ideas, their work – and start with the greatest! It's essential to remind ourselves that we're all dots within bigger circles. And that each dot, if we look closely enough, is itself a circle. Know thyself or whatever the Pythia says will sound dotty.

In a very down-to-earth sense, Ira could indeed be considered an oracle of theatre and clowning or acting and creativity. Remember though, that we mostly hear what we listen for. Ira wrote this book; it comes from his more than four decades of experience. But it's not about him. When you read the book it's about you and how you take it in – not just the book, but the world it came from, the world it connects us all to. The one physical world and the countless ones of poetry and imagination. Old stories. And from them new stories. Our stories. We're all history before we know it.

In the words of Jean-Louis Barrault, theatre is "entraînement à vivre", training to live. If we just look at those words together, it's all there. What it's for and how to go about it. It is not for life, taken as an abstract principle or a general phenomenon, but for living it. And the training is not to be executed just as a means to end, but to be lived, to be fully experienced, in and of itself. Here we can note that *entraîner* also means "to lead to" and "to carry away". Lived training leads to fully alive theatre which carries the audience away. It is material, real, ethereal, remembered, forgotten, gone. Not unlike our individual lives.

The gist of this foreword came to me this morning. While still in bed, I heard the familiar sounds of the garbage truck outside. Clonk. Clatter. Crash. Clonk. Beep beep beep. The world starting anew. No escape in sight from these annoying sounds inaugurating the daily onslaught on my nervous system, mind, spirit.

All of a sudden it switched. I started actually listening to the sounds, now hearing them within me, rather than resisting them as outside phenomena. Their source remained without, of course, but I felt and accepted them for what they were inside of me. Pure effects detached from the workings that caused them into being, existing fully as themselves – and free for me to grasp in their brief passing.

At peace now with the world just outside the window, my attention turned to the homely sounds inside. First the breathing warm body of the woman I will marry, then the motor of the refrigerator. Overtones and undertones. Back to the breath, my own this time. This I could both listen to and feel the workings of. Then all the sounds at the same time. Ah! The world! Oh! To be alive! Right here! Right now! From annoyance and animus to consideration and love in a heartbeat. A sort of quantum leap? Perhaps. At least human.

This experience was not a given. It was there for me to take. And if I was able to do so, to live that moment this morning, it was in large part thanks to the many, many hours I've spent working with the ideas in this book. I've learned to put reactions and personal feelings aside, see them, see through them, and come back to them. All in a matter of seconds. Sometimes even a split second. And on rare occasions simultaneously. That's like a miracle. And if there is a goal to strive for, I'm convinced that's it: to act from the living conscious human heart.

So. I urge you to really dig into this book. Engage with it. Don't believe it or disbelieve it. Read it. Think it. Feel it for yourself. At the slightest provocation, doubtful thought or spark of inspiration, put the book down and try something. Express yourself. Get up on the floor and dance or pick up a pen and write. Ask someone to watch or read. Expose yourself. Risk opprobrium to reach equilibrium. Rinse and repeat.

The world is never ending
Until it ends
You are reading this
It's not over yet. Go on

The *nothing new* remains
To be seen anew
Rise and shine! Be
The sun that you are

Good morning.
—

Caspar Schjelbred
Paris, November 2020

PREFACE

"This is a journal of a theatre artist. I have chosen to write in many voices and moods. Sometimes you may find offence with what I have written or how I have expressed myself. So I apologise now and say that my intention is to stimulate you to carry on to create a more fulfilling theatre for yourself and others. We are in this together. I hope this verbal acupuncture helps you find your own source of inspiration. I hope you can read this with a sense of humour as if in conversation with a friend who is sometimes too outspoken yet often has good insight with fresh thoughts." (1996)

That paragraph was written in 1996. Now it is 2020. Most of the essays in this book were written in 1996. In some cases I have updated a few minor details. In some cases where it may have seemed advisable to update, I did not do so because I want it seen that some things were foreseen as patterns then in 1996 which continued at least through today in 2020. This is a book of ideas and thoughts. Many of those, you will see, can have an immediate impact or inspiration to one's creativity on a practical level. The practical introduction to *Quantum Theatre: Slapstick to Shakespeare* is a chronological series of physical and creative exercises comprising a template called The Four Articulations for Performance. All exercises, are with step-by-step instructions, in chapter 2 of the book *Clown Secret*. *Clown Secret* tells many more stories that provide the context in my life and career in which the whole method evolved. This book that you are now reading, *Quantum Theatre: Slapstick to Shakespeare,* provides more of social context within theatre and society generally in which the method is located. *Clown Secret* provides the introductory template, whereas *Quantum Theatre: Slapstick to Shakespeare* provides the larger vision of the whole method. These two books complement each other.

In 1996 self-publishing was an expensive investment. I stored the manuscript on a floppy disc. I had moved residency so many times. I thought this book, *Quantum Theatre: Slapstick to Shakespeare* was lost. In January of 2020 a friend was moving house and found a box of mine that had been stored and forgotten. Inside was the manuscript of this book and the floppy disc it was stored on.

I hope you enjoy the book. It is quite a trip. It is simply me communicating my ideas in a variety of ways to stimulate your own thoughts about theatre and creativity, and maybe some other odd subjects that are part of life.

Why did I use the word 'quantum'? I am not trained in physics, nor mathematics, so quantum to me is an inspirational idea and a metaphor. Directors, teachers, and actors whom I worked with in the theatre saw that I could help others to 'make a quantum leap' that is to suddenly improve with no clear explanation how. After many years of such occurrences I wanted to know, how did I assist others to 'make a quantum leap'? This book is my attempt to discover and discuss the hidden dynamics which I had developed first intuitively and then more consciously.

I had already begun to develop my method first with a set of ten physical movements that I named "Core Mechanics". I was 24 years old and still a novice in the study of theatre. I created that series so that I could locate and practice the basic mechanics within larger physical methods I was being exposed to in my study of theatre. Core Mechanics ten movements are a part of Chapter 2 in Clown Secret.

Those ten movements start 7 that are while standing then 3 while on the floor. The very 1st movement involves the spine, the 2nd involves the legs, the 3rd combines the spine and the legs. Core Mechanics' 6th movement, The Creative Twist, with its outstretched arms, was based on ideas I had read about Leonardo da Vinci's Vitruvian drawing. For me, that particular exercise held the secret of the 'quantum leaps' that my colleagues had observed.

In the 1970s some, scientists wrote books, for laymen, to explain some of the principles of quantum mechanics and quantum physics. For example the influential *The Tao of Physics: An Exploration of the Parallels Between Modern Physics and Eastern Mysticism* (1975) by Fritjof Capra. That and others appear to have inspired books written by non-scientists who seemed to understand the metaphors such as: the observer affects the observed; quanta is the potential of energy; and, two perspectives occur simultaneously.

Then, in 1993, I found a strange book *Quantum Gods* (1976) by Jeff Love. I opened that book and read only a few sentences before shouting to my friend 'this is it, this is what I do, this is what I should call my method'. *Quantum Gods* is not a science book. That book's interesting idea is that the mythical and mystical kabbalah reminds one of quantum physics. And vice versa. For a layman, reading about quantum mechanics and quantum physics sounds like a myth, a creation myth like most ancient cultures have. Except that physics is based on mathematics, proof, experiments, and predictions. I use the word quantum as a symbol for potential and other matters that are explained within this book: *Quantum Theatre: Slapstick to Shakespeare*.

CONTENTS

ACKNOWLEDGEMENTS v
FOREWORD vii
PREFACE xiii

1.	QUANTUM THEATRE: SLAPSTICK TO SHAKESPEARE - BACKGROUND	1
2.	QUICK DEFINITION OF QUANTUM THEATRE	5
3.	CORE MECHANICS	7
4.	THEATRE HISTORY	9
5.	TRAINING THE ACTOR	13
6.	CREATIVITY AND THE ACTOR	18
7.	POPULAR THEATRE	23
8.	COMMEDIA: COMMEDIA DELL'ARTE: COMEDY	28
9.	MASK MASKS MASQUE MASKED BALL	33
10.	A STORY	37
11.	SHAKESPEARE	42
12.	MIME AND VOICE	61
13.	YOGA	64
14.	THEATRE CLOWN	68
15.	CLASSICAL ACTING AND STYLE	73
16.	DIRECTION	76
17.	MULTI-CULTURAL THEATRE	83
18.	MULTI-CULTURAL II. AN EXAMPLE	90
19.	MULTI-CULT III	96
20.	SHAKESPEARE II	103
21.	SHAKESPEARE III	112

22.	SLAPSTICK	117
23.	GENIUS OF THE THEATRE	121
24.	TEACHERS AND LEARNING.	124
25.	A SCHOOL OF DELL 'ARTE	132
26.	TRY TO QUIT THEATRE	147
27.	PROFESSOR CLETUS	149
28.	SHAKESPEARE'S SLAP SCHTIK	154
29.	HENRY THE FIFTH … A CAST OF TWELVE WOMEN	168
29a.	KING LEAR	183
30.	CRITICS	189
31.	THEATRE AS RELIGION	196
32.	COMMON SENSE, CLAIRVOYANCE, AND CAREER	203
33.	C C C 2	210
34.	CONCEPTS INSIDE QUANTUM THEATRE: SLAPSTICK TO SHAKESPEARE	213
35.	SPEAKING OF NOTHING. THE SHAMAN	223
36.	ALCHEMY	227
37.	HARRY HAYTHORNE, MBE (MEMBER OF THE BRITISH EMPIRE)	230
38.	BALANCE IN TRAINING AND PERFORMANCE	237
39.	STRUCTURE - QUANTUM THEATRE: SLAPSTICK TO SHAKESPEARE	241
40.	HEALING THE THEATRE FOR TOMORROW	258
41.	ORIGIN OF CREATION …. ORIGIN OF IDEAS	264
42.	QUANTUM THEATRE - THREE SYSTEMS OF TEN	269
43.	COMMENTS - NEUROSCIENTIST JIM PICKLE	274
44.	COMMENTS - THEATRE PRACTITIONER NAREE SHIELDS	281
45.	COMMENTS - THEATRE MAKER THERESE COOK	288
46.	COMMENTS - CHOREOGRAPHER, DANCER OONA DOHERTY	301

QUANTUM THEATRE: SLAPSTICK TO SHAKESPEARE - BACKGROUND

I came to the world of theatre late in life by coincidence. As a youth I had hardly ever seen "theatre" except for circus, television and movies. Yet my whole youth was theatrical, imaginative, explosive. What I considered as a normal youth, was that of playing games, sport, mischief, rebelliousness, curiosity, seeking some purity or truth to society and existence.

Quantum Theatre: Slapstick to Shakespeare is based on simple questions.

Question 1: What is Theatre? I have attempted a variety of approaches to theatre including thousands of odd situations as an entertainer. My answer to the question is in essence that theatre is the uniting of two opposing creative energies to create a new living entity. That living entity is a performance, a living work of art. It is as if theatre is a creative imitation of procreation. That is, the union which begets a child. To procreate for real or through the primal dance of sex is a base urge. To transmute this energy there must be a creative outlet. It can raise its baseness only by raising our consciousness.

Part of this consciousness raising would include the wisdom to understand the purpose of theatre. Theatre is a communal rite which in an infinite variety of ways re-enacts conflict between feminine and masculine energies.

In the rite these energies unite to create an offspring. That offspring is hope. In Shakespeare's time even despairing tragedy ended with a clown's jig or dance. In my own creations I love to create comic-tragedies which always end in Hope. Hope does not imply a happy ending. Hope is simply light at the end of the tunnel.

Quantum Theatre is bigger than my own creations. It is a way for each Theatre practitioner to clarify and purify their deepest and highest purpose of Creativity. Quantum Theatre allows for infinite and unique visions of theatre. To get to that infinite and unique expression the artist must expand their consciousness beyond what is fed to them in school, in the media, in specific interest groups. The artist must learn to make quantum leaps in their thoughts.

Question 2: Why are so many methods, schools, techniques perhaps inadequate? Schools which claim to train actors often fail. All the ideas and ideals are meaningless if they are not practical. All schools claim successes. What is success? Is it employment? Time again employment in the theatre often leads to conservatism without preserving the best attributes of group work. So many schools claim to train the whole actor. These schools whether private or state supported are businesses. They are caught up in pleasing unions, governments, parents, insurance companies, agents, friends, etc. Where is the space for spirituality, of practical business concerns of the future practitioner? Where is the space for the inspiration of the student? Where is the balanced discipline? It is time consuming to teach fencing to a student who cannot control their leg and arm coordination. It is inefficient to teach acrobatics once a week. It is superficial to teach voice and singing without allowing for the expression of spontaneous joy and melancholy of the actor. Many Western theatre trainings are in a rat race to get accreditation, approval, degrees, diplomas, more students, and funding. It is a system which fails to resolve the general apathy which unskilled theatre generates. It fails to create appropriate local theatre.

To expose people to theatre for one or more years is a positive life experience. All people deserve the opportunity to create theatre on a community level.

Theatre is valuable. Quantum Theatre follows on from the theatre ideas and work of: Konstantin Stanislavsky, Jacques Copeau, Jerzy Grotowski, Tadeusz Kantor, Viola Spolin, Peter Brook, Eugenio Barba; and, insists on the questions; What is theatre? Why are established trainings inadequate? Why are alternative trainings so weak?

Quantum Theatre asks: What makes a great actor, also a good actor? A great actor is usually robust, full of drive. It is hard for most actors to drive themselves. A simple, clean, expressive training will go a long way to encourage each actor to become good. Basic skills developed clearly to intermediate then to advanced are the main requirements. Next is the personal discipline of the Self. There are abundant philosophies to draw from; Buddhism, Sufism, the mystical philosophies of Christianity, Judaism, Islam, Patanjali's Yoga Sutras, the Fourth Way, Zen Buddhism, etc. Theatre is a spiritual path and yearning even in the most commercial situation. If you are correctly scared of religious or spiritual organisations go to Shakespeare. The texts are asking the primary existential questions. Examine the main plays of Samuel Beckett, of Arthur Miller, look at the Woody Allen play "God" !

Quantum Theatre goes directly to the issues of the Body-Mind-Spirit connection of the actor. This enables and empowers each actor to define in their own terms why they do theatre and what kind of theatre do they wish to create.

All work in Quantum Theatre: Slapstick to Shakespeare, stems from the Quantum Theatre movement technique Core Mechanics. Core Mechanics' ten movements introduce their application to primary movement techniques of dance, yoga, acrobatics, martial arts, mime, and improvisation.

The philosophy of Quantum Theatre is stimulated by the educators John Holt, Ivan Illich, A.S.Neill. Holt wrote *How Children Learn*; Illich wrote *Deschooling Society*; Neill wrote *Summerhill School: A New View of Childhood*. Quantum Theatre is backed by decades of practical application, examination, and development. Understanding the Self through daily Yoga practice and practical development of the Intuitive process has provided the insight necessary to develop simple, adaptable applications.

These are words and ideas. In practice I have baffled and surprised friends, peers, teachers, a large variety of experienced directors. In practice Quantum Theatre methods are perhaps advanced techniques for an integrated actor-teacher-director training. Actors enjoy the process as it helps them immediately identify the point of focus. It is not a cold logical approach. Quantum Theatre is organic, practical, fast, and detailed. Its essence is the Core Mechanics; centrally the sixth movement - The Twist Choreography, along with The Creative Twist. The practical, efficient approach is the foundation template: The Four Articulations for Performance that is explained with detailed instructions in the book *Clown Secret*. It works. It is a tough process yet the joy of results is immediate and continuous. Quantum Theatre accepts a belief in human potential with the common sense that each person is dealing with their own scoundrel. By scoundrel I mean the part of a person that leads them away from their inner conflict which is often the most creative point that is not to be avoided but to be engaged with on the spot. The Core Mechanics helps the actor to see the scoundrel. The Four Articulations, and, Quantum Theatre: Slapstick to Shakespeare help the actor to laugh at that scoundrel.

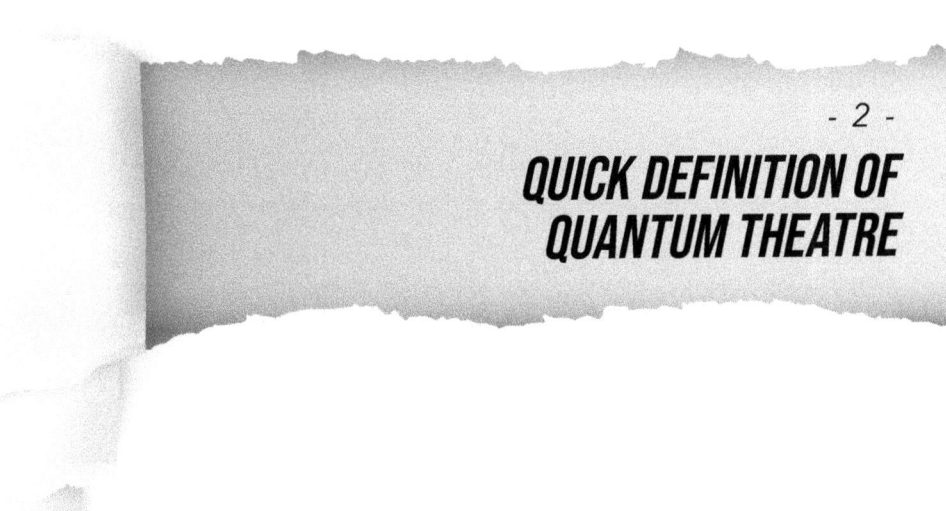

QUICK DEFINITION OF QUANTUM THEATRE

Quantum Theatre: Slapstick to Shakespeare is a complex of ideas which represents an instinct that actors, teachers, directors, and writers have always gravitated towards.

This complex of ideas which I call Quantum is the artists' attempt to construct a more refined way and purpose for theatre.

For example Brecht sought a stronger way to engage the spectator to think clearly and then take action in their own life and society. He directly attacked Church...all forms of religious and spiritual organisation, State... all forms of legal control, Business...all forms of financial control, Theatre... all forms of creative control.

Quantum Theatre: Slapstick to Shakespeare looks first at; beliefs, paradoxes, and, dichotomies inside theatre. This whole book, and much of the book *Clown Secret* cover those areas.

Second, Quantum Theatre: Slapstick to Shakespeare looks at logical training. That is training the body first yet at the same time engaging the actor's thoughts, ability to focus, and creative engagement of the mind. The practical starting point is The Four Articulations for

Performance. That is described in detailed instructions in chapter 2 of *Clown Secret*.

Third, Quantum Theatre: Slapstick to Shakespeare, offers clear ways for actors to communicate and pinpoint difficulties and to discover solutions.

Fourth, Quantum Theatre: Slapstick to Shakespeare deals openly with theatre as a path for the integration of body-mind-spirit. At the same time all classes are filled with traditional and classical professional focus upon craftsmanship.

Theatre is actually a spiritual calling. Like any spiritual path you must be anchored in the body. This requires training. It also requires practical ethics training in cooperation and collaboration and a focus for one's abilities and talents to serve in the community. Theatre requires a philosophical study of humanity and the higher purpose which is the creative nature in essence.

It is quite trendy today to laugh at and attack religious fundamentalists and religious and spiritual zealots, and anyone who thinks differently from "us". Yet the theatre is filled with fundamentalist preachers of intellectualism, education, and higher values of culture, and rescuers of the working class. Quantum Theatre seeks a middle path between the religious or spiritual zealots and the intellectual or cultural zealots.

There is no intelligent culture without the wisdom of the universe, anchored in the body and engaged in training higher spiritual values. Likewise the religious and bureaucratic ones must make way for the creative drive in the individual human.

- 3 -
CORE MECHANICS

Core Mechanics is a choreography of ten basic actions of human movement. The choreography takes ten minutes to do. Core is clear, simple. The simple things include; control of the leg, knee, and hip; articulation of the foot, expressiveness of the hand, focus of the eyes, order of efficient movement, counting moves, change of direction, changes of rhythm, details of the spine, control of shoulders, breathing, and, attention with awareness while moving.

Although I consider Core unique I hope that it integrates the common sense of Yoga, Alexander Technique, and Feldenkrais Method.

Core is based on learning problems adults may have with new movement techniques. Once patterns and sequences of Core are learned the student is challenged and guided to see how Core is hidden inside all movement techniques. We examine some such as yoga, dance, mime, acrobatics. The actor starts to see how advanced techniques are actually based on natural principles. Most importantly, the actor develops; an effective mental approach, focus, concepts for learning new movements, or skills for improving and developing technique. Then the actor gets to explore creatively via concentrated improvisation. With progress the warm-up is changed to create new patterns and challenges. In this way the actor learns to be creative, efficient, and flexible with their own warm-up.

In each project as an actor I create a unique warm-up to meet my needs of stepping on stage with the energy appropriate to the production and able to sustain the levels necessary throughout the performance. As the season progresses this becomes a ritual which I adjust as required.

Core is a warm-up for Acting. Once the body and mind are warm and focused the work of the Voice is begun. This work extends to the various Acting subjects. The corporeal work teaches the actor to understand their own work in a specific and clear way. Their learning difficulties in movement will repeat in the more creative and esoteric disciplines of theatre. This concept may be common to other techniques. However, the practicality, flexibility, immediate and long term results of Core are unusual, because Core's mechanical simplicity allows each actor to organically establish their own roots and branches, like a tree that will bear fruit. Core Mechanics is part of The Four Articulations; which are part of the bigger picture of Quantum Theatre: Slapstick to Shakespeare, that gives the theatre practitioner infinite possibilities to develop, train further, write, or direct.

- 4 -
THEATRE HISTORY

Did Theatre change History, or did History change Theatre?

Theatre is a small but essential part of life. For people like myself, Theatre is almost life itself. I love it. I live and work with it almost all day every day.

Yet I find it perplexing that so many people in the theatre suffer from so many false beliefs, illusions, acceptance of clichés, illusions about themselves and the very nature and history of theatre.

How has theatre this century evolved? We are hair away from the millennium 2000. Meantime the scientists are arguing when does the millennium start? January 1, 2000, or January 1, 2001. Something so explicit is completely unclear.

How clear are theatre people about Theatre History? Theatre history books revel in the birth of a new play. What about the birth of electricity, airplanes, smart bombs, telephones, telefax? How does it affect theatre to have beepers and mobile phones in the audience during a live performance? How has life changed since 1900 or 1901? What has remained the same since Ibsen, Strindberg, Chekhov? What has changed since World War I? How did war affect Pirandello, Max Reinhardt, Stravinsky, Martha Graham,

Chagall, Georgia O'Keeffe, Picasso? How does war affect creativity? I'm not sure creativity affects war very much at all. Chaplin, perhaps the most popular and therefore most powerful artist on Earth, created the film, The Great Dictator, of 1940. Nothing stopped World War II except military and economic defeat. This did not stop greed's natural malignancies of exploitation, pollution, war. When this book was first written, 1996, there were 52 wars on Earth. The Earth seems at war. How does the actor respond to this? Some actors are much closer to war than others.

After Chaplin the next greatest artist for peace was Marcel Marceau. We have overlooked this artistic angel in our history of the theatre. His mission was not his personal success. Yet his personal success has completely altered the dream of the consummate actor.

Marceau was active in The Resistance in World War II. He came out of the war with a mission of peace, every piece he created spoke of the common thread in Humanity. In many countries from Russia to Persia, to Argentina theatre artists have been snuffed out for their views, writings, actions. Dead. Murdered. Imprisoned. In America there were the McCarthy trials, J. Edgar Hoover, Mafia, Big Business, Big Brother to snuff or stifle the actors, writers, directors who wanted to change history. It is not so easy to change history and be a commercial success. Maybe it is impossible. The Living Theatre led by Julian Beck and Judith Malina probably affected a portion of public demand to end the Vietnam War. They tried. Many tried. Nicolai Erdman wrote "The Suicide" in Russia, he tried. Frank Capra attacked the mother of all wars, GREED, with films like "You Can't Take It With You". He tried. Shakespeare and Dante too. Steven Spielberg tries to raise our consciousness and hopes. It is not so easy for Theatre, or even its younger, more successful sibling Cinema, to affect History.

History is tough. It is like the ocean; you can not stop it. You can surf, swim, dive, and drown but you cannot stop it.

A tough lesson in History in the Theatre is that the legacy of Marcel Marceau has inspired a non-stoppable quest to create actors of our dreams. Actors who create without words, communicate directly to our spirit, to our common humanity, to our higher self. Or with words an actor has the often untapped potential to reach the audience directly. Notably, Marceau was inspiring when he spoke, and was an exceptional wit. His success started immediately after World War II. He responded directly to a public need for healing. Constantly he has inspired theatre artists. He created a demand for new actors. We all follow in his footsteps. As in the end of Hamlet we hear the devastating thud "and the rest is silence". *Tell my story.* I believe that the story of Marceau is a story that needs to be told. There are key characters who sweated with him such as his teachers Etienne Decroux and Charles Dullin, and Jean Louis Barrault. Barrault, earlier had been a student of Dullin and Decroux. No doubt the wives of Marceau shared his trials as did his long time touring associates such as Pierre Verry. Marceau created 16 mimo-dramas and Verry appeared in most. Marceau's stage manager and lighting designer travelled the entire globe as Marceau was giving, sharing, studying the global truth of theatre. There is a common language - the silence from the heart.

Our theatre history books need to be re-written with a new focus around actual practitioners, performers on stage, Decroux, Marceau, and Barrault. There needs to be a chapter on another war refugee Lotte Goslar the great German mime, clown, dancer, teacher and director.

There needs to be a chapter on the mime, pianist, painter Agnes Enters. The effective teaching of Viola Spolin and her inspired understanding of improvisation, comedy, and psychology of the actor's process.

There needs to be a correlated approach to the mothers of Modern Dance: Doris Humphrey, Isadora Duncan, Mary Wigman, Ruth St. Denis, Martha Graham. All of whom predicted greater creativity for the performer.

Our perception of theatre history is often nationalistic and usually needs clearer perception. Spielberg, like Woody Allen, Frank Capra, Fellini,

Kurosawa, Lena Wertmuller are amongst the most engaged auteurs of social critique cinema, but, who create in staged theatricality. Theatre practitioners need to face the music which has affected us like Jazz, Stravinsky, John Cage, Nino Rota, Michael Jackson, Madonna, The Beatles, Bob Dylan, Leonard Cohen. This area and its effect on theatre is endless. Theatre history, as framed by experts, is like most individual humans, it is self-serving. Theatre history, as it has been traditionally taught, and in the ways that most experts present it, undermines the truth. The truth is that theatre history is not a linear process, rather the history has overlapping influences and hardly seen tides of influences.

- 5 -
TRAINING THE ACTOR

Because of the variety of acting styles and the complexities of an art form which is about the person, actor training is difficult. There is a difference between teaching acting and teaching theatre. Acting will normally imply a more specific and more narrow approach. In theatre training, the actor would clean the floor, hammer nails, paint, rig, run and design lighting. In actor training, the main objective is to become a good medium with which a director can be the overseer of a creative whole. In actor training the actor learns union logic. That is if coffee spills on the floor, call a technician. Alternatively the actor could clean it and become a Humble Histrionic Hero.

Actor training. There are two great books by Michel Saint-Denis on the subject. Those two books are: *Theatre, A Rediscovery of Style*; and, *Training for the Theatre; premises and promises*. My own view is that there are several areas in Actor and Theatre Training which are illogical. In the beginning of training the actor needs a simple, basic period of one to three months with a simple, cold, logical training. Each day could start with a basic movement class which is mechanical, much repetition and explanation. This 1.5 to 2 hours could be immediately followed by an acting class. This acting class should emphasise speaking simple dialogue while improvising movement and playing with the sound of the speech rather than the meaning of words. Then with the rest of the day each school can offer whatever curriculum they prefer. The average acting student needs a steady program every day for four weeks of Body Mechanics, Discovery of Sound and Vocal Mechanics, Acting in the Body, with the Voice and Complete Freedom. "The Four Articulations for Performance" is suitable as a daily beginning training, and that whole template is in chapter 2 of *Clown Secret*.

An Introductory Training Process.

In a four-weeks introduction of The Four Articulations as a daily connected class for BODY-VOICE-ACTING most adults will clarify their own learning problems. Their enthusiasm will be natural, they will be alert to new details, new ideas, different styles and approaches. After this initial period one dance technique can replace the body mechanics class. The dance technique needs to teach the difference between classic, modern, and post-modern use of feet, legs, arms and torso.

Basics, basics, basics are the secret to actor training. Once the actor has basic mechanics, the elementary control of the whole body (heel, toes, achilles, calf, hand, wrist, posture, alignment, coordination) they can go on to another subject three days per week, and work ballet basics two days per week. During the introduction period of ballet (i.e., coordination of arms, legs, torso, eyes) the vocal approach should change to the relish and delight of words. Articulation with an emphasis on the beginning, middle and end of EACH word. Separating one word from the next and 'singing' the difference between consonants and vowels. During this second stage the Acting should shift to quick characterisation by the changing of body shape and rhythm.

Through all of this the actor must constantly be reminded to breathe, relax, focus on the essential points only; use energy with control, enthusiasm with clarity.

Around 1990, Actors Equity selected a small panel of experts in actor training. We were to discuss a way to establish a national standard for actor training. We were to discuss what elements such as skill and attitude are required for a professional standard. The musical producer Cameron Macintosh was there because he knew that Australia had the potential to exponentially develop its ability to produce many more major musicals drawn from London's West End and from NYC's Broadway. However, he knew that in order to provide enough qualified Australian musical theatre actors there needed to be a revamped national standard. One expert was speaking about relaxation as an essential aspect of actor training. I agreed, but, I said an actor can learn all that is necessary about relaxation in acting in three weeks. What should they learn for the rest of the three years? The actor needs have several years of learning to apply relaxation in their technique, skill, exploration, freedom. It is best to teach mechanics of the body, voice, acting first. With an emphasis on exploring; breathing, and relaxing while active. All the yoga, Alexander and Feldenkrais techniques will not make an actor. They need basic movement and acting skills and exploration followed by incrementally difficult practical challenges.

In addition it is not helpful at an early stage to teach actors too much technique in mime, dance, martial arts. Basic mechanics, gentle coaching and coaxing, much freedom - are the essentials. Then as the actor's confidence grows they will master new techniques and ideas with speed and enthusiasm.

Many of the so-called physical theatre trainings suffer from many hoaxes and complexes...

Most of them have very weak focus on the voice-speech-song-music. Almost all claim to teach skills like acrobatics. Yet after 1,2,3 years of training the actor cannot do a proper handspring. That is basic. After the first year of training with a basic clear program all actors could know three distinctive dance styles and be able to get choreographed quickly with detail and motivation, they should know all basic mime illusions and be able to improvise on any subject. Those should be essential basics in any actor training. In many theatre schools there are teachers of skills who were never experienced in the field. At the other extreme there are experts who are trying to cram a whole style down the unsuspecting student. There are also gifted, talented, dedicated teachers dealing with a subject professionally but the poor actors have never been taught the basics. Who is responsible? The theatre community is very gullible and wants to have people with names of repute, schools want to say they teach EVERYTHING. So their program includes mime but in three years the student gets only ten lessons. In actor training, national theatre institutions of the Chinese, Russians, Poles and Czechs lead the way, along with the finest conservatory programs in Western nations.

The TV and film industry constantly needs new, fresh, young talent. Every year, every week, every day. Like Dracula, fresh blood. So do not confuse success with good actor training. Verbally active and physically robust actors will come out of any American or English training like stars. There is still a rift between these two continents like the distance 'twixt Shakespeare and Strasberg. In Europe the East leads the way with the work of Grotowski, Kantor, the Yiddish Theatre, Pantomime theatres, Henryk Tomaszewski, and Jan Kott ... that is only from Poland. In Africa and many other places it is the genius of the indigenous storyteller which has long possessed all the secrets which the West seems blind and close hearted to. Peter Brook went with his acting company on a long journey to Africa to try to find what is universal in story telling and theatre. For example, in France, Italy, Spain, the culture and life itself provides the stuff which actors are made from. Other cultures which influence artist drive: Harlem, Brooklyn, East End, Farm-life, etc.

Training should not only purify the personality but should allow the individual personality maximum freedom. Today, too many trainings make their students into twee, well-behaved achievers. People who will do anything to complete training while knowing it is riddled with false work.

Actor training is complex. Stanislavsky asked all the most important questions. But he failed to resolve the problem. The Chinese resolved the problems long ago. Their clowns are consummate actors. Goethe said something to the effect of: "if only every actor had to tread the tight wire". As wild as Russian and Chinese acrobats seem, they would not dream of a wire walker without training basic body mechanics and then basic ballet. If you really want to train actors, study how the Chinese and Russians train acrobats. To them an acrobat is an *artiste*. An actor should be an artist. The actor's medium is the body. The body houses the voice, the mind, the brain, the imagination, the spark of life which is the soul which connects all spirits to one whole.

The training of the actor is a spiritual path. Its only anchor is the body. Actor training is about training the body first and foremost. The body carries the costume, make-up, and wig. Maybe we need to learn from Drag Queens in our society. Maybe. One of the greatest actors and artists of our day is Barry Humphries. With his team of alter egos (Dame Edna, Sir Les, Sandy Stone, Lance Boil) this is an actor, entertainer, clown *par excellence*.

The legendary Georgian actor Ramaz Chkhikavadze was often a comic actor in his early years. Towards the tail end of Sir Laurence Olivier's career he became a tragic clown in "The Entertainer". About this time a great English clown Max Wall became an actor in stage plays.

In other words I believe there is a strong relation between the training of a good clown and a good actor. The basic training is not necessarily the evolving path. The basic training is to dance, mime, speak, sing, to create through the power of imagination. To be, to do, to communicate.

- 6 -
CREATIVITY AND THE ACTOR

An actor should be a creative artist. It is my experience that even when actors are fully employed, well paid and in a good project, they get frustrated. In particular it is their frustration with not being creative enough even while employed in a production. My experience as a director has been to relieve this frustration as early as possible in rehearsal. How do I do this? The actor usually realises within two or three days that I am working with them. It is clear that as director it is only a role for me to play. I play this role to create a positive yet hard working environment. A no nonsense environment where laughter erupts spontaneously, where each actor at some moment is hit with the instinct of the Fool.

The actor knows early on they can try anything, absolutely anything. Though they know clearly I will accept no one being hurt physically or emotionally. Try anything. It does not have to work, you do not know where it will lead. Trust your instinct not your intellect. The hard part for actor, director, teacher alike is to find the difference between instinct and intellect.

I have seen a few pathetic actors who love to come up with "ideas". The sad thing is when these "ideas" are nothing more than acting school exercises.

A real idea should come as a spark of light, in a flash, usually simple and succinct.

Usually I will try their idea. Usually it does not work the first time. I say try again, perhaps with a slight change in focus. We continue this way. Something starts to work. The actor has learned to trust their instinct, to trust the director, the other actors witness the process. We have begun to grow into our own group creative process. Sometimes an actor will make a poor or even feeble "suggestion", still I will say try it. I will try with all my soul to make this suggestion work. Often the suggestion at least serves to get a creative dialogue happening.

Many successful actors have learned not to be creative but they have learned to get their way. It is part of a general education where people learn to get praise. In my class and studio I make a distinct effort to draw out the shy, weaker, most reserved people. Their hidden resources are always invaluable to my work. As this revelation happens over days and weeks, the more free and more dominant personalities start to open up and respect the choices of the less experienced or less articulate individuals.

I make a distinction between one's ability to articulate and their potential to act.

To be creative an actor must release their own blocks, problems, weaknesses. To take little risks, baby steps. Soon they will walk, run, jump, fly. It is the little things which count.

I have always been in absurd situations about casting. I am rarely involved in "cattle calls". Although as an actor I accept auditioning as a separate art form.

Once I directed a recent state school acting graduate. A very tough and gifted actress. At the first rehearsal I asked her to try something with two actors. She said, "I can't". "Why can't you?" I asked. "I can't improvise. I failed Improvisation at school...I just can't". "You can improvise. You didn't fail. Your teachers failed". Then I proceeded to "direct" her. To tell her what to do, when and why. It did not seem to be an improvisation. Then the process evolved step by step with support from the other actors. She improvised.

Each actor has to create and be creative in their own way, yet it must be a co-operative creation with the company as a whole. Each person's creativity lights up at different times and in different ways.

Deep inside the actor is a desire to create and to be accepted, loved, or respected. There are many possibilities. Much of the creativity of the actor is to pay attention to the detail of what they are doing, or pay attention to a new choice or new detail or new realisation about a word, moment, movement, beat, action, or direction. The actor's creativity is flowing with a partner, another actor, and other characters' evolution.

The actor is free to write, direct, produce or paint. Free to be as creative as any human in any given society. Sometimes when the actor is hired into a project it feels as if one is being paid to be not-creative. Odd as it may seem often an actor can be creative when unemployed. That is the time to be creative. Time. Time to write, train, study, read, dream, find other work, other means of employment, time to practice your own creativity. Then the next time you are employed as an actor you can be more creative within whatever restrictions are dealt to you.

To my surprise when I started work as an actor in commercials and business events the businessmen and women were found to be more creative in their thinking than most theatre actors or directors. Quite a shock. How can this absurdity be true? In the theatre there is too much freedom, an illusion of creativity. In the commercial world the restricting goals are obvious. Profit. With restrictions the creative juices can become more intense. When a painter cuts a canvas to be a certain size a restriction is set. Theatre has the illusion of creativity.

It is often very conservative people looking for a creative outlet who end up in theatre. The social aspect of theatre schools and rehearsals is to be well behaved, sociable, conservative. The creativity of the actor is effected by the social aspect of proper behaviour. Like children of conservative environments actors will sometimes rebel like extremists outside work. They will indulge in anything taboo or go the other way into purity simply because they are not using their creativity. To be creative is a primary urge. A computer programmer wants to create programs. The urge to create is basic to human nature.

The problem of creativity and acting is that acting is the illusion of creativity. It is standing up and pretending to create. Too often it is just plain business. Business can be creative and the business aspects of acting can be more creative than the artistic. An actor will think they are happy and creative when they have a lot to say or do. A dancer will think they are happy and creative when they are sweating.

The question is: What is the nature of Creativity?

The simplest answer is to say creativity is being in a flow and making choices. Creativity is like rafting down a river. You can stop at any point and pause for a swim, rest or picnic. Creativity is an attempt to reveal the unknown or to use the known in new ways or new combinations. To be creative is to release a light or energy.

Creativity in art is a metaphor for creativity in life. That is to procreate. In theory the first element is love (attraction) then a merging of Yin & Yang energy, a gestation period, birth, nurturing, trials and errors of life, old age, death, rebirth.

The origin of theatre is connected with nature's seasons and with a divine calling which at once connects and separates mankind with and from nature. Theatre is meant to harmonise mankind's higher and lower selves. It is an act of purification. The actor is the medium. Halfway between God and the Devil, that is, halfway between the forces of the Universe and the forces of the Earth.

All cultures have Creation Myths. Perhaps actors need to go back to the origins of theatre and restudy Creation Myths. Within the myth of Genesis the actual meaning is encoded in Hebrew. That myth/book is Bereishit ('in the beginning'). Some consider that the seven 'days' of Creation are nearly precise for the seven aeons of The Universe's evolution since The Big Bang. Human intuitive wisdom is encoded in that book and myth, just as such intuitive wisdom is encoded in Taoism, Vedic, and Indigenous myths.

The actor must work to create a satisfying myth from their own psyche. It is a deep and profound problem. It goes with good business sense, with creative particularities of co-operation. It goes with a sense of humour, joy and enjoyment. We need each actor to heal their own creativity. It is a matter of balancing the spirit, personality, life, and work. That is enough to keep all actors creatively employed full time.

- 7 -
POPULAR THEATRE

Popular Theatre? Is theatre popular? Popular? Sport is popular. Current or pop music is popular, Movies and TV are. Newspapers, magazines, gossip, are popular. Theatre is not. Well, perhaps Musical Theatre is? Not even ten percent of a city or town's population will go to the theatre. Actually in most Western countries only 1-3 percent of the population goes to the theatre. Popular theatre is free theatre wherever it appears.

Sport events fill stadiums with tens of thousands of spectators … paying customers, fans, a complete spectrum of the population. While the most popular theatre tries to fill a hundred or a thousand seats. What is the most popular indoor theatre? Musicals. Why? They do the basic job of theatre, telling a story. But the musical does it with panache, with charm, with beauty; and skill. The musical is presented with the greatest professional care, with the top talent in dance, song, action acting, music and choreography. Musicals are popular because they entertain people with skill and allow the audience to pass through a range of emotions and leave the theatre fulfilled, uplifted, positive, and feeling that money has been well spent. Much of what teachers and scholars profess as "popular" is little more than wishful thinking. However there is a trend now for theatre to use the secrets of musicals like action, skill, music, song.

The problem is that the public, NORMAL people, love to be entertained. Even if the story and acting and directions and choreography are not so good, the public will still be most appreciative and thankful if they have heard some decent singing and seen some tricky movement. This is actually why many groups today are starting to succeed.

They are not successful because of the merit of their artists, visionaries, or social luminaries but because they entertain. The same is true of the many wonderful New Circuses. They may not be as good as their success would lead one to believe. They entertain whether it is by sweat, colour, light, music, anarchy, beauty, or grotesque trickery, or physical skill. To be popular in the theatre you must entertain and delight. Now that secret is out, how can theatre become more popular? Ask Andrew Lloyd Webber, Stephen Sondheim, or the great director-producers Hal Prince or George Abbott. Mr Abbott was over 100 years old and still working and must have known what was popular. He was commercial. He gives the public their money's worth.

A clown at a birthday party must entertain. The clown can be great or awful but if they entertain there is a paycheque, a thank you, and more work. (WARNING: The next comments were written 24 years before the 2020 pandemic. So the comments are not reflections on the tragic loss of work that commenced in 2020.) Believe it or not, so many actors, directors, writers are out of work because they have false beliefs taught to them by fully employed teachers. They are taught false security and idealism which has nothing to do with the hopes, dreams, needs of the general population. Even the greatest stories in the world like Aladdin, or from the Bible, Mythology, histories, need to be well told.

Today of course the most popular story teller is TV itself, the medium.

You have it in your home, where you have control, comfort, safety, food, friends, relatives, or solitude. The medium itself works on some understanding of human psychology. Theatre works by a different psychology. Theatre does not work when its psychology is based on a psychological myth, the myth of the actor as a healer for society. Healer heal thyself! How? First be honest and face your false beliefs. The idea of popular theatre is already a myth, a false belief. Theatre is not popular except in the forms already mentioned as TV, film, rock bands, sports, entertainers hired for private comfort, or free entertainment. Musicals in other words are the only indoor theatre which is close to being popular and they come a distant second to ... guess what ... circus. Why is circus more popular than musicals? It is more entertainment and less story. Plus it is usually cheaper, plus you can take the whole family . That depends on the family and their views in an array of current social politics.

How can theatre become popular? Number one you must entertain, number two your group or theatre must entertain consistently, number three if you have been giving your public music, song, dance, tricks and jokes, you can not say "Now is the moment to reveal the TRUTH and EDUCATE the public". The public is not to be fooled except by politics, advertising, and manipulating their sense of security. The public is either entertained or it is not.

Now we need to see another thing with very clear lenses. Those who like one popular form may not like another. So we in the theatre must find our niche. For example, Shakespeare appeals to school teachers, those who fancy themselves as actors, those who identify with the Glory of the British Empire, those who cherish the written word, those who wish to be educated. So if you want to prove your popularity through ticket sales you must simply make good business choices, correct approaches to advertising, correct choices in a director/producer who will fulfil the (your) public's wishes. Colour, costumes, action, music will help. Bad acting does not matter if you have the pretension of High Art with enough entertainment elements. In other words if you give the public what it wants you will be tolerated to do what you want within reasonable limits.

All of this may be very difficult for the dedicated theatre practitioner to swallow or believe.

Just to make a point ask yourself: Is theatre as popular (as loved or as well attended) as sports? Obviously N - O. Ask yourself the same in relation to TV, film, rock music, circus. Of course theatre is second. Free theatre is popular theatre. Not because it is good, but because it is free and it is part of the bigger scheme of life like streets, fairs, festivals, celebrations, conventions. So don't confuse popular with good. Popular theatre means only that people like it first because it is free, it is part of the whole of life, and it is an entertaining diversion from daily work.

Popular theatre can also be of such quality that it rivals indoor, State, National theatre in quality of communication.

Should theatre attempt to be popular? I think it should but at the same time work of the avant-garde should be respected even though only a few people may view a showing.

There was a period when I did a solo performance prior to the daily opening of a theme park, "Wonderland". Many thousands of people waited each day for the gate to open. As a solo jester I entertained in my own ritual coming from a hill top forest playing my flute as I danced towards the mass of people. At night I played my solo theatre show in an inner city theatre which held a maximum of 200 people. The house was never half full. But these two experiences in a single day always taught me what popular theatre is and what it is not. Mine is not. Wonderland is.

Once we understand the difference we can proceed according to our desire.

On a recent trip to Prague I wanted to see both the famed Black Light Theatre and Magic Lantern. These two famous theatres now had many copies. These small theatres had one or two persons at a table in front of the theatre each day selling the show on the street. Inside there were 6-9 employed actors and in the evening full houses, through the same business cunning required on Broadway, LA, West End, or any National Theatre these skilled mimes, dancers, actors learned to make popular theatre. From the Czech trained actors we can learn not only some excellent techniques of Commedia, mime, movement, tricks of the trade, but also the authentic show business. At the time of writing several years have passed since the Berlin Wall was torn down in 1990. There are thousands of the best trained acrobats and clowns from Russia now on the loose. They are touring everywhere possible to earn a living outside of Russia. There are many troupes just like the Commedia who are seeking a public and winning. Their strategies are changing as quickly as politics. Perhaps the first art of theatre is to survive. To entertain is to survive.

- 8 -
COMMEDIA: COMMEDIA DELL'ARTE: COMEDY

There are numerous reasons to study and to understand Commedia Dell'arte (CDA). CDA was a form of theatre developed in Italy. Its peak period was from the late 1500s to the late 1700s. During those two hundred years it changed and evolved in many ways.

When we discuss CDA and what it was really like, remember that it varied dramatically in different periods and in different places.

Let's look at what did not vary. It was popular theatre. That means it was not only intelligent but it used a high degree of skill and tricks, outdoors.

It used not only the usual skill of the actor (voice, characterisation, timing) but also techniques of singing, music, acrobatics, slapstick, dance, mime, and improvisation.

Why study CDA? It is a symbol and metaphor for the dream of a skilled popular troupe who can also deliver a message, and create their own dramatic texts.

Where to find Commedia Dell 'Arte today? Almost nowhere. Perhaps it never existed as we imagine. Perhaps as would be normal today in any given troupe one actor might actually be an acrobat, another might excel on several instruments, someone else might be a writer, another a mask maker and perhaps everyone could do a little of the others' skills. Yet as an ensemble it would appear that everyone could do everything. Also CDA in its purest form relied on text and language. Not only were they speaking in Italian but in a variety of dialects. With different characters speaking sometimes different languages. In addition the troupes would change dialects as they played different regions of Italy. No doubt once a troupe settled in a new country they would quickly learn to speak the basics of the new mother tongue of English, French, Danish, German or Czech. It is normal for the clowns of traditional European circuses to speak at least five languages to allow the clowns to work in different nations.

The romantic view of the CDA's popularity is questionable. They were like any travelling troupe today, itinerant. Maybe if lucky they were welcomed by some patron for one day and one bacchanal dinner. It was then as it is now best not to wear out one's welcome. In some cases the Church, local merchants or local actors strongly opposed the arrival, playing, or staying of the CDA. Also some people may have preferred other acts. Today rather than theatre, people prefer TV, film, circus or sport.

The real true Commedia Dell'arte with dialects, travelling troupes, rich patrons, troupes which stayed together as families through generations, with an actor playing a role for forty years then passing it on to a twenty year old child of theirs ... these ideals are long gone. And imagine playing a character for forty years. Long gone. Are they? Well, the transmutations of the CDA are alive and kicking. The spirit of Commedia has never died and this spirit preceded Commedia Dell'arte and lived in all cultures. The CDA is a historical fact of Italian culture. The spirit of Commedia never dies.

This ties back to the previous essay dealing with the creation myths coming from intuitive wisdom. The actors need to create their own myths. Commedia Dell'arte has a factual history but it is also a myth, yet, at the same time its creative instinct has a natural human social-psychology found in most cultures. The social-psychology of creation myths is the same layered process as in the Torah, or Taoist or Vedic scriptures, or, in Indigenous knowledge and folklore that is layered into myths. The evolution of physics from Plato to Newtown to Einstein to Bohr to the evolving present has a similar layering mix of fact and fiction that moves beyond friction, fractions, and factions. More fission than fusion.

Let me give some examples where you can find Commedia.

First of all the Keystone Kops, Sennett Studios, Hal Roach and the heyday and mayhem of Hollywood. Fred Karno the English genius sent many troupes through the world. Two of his young players or comedians were Stan Laurel and Charlie Chaplin.

Etienne Decroux gave artistic birth to the actors; Jean Louis Barrault and Marcel Marceau. Both of whom were physically brilliant, inspired, hard working artists, who understood deeply the comic/tragic balance.

Beginning in the late 1940s, into the 1950s and 60s 'sitcoms' i.e. situation comedy began to develop in television in the USA. Each capo comico or head comic in the "harlequin" role would develop a team or pool of actors and writers with whom they could develop scenarios or sketches. Some of those comedians were Milton Berle, Jackie Gleason, Phil Silvers, Lucille Ball, Red Skelton, Molly Goldberg, Charlie Weaver, Jonathan Winters, Sid Caesar, Dick van Dyke, Amos 'n' Andy, Bill Cosby, Candice Bergen, Rosanne Arnold.

Internationally in film there were Max Linder, Jacques Tati, Toto, Nils Poppe, Danny Kaye, Fellini, the Crazy Gang, Carry On, Monty Python, Woody Allen all seriously infected with the commedia bug.

More keys. I have mentioned previously actors in the film "Les Enfants du Paradis". Here you can see Decroux and Barrault, as actors. Barrault in one of his auto-biographies mentions how his acting teacher Charles Dullin was obsessed by Commedia Dell 'Arte. In Paris Dullin was preceded by the key figure of Jacques Copeau and his protege Michel Saint-Denis.

In Moscow the spirit of commedia was alive and well in the work of Stanislavsky, Vakhtangov, Meyerhold, and Tairov. Formally in the 1920's a school was founded for technique, artistry, popularity, and educated political messages, that was the Moscow State Circus School. This school may know more about training commedia than anyone.

Which brings me to another point. There is a key to the CDA which most scholars, intellectuals, actors and Commedia teachers are yet to turn. The traditional European circus families. Remember above all the CDA were actually families. Famine, as Carlo Mazzone-Clementi pointed out, was related to familia, fame (the Italian word for hunger), family. It is normal for the circus families to pass on traditions and secrets, to know the art of popular entertainment, of skill and training, of multiple skills, multiple languages, travelling as a troupe, and dealing with municipal authorities.

The commedia lives in its purest form in the circuses with the clowns and slapstick acrobats. The biggest find to this day is any Italian acrobatic family. They are often the direct descendants of the CDA not only by culture, but by blood.

Where else can you find commedia? Not only in a library but at conventions, birthday parties, weddings, business lunches. There you will find entertainers carrying on with popular entertainments of jokes, tricks, magic, music, mirth for a good fee and free food...

Anywhere else? Folk dance, folk theatre, puppet theatre, particularly Punch and Judy and the Kaspar traditions. It is in the ancient customs of most native or indigenous cultures. The Yiddish theatre sprang up in Odessa and Bucharest after the commedia-like Klezmer bands passed into modernity. The Chinese Opera comedy tradition of Szechuan.

Too far to travel, too much to study? Get some DVDs or youtube videos of cartoons and you will see a level of imagination, colour, life, joy that all of today's commedia actors should study and emulate. The cartoonists know about commedia and its key elements: music, movement, timing, slapstick, skill, technique, a hidden message in open entertainment.

Now to be fair we need also a scholastic approach to CDA and that is why we have professors and scholars. But for the spirit and skills of commedia hide your scripts, books and masks for a year. Try a street improvisation for 20 minutes, then 30, 40 then ... go back in the studio and train the body in dance and acrobatics, ...sing. Next year go to the library. This year go see a dozen professional musicals. You will see consummate actors of today, they sing, dance, flip, act, and communicate directly with the audience. That is commedia.

- 9 -
MASK MASKS MASQUE MASKED BALL

Comedy/tragedy Masks. The most ancient symbol of the theatre is the mask. In the Western theatre it is the ancient Greek pair Comedy/Tragedy. In each Eastern culture there is a unique mask symbol. Many native or indigenous cultures use animal masks. In modern terms a symbol of theatre could be a painting or production photo of King Lear in the storm scene or Hamlet with the skull of Yorick. Many artists have attempted to create a mask or metaphor for theatre seeking a comic/tragic theme. As with King Lear the storm scene highlights the character's two masks and often to make the point the Fool is by Lear's side. The jester Yorick gives a bittersweet memory to Hamlet in the midst of one of the greatest comic-tragic scenes in the graveyard. Many artists in the 20th century tried to conjure the masked character Harlequin or his ancestor Arlecchino.

One great painting is the David Hockney portrayal of Harlequin. Here we see so strongly not only the FACE MASK, but the mask of the whole body. We see Harlequin upside down like the ancient fool with a natural balance in action rather than a stagnant over-trained technician.

The mask is not just the covering over the face or part of it. The Mask is the whole body. The whole being is energised and revealed. The Mask is from the top of the head to the sole of the foot, it is front and back, 360 degrees.

Left and right. With this awareness then we can allow the oval, the face mask to reveal the secret of the character's soul through the enlivened eyes. The whole being and body must be coordinated to focus our attention at random or at will on the face of the mask and then to the eyes. We meet eye to eye. Masked player and audience. With each member believing the Mask is looking right at them or may in the very next moment.

The practical training of Mask acting is of course a subject of debate. It is a highly trained, skilled, and free body which can fluidly punctuate a mask performance. It is what is below a mask that counts; the body's imagination.

All people should have a chance to experience and experiment with their own discovery of mask. Not just actors.

There are so many trained mask players who have the most superficial training and now are officially recognised simply because they have trained at schools of "good reputation". Those trainings are usually only a few weeks and totalling only a few hours of practical work on the floor. Unfortunately it is often a case of the Emperor's New Clothes. Many experts use a small variety of gimmicks. First they handle the mask mysteriously rather than carefully. Acting like a good charlatan. Then they speak philosophically or romantically. Then perhaps someone can don the mask to make their feeble attempt to correctly allow the spirit to take them and to be correct about this particular mask's characteristics. Then the mask teacher or expert gives a coded message about mistakes.

There are some very simple truths which can cut through the red tape of mask discovery and performance.

First if you want to discover a mask, put it on and try it. Many times. If you then want to understand it try it with many different objectives such as free play, stillness, move only the head, move only the torso, or only the legs, look in a mirror, do not look in a mirror, have an audience of one or more people and feel what communicates, or ask what people saw or felt, and maybe but lastly ask for criticism. If you want control, train your mind, free your mind, and practice following your intuition and impulses. Practice a physical discipline.

It is good to practice 360 degrees mask work where anything goes. It is also good to understand basic Western mask technique. If you cannot see the audience, the audience cannot see the mask. That is basic. Then only you can find what barriers and beliefs you can break with a particular mask. Often less is better. But that is only a conservative and practical truth which is not all possibilities. You must constantly remind yourself of three different viewing lenses: the mask is the whole top of the head to the sole of the foot. 360 degrees. Then it is the refined articulation and of the use of the neck and inclination of the head. Etienne Decroux Technique is ideal as a base for mask control. Lastly, it is the eyes and the gaze of the mask which reveals the soul.

For a one sentence lesson in Teach Yourself Mask Performance: Move the legs separately from the torso and the neck, then move the torso, then move only the head and neck. Lesson two. Breathe and relax. Lesson Three. Use lots of energy then suddenly freeze, then move in slow motion. Lesson Four. Find a partner or someone observant to play in front of. Lesson Five. See as many mask performances as possible, particularly traditional mask performances from various cultures.

There is another level of mask which is your actual face and its infinite possibilities. Here I am not referring to being a Rubber Face, or Face Acrobatics but to the subtle changes of "mask" when you change your psychic or emotional realities. Buster Keaton was supposed to be a stone face... look again and study only his face and eyes, do the same with Chaplin, with the Italian Clown Toto (Antonio de Curtis), Marcello Mastroianni, Giulietta Messina, and one of the greatest natural masks - the face of Harpo Marx. Look at the films of Fellini and study the face and eyes of the actors.

See those actors then you might understand why the Commedia Dell'arte dumped their masks. They took up the God created mask, the face. It is a phenomenon of nature. Feel the energy swell up, change, release and flow in your own face. Get a professional Facial where your face is cleansed and massaged and healed with natural oils and herbs.

When using a mask some people use their face a lot underneath the mask, some people work cold technique of the body. See what works but be open to both. Try both and maybe mix both. Try many times.

- 10 -
A STORY

I was to start my first contract with Australia's great classical actor John Bell. My assignment as "Resident Teacher and Choreographer" was to "build up and open up" the national touring company. As an actor I was to assume minor comic roles and extra roles in all productions. Alongside John I was to co-direct Richard III also with dramaturge Dr Adrian Keirnander.

There was a known company in town playing Shakespeare, Theatre de Complicite. I had heard of them and thought this would be inspiring to see on Friday and start my assignment on Monday.

As it turned out on this Friday John and his wife Anna Volska came to see the show, as did a few other members of our company. I thought now they will see what can be done.

Within the first minute I realised that this show was full of misplaced energy, poorly directed, and what I consider lousy ensemble work. Oh they tried. Yes they gave a lot, sweating, shouting, running around doing funny i.e. odd things. However compared with my own experiences this "wonderful"/"successful" show was a big nothing.

At interval I tried to avoid my peers because no doubt they would love this. I should have stayed in my seat. One of my new cohorts came up with a delighted smile, "Isn't it great"? I did not want to ruin his night but I did not want to spend the next year holding my opinion. Especially when I was asked to change things in our company.

I squeaked out, "Yeah, It's Okay". It was obvious what I really felt. We talked about it. John and Anna walked up smiling. "Isn't it wonderful? Do you like it?" Sean said, "I love it and Ira hates it". John and Anna are tough, honest, open. "Why"?

Again I did not have any desire to bring down their pleasure. I centred myself and said, "I would like to do much better than this and with our company we can".

I almost never leave a theatre show before I see the whole thing. The second half had some better moments and the tiny actress that was interesting in the beginning was still interesting.

At the close of the show I attempted a quick departure. One of our technical designers beamed, "Wasn't it great"? "Not for me". He looked, no, he glared at me that implied our professional past was now null and void.

The big first day of work came. John spoke eloquently to "we happy few"; sixteen actors, designers, admin personnel, stage managers, board members and others. At the end of ninety minutes we were to take a break: "Oh, one more thing, there is a production on at the Seymour Centre and I would like everyone to see it. I saw it and loved it, Ira hated it. Please be sure to see it". Nice introduction. I sat dumbfounded. One of my former students was sitting next to me, Chris. He was the new Hamlet. He gently eased the pain of this Yorick's alienation and asked, "Why didn't you like it"? See it and then we can discuss it. The same I would say to anyone about any show. See it first, discuss it later. In fact if you are the type of actor who discusses shows which you haven't seen then you are a gossip. Over the first few days each actor quietly on the side asked me "why"? The same with members of the board and crew. We had easy going discussions as I hoped, but, I continued to suggest they see that show then we could have a proper discussion about it.

After the break on that first day, after John's introduction talk, we started to work. As a warm-up John started with the Players' entrance in Hamlet. A scene which was to involve all sixteen actors including John and myself. He started pacing with the text in his hand. He asked all actors to stand in a large circle. He continued pacing within the circle with the text in his hand. He started to say something but he kept darting an eye at me. Now what did I do? This is the first minute of rehearsal. Then he just looked at me and appeared to be stuck. I asked if he would like me to try something. Yes. On the spot I started to give a very simple structure for sixteen actors. We did it. Then I added some detail. We tried again. Good. More details, some clarification, some encouragement. Good. And again. After forty-five minutes the actors were sweating, flowing, adding nuance was happening naturally, the dialogue fit in, the music too. An ensemble was born. John is that okay for today? That's great thank you. This was already better than the visiting troupe.

I could not rest that evening. The entrance is not good enough for me. I'll call John at home. Ira no! I tell myself it is only the first day. Do not call. I didn't. But I arrived at rehearsal early gunning for John. We have to work on the Players' entrance again. Not today it is fully scheduled. On the following morning, John asked if half an hour is enough. Fine. The scene became richer. John and I would jump in and out to have a look and add touches. As I was to act in this scene with the other 15 actors, at final period of choreographing and directing this Players entrance, I asked the Stage Manager to play my part. When we finished I offered to coach the Polish actor Marion who was the Player King. Yes he would love that. He got his best accolades for that role. John and Anna were great as Player extras. Hamlet by Chris was a dream. Some of the text work of the actors drove me up the wall and made me feel sick. I was able later to try my method via "suggestions" on several volunteers early in rehearsal.

Then I was asked to take the part of Ol' Gobbo the clown's father in the Merchant of Venice. Carol Woodrow directed this play. She gave me two days to work on the scene with Launcelot played by James Wardlaw. James was an excellent comic actor whom I taught at the national school. He was open to let me direct, as he put it "You direct". Then as always it became more of a team effort. A few days later Carol was very enthusiastic when she saw the first run. Then we began to discuss and analyse the scene and work on motivation. We showed our scene to the whole company. Much applause. This was five weeks into overlapping rehearsals of three plays. It was the first and only scene to receive applause in rehearsals. John came from his distant seat, hugged and congratulated me and said it was the first time he had ever seen the scene actually work. Then one of the young actors approached. A tough nut. He threw his arms around me and said, "I owe you an apology! When I saw Complicite I thought that was the best Shakespearean clowning, but you're right it is nothing compared to what you can do". Am I vain? Perhaps. Probably. But I had some great teachers including one with fifty-five years performance experience and another with forty years as a performer.

The point is not vanity at all. The point is I consider some of the famous front runners of the theatre very low on the scale of possibilities. Here we are stuck with words. Am I the only one who can better the famous groups and teachers? Not at all. Check out the work of the Russians, the Poles, the Czechs, Japanese, or Chinese or many others.

This little scene from The Merchant of Venice (Act 2 Scene 2) was applauded every time we ran it for actors. That was the only scene that received applause throughout the tour. John always gave good and helpful suggestions. Carol ensured that it was an integrated scene. It took a team to make the scene what it was. But the director did the right thing and handed it to me trusting that I can not only craft very well but absorb directions and suggestions. I am a strong personality but totally a team player. The scene had five actors and each added to the dynamic.

I question what our theatre calls a good ensemble. I question the reasons why a theatre company is seen to be good, successful, or great.

This story ends on a flat note, minor key. My congratulations to all theatres which succeed and survive. But I question what we perceive these days as great theatre.

- 11 -
SHAKESPEARE

I am not a Shakespearean scholar. Nor, am I, a scholar in the English language. I am a player.

Most of the theoretical and rhetorical books about Shakespeare which I have read have been thoroughly enjoyable. Most of the people I have met who earn their PhD's in relation to Shakespeare, English, or renaissance theatre have proven to be worthy of scholarly and practical respect. Most of the actors who have accumulated experience playing in many Shakespeare productions, seeing many more, and reading the plays, sonnets, theories are worth respect. Directors can bring a lot of knowledge to a production.

However, I find it shocking how poor so many productions of Shakespeare are. Primarily in terms of language, oratory and the power of the spoken word. Secondly, in terms of movement, staging and imagination.

It is odd given that there is no lack of scholars nor experts around. It is odd too that audiences will give enthusiastic applause even to a poor production.

Do they applaud the actors, the director, the production, the play or the playwright? My theory is that they applaud, or give thanks first for the effort the group makes to present a great play. Second they applaud out of social etiquette.

It is a relative opinion whether a show is of a high standard or not. What I am presenting is a method which is guaranteed to improve the standard of playing for most or for the average actor, ensemble, and director.

I love Shakespeare. The words, the ideas, the structure, the themes, the musicality, the humour, the legacy. I am not alone in this love. Mention Shakespeare and it will invoke a passion of love or loathing. But the response is never neutral.

An audience comes under a spell in even a poor production of one of his plays. It is a social agreement to try to enter an ancient magical kingdom of words. We enter a lost world of bards. It is like going to a place of worship, we agree to try our best to be in a receptive state for the spirit of holiness to enter our souls. We agree to be unusually receptive to an individual's idea. To be touched by a sermon when we would normally interrupt or disagree. When we walk out at the service completion we may not have felt a spirit enter us. We may not have understood or agreed with the sermon. But chances are we will leave in a better state simply because we made the effort.

It is similar with Shakespeare. If it is a comedy we try to be receptive to laugh at even ancient wit or dull execution. If a tragedy, oh what joy to be in control of sadness. The catharsis of induced sadness.

The structure of Shakespeare is an introduction, then a madcap journey through the senses and if you are willing to go the distance, there is always light at the end of the tunnel. The Holy Wait-for-It and a burst of sunlight as the doors to a new beginning. A rebirth. It is like a symphony.

Then why is it that only occasionally does even a single player stand out amongst a cast of 9, 12, 16, 20 actors? What is this actor doing that the others aren't?

As Hamlet's in his speech to The Players says: "Oh there be players I have seen play and heard others praise, and that highly, not to speak it profanely. That having neither accent of Christian, nor gait of Christians, pagan, nor no man. Have so shouted and bellowed that I had thought some of nature's journeymen had made men and not made them well they imitated humanity so abominably".

No doubt if you saw a Macbeth played by Gielgud, Olivier, Richardson, Wolfit, McKellen, Branagh, Sher, Rylance, Beale, you would have a preference of style or interpretation. In fact, you would have a passionate response.

How can I dare claim to be able to turn someone into a great Shakespearean actor? This is not my claim. My claim is that there is a relish for words which a great executor of text must have. You may have a preference of how they use their "treble, pipes, and whistles". But I claim there is method to their madness and uniqueness.

I shan't be brief.

I do not claim to be a great Shakespearean actor. There is no indication that Shakespeare was so hot himself. Of course he was busy writing. I have been busy myself. Writing plays, performing as a mime, acrobat, dancer, clown. Not a bad premise for acting Shakespeare. In spite of having 'imperfect' speech I have no trouble being heard very clearly and with subtle nuance.

I worked in a Shakespeare repertory touring company. My year of visitation meant I was hired as actor and as the "Resident Teacher and Choreographer". I was also given leeway to assist in direction of Richard III, and to assist the director in all of our four productions.

Tell someone you are in a Shakespeare Rep and they will no doubt quote you some Shakespeare and tell you about their own close encounters with the Spirit of the Bard. Some of these encounters were beautiful, some boring, some inspiring.

To understand how and why my system works it may help if I can psyche you up a bit. Playing Shakespeare requires acting with Psyche. You must go back to a time in your mind. A place where you are aware of a mythology in your subconscious. A respect for bards, Orators. A knowledge of itinerant players, mountebanks, minstrels, troubadours, fools. Just imagine when Shakespeare wrote and acted, royalty around the world had Court Fools. Telepathy, fears, dreams, listening were primal experiences. Apparently politics, relationships, families were however the same in Shakespeare's day as in Euripides' and Moses' as today.

Some things change, some things don't.

Let's face it, if you want to speak Shakespeare you had better find out about Iambic Pentameter, Diction and Articulation. And how to put them into action.

I "did" Shakespeare first and studied things later. My experience as a teacher, director and audience is that, even though most actors have studied Iambic Pentameter, Diction and Articulation, these actors still haven't found the missing link. Nor have most teachers nor directors. This includes a great many actors, teachers and directors who claim to be particularly good, knowledgeable and experienced with Shakespeare.

Iambic Pentameter, Diction, Articulation are the Big Three for acting, i.e., speaking Shakespeare. There is also breathing, pitch, projection, and other factors which an infinite number of voice teachers' methods and books can help you with. Some fine books are from the big four: Cecily Berry; Patsy Rodenburg; Kristin Linkletter; Arthur Lessac.

The Missing Link is what concerns me. Why is one actor clear and another not? Why are the great actors good? Why does so much Shakespeare sound like gibberish? Why do actors who think they know what they are doing communicate so poorly?

Many actors of Shakespeare claim to have some odd direct link to the Bard. "I spent a whole month at Stratford". "I did a month-long workshop with

RSC". "I've seen all the BBC Shakespeare video collection ... twice". "I've seen it thrice". "I played Shakespeare in a play". Yes actors are only human. I want to join my peerage in their silliness and tell snippets of my encounters with the Bard. I shall be brief.

I joined the theatre by fluke. But decades in the business reveals some form of pattern. Perhaps even destiny.

What I am about to tell you, will hopefully make you laugh. At best you'll get an insight into an authentic fool. At worst, your sense of superiority will soar so high that you won't try my method.

I did the Henry V project because I had a dream to do so. I tell about that in the book Clown Secret, and also in the autobiographical show Harlequin Dreams that is on Youtube. Although Harlequin Dreams is only about 45 minutes it is listed with Parts 1-4, and the 5th Part is listed as "Final Part". But prior to that Henry V production I had never read nor seen Henry IV Part 1 or Part 2; the plays which preceded Henry V. In other words really my insights into Shakespeare are about my intuition, not my studies in libraries. However, it was my colleague, Professor Tom Bishop, Co-Editor of the Shakespeare International Yearbook who suggested that I start to study Falstaff the clown in Henry IV Parts 1 and 2. Prof. Tom Bishop is a Patron of I.S.A.A.C. (International School for Acting and Creativity).

You can not do Shakespeare justice unless you tap into the vein of insight. Libraries and scholars will help.

I'll tell you a few more personal anecdotes about Shakespeare so you can know more about the teacher you are about to trust. In so telling I hope to hit your vein of insight, your lost memories of Shakespeare, playing, oratory (oration, ora, aura, aural, oral).

My father was a travelling salesman who had a few "gifts" but really he had wanted to be a writer. His favourite writer was William Makepeace Thackeray. My father always called me Thack. On Saturdays we sometimes went to the library. Carnegie Library in Oakland, Pittsburgh. There were huge, god-like statues in front of the combined museum & library. My father would lift me so I could sit in the lap of one. Shakespeare.

At age fifteen while attending Richard Montgomery High School of Rockville, Maryland, I had an inspiring English teacher who was a pure orator. She was a Black American from the South. Once she read to us part of Shakespeare's play Julius Caesar. When she hit "Beware the Ides of March" something in me opened up. She was astounding.

2 years later at Taylor Allderdice High School in Squirrel Hill, Pittsburgh, in my senior year, by some fluke I got stuck in the class for the top students. Who me? I sat quiet as a mouse as these discussions bounced around the room all over my head. Then one day we were taking turns reading Shakespeare. When it came to my turn in seconds I was flying with the language. Totally taken, it completely stunned the class. The teacher congratulated me and admitted he had no idea what I was capable of. Nor did I.

Four years later I was 21, fresh out of the navy and through coincidence I fell into the theatre. An art student needed another actor for her student production. The theatre professor at college watched the performance and afterwards said I was to act in her coming production. That was "A Midsummer Night's Dream" and I was cast as Lysander.

There were a couple of guest professionals in the production. At the first play reading there was a fat old gentleman, Tony Yenias. We sat in a circle. Tony had no script. But he knew all the cues and lines, and corrected the actors' pronunciation. He knew the play back to front. Tony had "Done the Dream" five times, he had also been an Opera singer, and had taught English, French, Greek, Latin, German, and Italian. He played Peter Quince and Egeus. He was inspiring. Another guest professional was an English teacher; comedian, clown and juggler - Art Jennings, Jr whose Father started the International Jugglers Association. Our director, Professor Trudy Scott, was an ex-Broadway hoofer and musical actress turned academic. One day I had an hour to myself with the director. I went through my lines but decided it was ridiculous I didn't know how to act and this stuff (i.e., Shakespeare) doesn't make any sense please get someone else. I can't do this, I don't know what I am saying. It doesn't sound right. It was awful. I felt awful. She was patient but adamant that I not give up. I pleaded for her to let me out of the production. She pleaded that I just relax and come back tomorrow. She was a better actor, so she won.

The next day as I went to speak my first lines it was as if a spirit took me. Like I was speaking in tongues. I was away and flying. I felt the language. Wow. That was it, my life was turned to theatre. I learned to juggle, act, tumble then apprenticed an old clown Danny Chapman. Next step on the journey was to study mime and Commedia Dell 'Arte with Carlo Mazzone-Clementi. He loved Shakespeare and Dante. Carlo's dream was that one day his students would act Shakespeare. So, I created a Shakespeare act based on a soliloquy but I improvised Shakespearean speech. It was performed on Friday and Saturday nights in taverns in three towns. I earned my living by passing the hat in working class bars doing Shakespeare. To quiet and control the pub audience through language, action and performance was a great teacher. I never used a microphone and was never scheduled or announced. The piece was comic and tragic.

Now let's talk about you. You must feel Shakespeare. Intuit the language. Control your senses to drive the audience. Command their attention, take them on a flying carpet with speed, clarity and dexterity. Move and entertain your audience. You are your audience, your teacher, your pupil. If you are already an actor, you must improvise, grow, study, and take risks.

PHASE 1

Select any soliloquy or monologue from Shakespeare. Learn the whole speech. Memorise. You can take any play and any speech of at least 25 lines. For my purposes and method you do not need to know the play back to front, nor the character inside-out. But you must know what each word means so you will need the notes for your particular speech. So you may as well get the whole play. Who knows you may want to read it. And re-read it. I recommend the following publishers' versions of Shakespeare's plays: Arden, Cambridge, RSC. The RSC is more convenient but the Cambridge and Arden editions have more extensive background notes. The RSC is better in your hands working, but the other two are better at your desk.

Memorising is not only mental but also physical. It is like choreography for the tongue and lips. Eventually you choreograph the breathing. I mean choreograph loosely. However I did work in one project with Alex Hays who told me that he knew every bit of Shakespeare including all of the grammar and breathing. Alex taught at the national school and amongst his fine students were Mel Gibson and Judy Davis. Alex taught primarily by telling stories in the classroom and by simply rehearsing on the floor.

There is not one way to do a speech, a character, or a play. It depends on style, effect desired and aesthetics. Just as your life can be different day to day so too can the feel of the speech.

Different actors have their own ways, needs and tricks of memorisation. You must find what works for you. And what isn't working requires a creative solution. Make one up.

Here's what I recommend. It is not gospel. But it will work.

Stage 1. Spend one hour a day saying your speech. Do it five days in a row.

The question is how to spend the hour and how to say your speech.

Read it aloud. Stand up. Feel it. Feel what is good, what is odd, what is interesting. Play with it. Act out. Use your imagination.

After working an hour on the first day, you will then with pen and paper, write out your monologue/soliloquy three times. Line by line, including all punctuation.

Stage 2. You are familiar with the text. Now you must be free from holding the book.

Here is a half-way step which quickens your ability to be word perfect. Use this after you have worked at least three days in a row, working one hour on the floor each day. "On the floor" means standing, moving i.e. working actively up on your feet.

Copy your soliloquy on a sheet of paper in the following manner. Keep the first letter of each word, keep all capital letters, keep all punctuation. Keep to a line by line copy as it is printed in the text whether it is prose or verse. Single letter words such as "I" and "a" write the whole word. Print rather than use script. For example: from King Lear Act II Scene iv.

> *I prithee, daughter, do not make me mad.*
> *I will not trouble thee, my child; farewell.*
> *We'll no more meet, no more see one another ... etc.*

thus becomes

> *I p------, d-------, d- n-- m--- m-- m--.*
> *I w--- n-- t------ t---, m- c----; f-------.*
> *W-'—n- m--- m---, n- m--- s-- o-- a------.*

Test your memory by this Half-Way. Naturally as you need to refer back to the fully-printed text this will not only point out what you haven't memorised but what you need to study in terms of meaning and understanding.

An hour with this Half-Way for three days and you should have any soliloquy well memorised. I am in fact talking about an hour of rote learning. Remember genius is 90% perspiration and 10% inspiration.

Each person works with memory in a different way and different speed. It is true that memory will hold quickest and best when you understand what and why you are saying something. But it still requires some form of rote, conscious repetition.

After three days of working "Half-way", sit and write out the whole speech without looking at the printed or previously written text. Then compare what you had just written with the book's printed version. NOTE: The one caution with "Half-way" is that the word 'that' and 'this' and 'then' and 'thus' each begin with the same letter and each is the same length of four letters. You must check early in the process that you are saying every correct word in a speech.

Stage 3. Eventually you will mix this stage with stage 1 and 2.

Learn Line by line. LLL. Each line should be a single breath. Practice this with a complete pause and breath between each line and a bold fresh start at the beginning of each line. The line is not a sentence. There can be three sentences in a single line. Or a line may be a single complete sentence. But for this step it is to Learn Line by Line. We will get to sentences and punctuation in a moment.

Eventually you will attempt to develop your breathing so that you can say several lines clearly in one breath. To do this you must speak very quickly without sacrificing clarity. Tyrone Guthrie insisted on 7 to 10 lines in a single breath, which seems to me daunting. In performance this may not be necessary or appropriate.

Your breathing is important to find the rhythm and flow of speech.

Stage 4. Breathing, Diction, Articulation.

Breathing. Let your jaw relax. Allow your jaw to hang naturally so that your mouth is slightly open. Focus your inhalation. Cool soft breath in. Warm soft breath out. Let your face soften and relax. Let your eyes and eyelids soften and relax. Let your tongue soften, lengthen and widen so that it softens forward. Let the back of your tongue relax. Deepen your breathing, picture an open cavity from the part of your mouth to the bottom of your spine.

Diction. Imagine that each word has a beginning, middle and an end. That is also a good speech exercise, saying each word separately: "Every Word Has A Beginning Middle And An End". Imagine that each word starts and ends with a percussive sound or consonant. In between is a long sound or vowel. For example, "end".

> *eh*   begin
> *na*   middle
> *da*   end.

the basic vowels to practice are

> *ah ay ee eye oh oo*

Rediscover (with the same breathing relaxation we just used) how each vowel sound feels in the mouth, chest, torso, and head. Say each vowel with an open mouth. Let each vowel last 4 seconds. Feel how the mouth shape is different for each vowel.

Now combine each vowel sound with each consonant in the alphabet. For example:

> B: *B-ah B-ay B-ee B-eye B-oh B-oo*
> C: *C-ah C-ay C-ee C-eye C-oh C-oo*

Once you go through the alphabet let's look at the sounds of B-D-G with a vowel sound uh as in "ugh" thus you have:

B-uh D-uh G-uh. These three sounds link B-D-G being the Front, Middle and Back of the mouth. Try to use an active percussive approach B-D-G and reverse G-D-B all with the uh sound. Then do the same with P-T-K which is also Front-Middle-Back. Then Back-Middle-Front P-T-K.

Articulation. Imagine that each word in a line is a separate life force, completely separate from the previous or next word. For example:

i/prithee/daughter/do/not/make/me/mad.

Find the beginning, middle and end of each word.

Then find the primary percussive sound B-D-G, P-T-K in the line. i/Prithee/DaughTer/Do/noT/maKe/me/maD. Read the whole line emphasising these sounds BDG, PTK. Repeat this several times.

Say the line again in one breath, flowing as if the line were one word.

Now say the line as if you were already mad. Mad angry or mad crazy? Try it each way a few times.

Next look at the word prithee. Say the whole line as if you were pleading. Then as if you were praying.

I mix this last creative part i.e., emphasis on the "mad' and "prithee" with the Breathing, Diction, Articulation because the words are reliant on a vehicle called the actor. The actor must as often as possible, as soon as possible engage their own creative, imaginative emotional faculties.

Stage 5. Punctuation. Pause and Breathe at each punctuation mark, i.e., comma, semi-colon, period, question mark, and the end of each line.

Do that, now, line to line. This process should start to give you new insight into the character's emotion and unique rhythm of expression. Take your time. Note any subtle insights.

Repeat this process through the whole soliloquy. Take your time. Repeat a few times starting to go with the flow. Follow your feelings and ideas. Play with the ideas. Let go of any preconceived notions of the text, character or play. Discover what the character says. Discover what you would feel as the character.

Stage 6. Sentence. Read each sentence. Each single sentence as if it was the only thing you were to say. Relax and let your thoughts and feelings come to you. Play with your delivery of each sentence in the following ways: Neutral, with Vehemence, with Nonchalance as if it was Noel Coward, with Humour as if you were a clown in a circus.

Now, try the whole soliloquy only pausing for breath at each full stop.

You may find that one publication prints a period where another puts a different mark. I have always found new insight from this slight difference. It is rare however to find such a difference. This brings up the important point about punctuation. How long you pause at each mark is relative to the speed and intention of your delivery and interpretation.

As a guideline though let's just look at the four main punctuation points - (.) (:) (;) (,). It is similar to a musical whole note, half note, quarter note and eighth note.

Put another way, imagine (.) = 4 seconds, (:) = 2 seconds, (;) = 1 seconds and (,) = half a second. (?) and (!) are the same as (.).

Punctuation as we have looked at it gives an indication of a change of thought, pace or rhythm. It does not really mean a pause at all. The pause and breath approach is a very important technical aid to assist with learning or performing a speech. Shakespeare requires above all speed, rhythm and clarity. It is awash with images which catch up and become clear on a subliminal level. Perhaps more so than on a conscious level. This is really where the power of words and language lies. This is the power of Oratory. The Bards of Ireland studied for twelve years to learn the power of words in their poetic rhythms. That knowledge is dominant in Shakespeare. It can only be released when we open to this unknown power. The technique of voice, breathing, diction, etc are to clear away obstacles so that something more divine can flow through the vehicle of the actors. The actor is not the source. Perhaps Shakespeare was not the source as much as the vehicle. A very great vehicle. There is a saying "Let go and let God". Whatever your viewpoint of Universal Laws, it is important to clarify your use of language to your own, individual potential.

Stage 7 Soliloquy.

Say the whole soliloquy. Imagine it as one single clear flow. Imagine that the single point and focus is really the last line. Try it.

Next time try it with the same flow and focus yet being more conscious of each sentence and the idea-feel-emotion behind it.

PHASE 2

Each stage of Phase One is important and completely necessary to allow the richness of language to flow through you.

The necessary questions for the actor about the character, meaning of each word and phrase, the sub-plot, relationships, etc will mostly arise spontaneously if you approach the text honestly through each stage.

This is not to negate any acting methods or techniques you wish to use or try.

Beyond any method, the demands and richness of Shakespeare's language require a joyous discipline of words.

Stage 8 Retreat to Advance.

Pick up your book again. Walk in a circle reciting each line with a pause for breath at the end of each line.

Do the whole speech while walking. Repeat this a few times.

There are several reasons to do this.

But first, what do you feel? What do you become aware of? What do you re-discover?

Some academics say that a normal pace or step is a metre. The speech rhythm of Iambic Pentameter can be felt in the body if you take a normal walking pace. Try to blend the rhythm of speech with the rhythm of your pace.

The walking will also help to flush out any breathing mistakes or it will help you to find rhythmical breathing. It will also help you to understand that delivery of Shakespeare is very physical, it is athletic. Just as Operatic singing is a very physical activity which engages the whole anatomy. It is not just a focus of a talking head. Engage your whole self and you will begin to engage an audience.

Stage 9. Sit down and have a look at the words again. Are there any words or phrases you are still not clear about? Have another look at the words. Back to King Lear Act II scene iv.

I prithee, daughter,

"daughter". Why is it not "son"? Why did Shakespeare create that King Lear has three daughters and Gloucester has two sons? That single word has the whole play behind it. Lear has "sons" which in a sense he cannot see, the Fool and Kent. Gloucester then loses his sight. Sight is a theme in the play mixed with various disguises and illusions "...no more see one another". This "see" takes on a much weightier quality.

I am not proposing that this is what King Lear, the play or character is all about. Simply, I pluck two words which ring a bell with me about the themes in the play concerning children (loyalty), sight (illusion), madness (fools, disguises, anger).

Stage 10 Soliloquy Structure.

King Lear Act I Scene ii - Edmund

I chose this for several reasons. It is a quite standard audition piece which means it is heavily laden with precedence of what "the character is all about". It is interesting to me because it has a tension, even a conflict, between a line reading (i.e., attempting to find or follow the meter) and a sentence (sense) reading. You must resolve this for yourself. It is also interesting in the context of Edmund being "caught" a moment later. In that moment he must shift from pleading (perhaps mad or angry) about the spiritual and emotional dilemma of his birth. His innocence. In the next moment we see him act out the illusion of innocence (play the fool) so he can plant a rather nasty seed. For my money, I love seeing Shakespeare characters "act" in order to get their way.

That Edmund speech. The words. Simply as they appear on the page.

Thou, Nature, art my goddess; to thy law
My services are bound. Wherefore should I
Stand in the plague of custom, and permit
The curiosity of nations to deprive me,
For that I am some twelve or fourteen moonshines
Lag of a brother? Why bastard? Wherefore base?
When my dimensions are as well compact,
My mind as generous, and my shape as true,
As honest madam's issue? Why brand they us
With base? With baseness? Bastardy? Base? Base?
Who, in the lusty stealth of nature, take
More composition and fierce quality
Than doth, within a dull, stale, tired bed,
Go to th' creating a whole tribe of fops
Got 'tween asleep and wake? Well then,
Legitimate Edgar, I must have your land.
Our father's love is to the bastard Edmund
As to th' legitimate. Fine word, "legitimate."
Well, my legitimate, if this letter speed,
And my invention thrive, Edmund the base
Shall top th' legitimate. I grow, I prosper.
Now, gods, stand up for bastards.

How many sentences are there? Seventeen. Ten of which are questions. Seventeen sentences in such a short passage is a lot. And so many questions. What else is in the structure of this particular soliloquy? Always look at the first and last line in a speech. This is a big hint.

In this passage the first line invokes "goddess", female, mother. The last commands "gods" male, father. Look at the idea of law, custom, legitimate. Law, legitimate, "L" what other "L" is in the passage, Lag, Lusty, duLL, staLe, Land, weLL, Letter, shaLL. Say these words and languish the "L"s.

Look again at goddess and god. Savour the "s". Look at line 10, try the line for the "s", think of the animal snake.

With base? With baseness? Bastardy? Base? Base? Look again. Say it again. "With". Consider the "th" a cousin to the "s". Say the line again.

Try the whole passage again.

Look at one of the longest sentences in the text. In the middle. It is perhaps phallic, Freudian, natural, sexual. It is located between "goddess" and "gods". Male and female. It comes just after a line about baseness. What does baseness mean, nature, tribe, got 'tween asleep and wake?

What child hasn't wondered about their own creation? How their parents met? About the procreation which gave birth to this child. Even a grown child, an adult wonders about creation and station in life. Edmund questions his own creation which was out of his hands as opposed to his future which is in his hands, in the letter. He has a letter in this scene. What is in the letter? What is his plan with the letter? In his mind is a lust for land "if this letter speed, and my invention thrive".

Read the whole speech again. considering his change from confused child to aggressive adult. "I grow, I prosper".

As you work the text you know how complex one small passage of Shakespeare is. It is not complex difficult, it is complex rich. It is like a detailed richly woven rug. We can either put it on the floor, the purpose for which it is made. Or we can put it on the wall for display. This is an aesthetic choice. I prefer the rug on the floor, but you must care for it so it will last and stay beautiful. But for its true beauty to come out it must be placed in the right spot.

Now that you know a soliloquy you must look again at what precedes and follows it. You must follow its many thread-like connections to other characters, themes in the play.

But you must also pursue two other things. First speaking with gusto, bold, strength, clarity and relish. Second, act it out. This is the opposite approach, take more time. Take all the time in the world, respect a word or phrase. Act out whatever comes to you. Try to feel your impulses to act. Feel, act, do rather than think out what you will do or try. Follow your most subtle impulse.

Try the whole passage again allowing your most subtle impulses, emotions to surface. Take your time again.

Good luck. You now have most of the keys and hints to open your enjoyment and ability to play Shakespeare.

My approach is unorthodox but it works very quickly and well. Cicely Berry books recommended are: *Voice and the Actor*; *The Actor and his text*; and, *Text in Action*.

Be sure to study more about voice, metre, text, acting, the body, etc. Have fun.

- 12 -
MIME AND VOICE

Actor training would benefit by having mime as a central subject. During all of the early stages of rehearsal the necessary props, furniture, costumes, even the other characters are not available. But you must pretend they are. In most auditions it is the same situation. The better you can act with nothing, the stronger the illusion to whomever watches. The words an actor speaks must come as if from their inner being. The more an actor becomes involved in the total picture the more true the words will seem. Mime is the grace, ease, and technique of the imagination, not just the technique of the body.

All of the basic illusions could be taught and also de-structured by combining movement improvisation with technical movement. For example there are two basic mime walks for the illusion of walking forward while actually staying on one spot. Those two illusions are: walking facing the audience; and, walking perpendicular to the audience. Once the actor can control the basic mechanics I have them play with combining or shifting from the forward then turning and then doing the sideways and back and forth and changing their turns left and right. Then do a few steps of a normal actual walk and turn that normal walk into, and out of, either sideways or forward mime walks.

Coordination of eyes, hands, feet, breathing, spine articulation, open joints-hips-elbows-shoulders, the whole body is the essence of mime. Ballet gently taught for adults is an ideal foundation for mime. Next level of technique is the technique of Etienne Decroux, or that of Henryk Tomaszewski. Tomaszewski's company trained in ballet at the start of each day. Decroux's method is a four-years course, but he said any ballet dancer could learn his method in six months.

Any of those three techniques combined with free movement, free improvisation is the most beneficial way to teach technique. Tomaszewski's company followed their morning ballet class with Commedia dell'arte style improvisations before rehearsals.

If the body is trained and the imagination is free then mime is quite natural. There are many problems with mime or physical theatre schools. I discuss those in the first chapters in the book *Clown Secret*. Train the body, not the imagination. Too often in mime/physical theatre training what is called creativity is a definite bias of style. Good mime training implies that the actor can perform, some basics of pure mime technique perhaps of Decroux, but also Pantomime of Marceau, or of the silent film clowns. It can be helpful to imitate Chaplin or Keaton by taking just one minute sections when they appear in a solo scene or moment.

Much of the training of mime using elements, colour, motive, is subjective or relative to the teacher's dogma. Mime training should be purely objective. Interpretation of elements, colour, etc is subjective and depends on culture, education, social, and relative perspectives. Thus in one culture black is used for some events for which another culture would only use white. Beware of any training of mime which mixes objective physical control with subjective aesthetics!

The good mime training harmonises the physical expression of breath, body, imagination. Add to that some very basic voice work and you will have the basis of a very expressive actor.

The voice training also needs to be very physical and practical. Stretching and relaxing, articulating the tongue. Strengthening yet relaxing the throat and vocal cords. Learning to pitch and tone the voice just as with mime you control your tempo, rhythmic energy. Also voice work needs to be expressive and playful thus plenty of improvisation following each technical session is imperative. The more interesting voice work today is related to overtones, falsetto, open throat shouting. Here again we can see in the work of Chinese, Japanese, and Polish training that they have known all along the secrets. Classical diction, volume, articulation are not to be thrown out. It is just that traditional speech control for speaking nicely and properly based on the English "speech and drama" is not the be all and end all of the theatre. There are many good traditional and classical voice methods. In chapter 10, Shakespeare, I have expressed several ideas on training the voice. Now you must practice.

- 13 -
YOGA

The word yoga means union or to join. There is also an older definition which means to harness, as in a yoke worn on a beast of burden to pull its burden.

When I speak of yoga I do not mean to imply that I am a yogi nor am I a guru nor am I an expert on yoga.

I did practice and study yoga for twenty years. I did train as a yoga teacher. Yoga for me is not a religion, not a spiritual path and not physical exercise and not meditation.

During my life yoga has been a tool for me to observe myself. In this sense it has helped me to harness my different energies into a better harmony of living. I can't say that I achieved 'harmony'. It is just that I tried and still try. Yoga was one tool for many years. I still enjoy yoga when I occasionally practice or when I read or study some aspect. Perhaps two of my favourite books are B.K.S.Iyengar's *Light on the Yoga Sutras of Patanjali*; and, the book *Awakening the Spine* by Vanda Scaravelli.

As you sit and read just now you can practice yoga. Be aware of your posture, be aware not to hold your breath but to let the breath flow naturally. Allow your face, eyes, and space inside your head to relax. Become aware of your thoughts but not attached to them. Let your thoughts disappear.

This then is the beginning of yoga. Conscious awareness of yourself, just as you are at this moment. Once you have a relaxed, quiet, awareness then you need a focus.

The focus of yoga is a duality of action - non action. For example if you attempt a posture of just standing you must examine what it feels like to stand as if it were the first time and perhaps even the first human. Just stand, but become conscious of the posture, breath, balance, lightness.

Balance in yoga is not a still body. Balance implies adjustment of the body and stillness inside. Balance is the relation of muscles, bones, joints, ligaments, tendons to the pull of gravity and the system of weights and pulleys in the body. In other words one of the first steps in yoga is to become grounded in the body. To experience the union of the body and the Earth via the mind and breath.

This very simple practice can naturally lead us then to elevate our consciousness to other levels of our existence. Linking us to the whole planet, the solar system, the galaxy, and beyond.

Yoga is a very obvious, practical, direct way to experience the magic and mystery of life. Perhaps not to understand it all but to experience it directly through our body and consciousness.

Yoga is not to be confused with exercise, aerobics, sport. Yoga is about humanity. Yoga practise which has a strong focus on the body or prayer or meditation is true yoga only when connected to ethics and service to other humans.

Naturally there is a vast array of beliefs about yoga. But here let us contemplate a triad DISCIPLINE, ETHICS, SERVICE.

You must resolve the triad of yoga yourself. That is life. Perhaps a teacher can guide you. But in the end we each must practice DISCIPLINE, ETHICS, SERVICE.

The practice of yoga postures (asanas) is to help you to live your life. In the process you may very well become healthy, strong, joyous, creative, giving, tolerant, energised.

Some practical advice about yoga and the theatre. Balance. Balance your yoga practice with your training in all aspects of theatre. Find the yoga inside theatre. Again the triad of Discipline, Ethics, and Service should be applied to all aspects of theatre life. Good luck.

In your practice of yoga postures here are some keys which are quite helpful and important.

1. Relax your face
2. Work with soft eyes
3. Your teeth should be parted, tongue relaxed, lips barely touching
4. Breathing should be light, deep, relaxed, & flow naturally

Particular attention should be to observe the natural movement of the rib cage, chest, diaphragm. Here is a general principle of two halves of the body divided by the waist. Find the anchor in the body, often the legs. The hands and feet are always active yet relaxed. The placement and relation of the pelvis and neck needs gentle awareness and caution at all times.

Five minutes of yoga is better than none. There is a saying that any posture done well has the benefits of all postures.

Where to turn for guidance. Try the library, read a bit, practice a lot. Some books that I recommend are: *Yoga the Iyengar Way*; *Awakening the Spine*; and *Light on the Yoga Sutras of Patanjali*. The benefit of books and practice is that you can organically come to your own understanding and conclusions. Iyengar pursued a scientific and anatomical approach to the body and practice of yoga. His system means that their teachers are arduously trained. Vanda Scaravelli, who wrote *Awakening the Spine* has a softer approach. Though the approaches are opposites, those are equally valid as are many other systems. *Light on the Yoga Sutras of Patanjali* is a superb guide to Patanjali's ancient masterpiece. *Light on the Yoga Sutras of Patanjali* by Iyengar, I also consider a book that offers a great insight into my method's integration of mind and body.

There are many yogic organisations. Beware. Each has a different focus, often a broad focus in many spheres of life. They claim to be the true way, the new way, the best way, the only way, the way of light, of love etc.They claim that their guru is the authentic teacher. They claim their guru is the Messiah. Maybe they are all right. Who knows? I don't. These organisations are <u>very</u> well run businesses. Beware. Enlightenment is free to all. But you must practice. These organisations create excellent facilities to practice in. Beware, but do not be cynical. Beware of sweet talking bait. Sad but true, this is just the art of salesmanship, the real teachers are often more close to a lion than a lamb. If you find a group to be a part of, good. But beware if your group is against or antagonistic towards other enlightened groups. This is part of human nature as we know it. It's the same human responses in theatre, business, politics, religion.

Yoga is a practice which can slice right thru all human conflicts, it is a very powerful tool for human revolution/evolution. However, always within an organisation yoga becomes a religion i.e. a dogmatic cult that is anti-religious yet is itself fundamentalist in its own entrenched belief system.

- 14 -
THEATRE CLOWN

The clown /fool is not only a part of theatre but the keystone and primary secret of theatre craft. Clowning is a very big field to study. There are many types of clowns. The clown is a central figure who keeps popping up in theatre. Why? How?

If we take the works of Shakespeare as a great body of theatre literature, ideas, craft and history. In those plays we see a lot of clowns! In his greatest works there are a variety of clowns. In King Lear, the Fool is as prominent as the King. In Hamlet there is the placement of Yorick, Rosencrantz and Guilderstern, the players, in fact Shakespeare seems to like clowns and clowning a lot!!! The rustic clowns in A Winter's Tale, or the devilish clowns of Puck, Caliban, Ariel, Launcelot and Ol'Gobbo, or the old Pantalone figure of Desdemona's father. The evil bastard clowns who like to lie and cheat, such as Iago, Richard III, Buckingham, the Comic Murderers. The central 'clowns' such as Menenius, Fluellan, Richard II, Falstaff. The clowning antics of Prince Hal, Henry V, Romeo. The working class clowns in Feste, the whores, priests, maids, politicians. Shakespeare is filled with clowning, stupidity, foolishness, the twists of language.

To understand the place of clowns and comedy is to understand theatre literature. Without this understanding you'll be left with a most boring, tedious, uptight, conservative understanding of our theatre heritage. The acid tongue clown is central to Brecht. Only the bigness and brashness, and full dimension of a clown can fill the boots of Mother Courage's tragedy. (Note: Brecht's great early mentor was the theatre and musical clown Karl Valentin. Brecht was in Valentin's troupe for two years). The clown is a tragedy. Humans must joke to survive. Soldiers have always rollicked to remove the stains in their hearts. Can you imagine the cackle of humour from a harem of prostitutes? How long has Commedia portrayed the pomposity of professors, doctors, lawyers, religious ones, political creatures? Strindberg is filled with the absurdities of the human drama. Anton Chekhov, Nikolai Gogol, Lope de Vega, Ben Jonson, Jean Racine, and Molière are filled with the trash of human foolishness. The ancient Greeks had to be able to write the most outrageous ribald comedy to accompany the blackest tragedy. Even Oedipus Rex can be seen as the blackest and saddest fool ever written.

We see the breadth of clowning that shows up wherever we look in our noble theatre. But not every clown character ever created has the title clown.

You are a clown if you are human. It is a part of humanity. Simple.

A clown implies tragedy as well as humour and bad taste as well as laughter.

How to learn more about clowning? The art of clowning? First the physical expression. A clown must be able to dance, mime and fall. I would go first to dance as a discipline for clowns, Technical and expressive & creative. Train the body first, put it in a comic situation second. Those are the seeds of mime for the clown.

Then there are gags. Mechanics of comedy which can be learned, studied, adapted. Certain few books mentioned in a moment below can help. The Four Articulations for Performance will give you the solid base. The masters of gags are the Russian circus clowns, the American circus clowns, and the Traditional European circus clowns. Old retired nearly dead clowns know the most. The young clowns have received watered down information and watered down experience and watered down technique. Even Chaplin relied on a gag master Henry Bergman for thirty years. When Buster Keaton "retired" he was the gag master in Hollywood. Woody Allen's gags are straight out of ancient Greece by way of the Ghetto. Gags are great. But gags were really part of very elaborate routines which were completely logical, creative, and relied on good acting, clear movement, articulate voices, and technique of mime, dance, acrobatic, juggling, or music.

Now we are warming up. Clowning is knowledge of gags, routines, techniques. It is a very solid art form itself. It is not a red nose and improvisation, these are simply two tools.

Clowning in the theatre is often within a well written play. Can the clown play according to the rules of this play, this director, this production? A clown in the theatre must know the technique of grammar, voice, mime, and classical acting.

What about original clowning? What about it, are you kidding? In the world of clowning nothing is original. The combination of elements, techniques, characters, personalities is likely to be an original mix. The gags, routines, and techniques are O-L-D, traditional. Clowning is based on tradition. The audience knows the tradition and the clown knows how to hit the right buttons: happy, sad, surprise, silly, absurd, dirty, cute, good, bad, angry, loving, peace, war, confused, abused, lyrical, metaphorical, rhythmical, arhythmic. This can all be written, structured, improvised. Improvised in this case means like cooking a meal at home. You take what ingredients you have, but you already know how to cook. You already know what is too hot and too cold. But maybe today you try a surprise ingredient. Voila! Well I won't try that again. You learn by experience. Traditional clowns had a chance to make lots of mistakes. They had the chance to try out their skills as they developed. Now clowns learn how to imitate dildos which are things that are already fake, not the real thing. Recently I looked at the first 20 or 30 Chaplin films (now available on video). He did some really awful stuff.

He was nasty. "You have to be bad to be good" is what Jango Edwards used to tell audiences.

Where does all this leave you the actor or theatre director. Even a very good book is not complete. Books collectively comprise a more complete picture. The books mentioned above: *Clown Secret* by Ira Seidenstein; *Clown Scenes* by Tristan Remy; *Clown for Circus & Stage* by Mark Stolzenberg; the two books by Barry Grantham on commedia are excellent 'clown' books. Importantly, my basic method The Four Articulations for Performance will assist you immediately to be able to actually understand and interpret those books. Note that chapter 2 in *Clown Secret* provides clear, simple, step-by-step instructions for each exercise of the Four Articulations for Performance. In the past the best training has been the Moscow Circus School. That school covered the whole range from tradition to modern with clear technique.

With the few books I've mentioned and specifically with The Four Articulations, you also can study, learn, and practice magic, juggling, music, dance, voice etc. When I was getting very curious about clowning I met Lotte Goslar. She had been a clown over 40 years. She warned me about schools, and I'm warning you. Lotte said "A clown must create their own world". The Four Articulations will directly assist your own discovery and self-knowledge. Goslar had been a dancer with Mary Wigman. Years later Lotte took about six dancers every year and trained them in mime and directed them in a show called Lotte Goslar's Pantomime Circus. They learned the right way: technique, gags, routines, performance and the guidance of a loving disciplined teacher. A similar process was run by the Royal Lichtenstein Quarter-Ring Sidewalk Circus created by Nick Weber.

There are many plays written with clowns in mind. How good the productions are though depends on the actors and directors. There are also operas and ballets with clowns. Traditional folk dance from many cultures have clowns in some of the dances.

Sorry, I'm not more help here but it is simple. But, get *Clown Secret* and start practicing with chapter 2. See as many different types of clowns as you can.... even if you don't like what they're doing. Remember clowning is technique, gags, routines, imagination, and love.

- 15 -
CLASSICAL ACTING AND STYLE

Classical acting is the type of thing of which one can say "You'll know it when you see it".

Classical Acting implies that the players are reliant upon technique and craft. They rely on the craft of the director. The director relies on the craft of the playwright and the actors. The actors use their voice, speech, and body language to express precisely what the playwright intended. No more no less.

In my eight years of seeing as much theatre as I could in Australia it became clear that playing a style well and classically well is quite difficult and rare.

Some modern plays create their own classical form. So in Australia a play such as, "The Summer of the Seventeenth Doll", has it's own classical form. In the USA the plays of Tennessee Williams, Arthur Miller, Neil Simon have their own classical form. Likewise in France there is an unbroken traditional form of Molière and in Sweden there is some classical form for Strindberg's different works.

In all of these cases the discipline of delivering the text and giving shape to the production is within a clear framework. However, many young actors do not know how specific their technique must be except in plays written one or two generations ago. There is a problem and actors must learn that classical discipline and conscious understanding of behaviour on stage is not just exuberance.

In truth exactly what makes one popular on TV (personal idioms and exuberance) can be diabolical to classical acting. They do not necessarily cancel each other but often they do. Classical acting is very much about grammar and mannerisms both of which must be respected and understood.

In Australia for example there are plenty of young and middle aged and older actors who could and would act classically given the right circumstances. Rarely would one see a cast 100% acting in the same classical sense (except in musicals). There will always be someone acting out James Deanishly in a tragedy, or being Mr. Bean in a comedy, and getting laughs everywhere 'cept where 'twas written.

I am certain teachers think they are teaching classical acting, actors think they are acting it, and directors think they are doing the best they could. Often, that ain't necessarily so.

The acting teachers who teach the tradition must also educate people who are lost in a world of techno, video, designer drugs, and liberalism. Classical acting is not liberal. Everything has specific value, need and meaning within the context of the play. It can be a lot of fun, but you can not James Dean your way through. You cannot just say your lines with deep meaningful looks. It must all be correct. The way you walk and the way you talk. It is tedious and time consuming. But that is the only way we hear the eloquence of the writer's voice.

I have seen many an iconoclast production of a classic text with unlimited virtue in concept but the reality is a gross work of art rather than a refined one.

When doing a classic today we must know what to update. But when doing an iconoclast version we must know what to keep. I am all for chopping, changing, playing with classics. But there is a lot of craft being lost over an immature need to be free, modern, contemporary, original. Brecht has a classical style, musicals do, a rock concert does.

I started to understand this classical problem when I assisted a walking theatre encyclopaedia Mr. Lisle Jones. He knew style, almost every style in western theatre and could articulate the differences, virtues, and values. He directed Noel Coward's "TONIGHT AT 8.30" a group of one act pieces each in a different style. The language differences are the guideline.

When crossing over the ideas of classical acting and style we can look at another giant, Mr. Shakespeare. In a given play the language of characters is often drastically different and implies a very different style to be acted. You cannot have James Dean playing Prospero and a look-alike act-alike playing Ariel. You could have Ariel by a Michael Jackson, Miranda by a Madonna, and Caliban by a Gerard Depardieu. But would they pay attention to the grammar? No doubt Depardieu would, I'm not sure about the others. Then again he has the advantage of spending time in jail. Briefly, 3 months in jail for stealing a car. So he has an insight into what freedom is. To many actors playing a style or acting classically is to be imprisoned. Everyone in theatre, film and literature worlds can argue over Depardieu's version of Cyrano, but maybe it was the ideal version of a classical done well for today's audience. So doing a classical is not meant to please the critic and professor yet leave the public snoring.

You can do a classic however you want. I am concerned because actors appear not capable to do it well no matter which way the production is set. They can't handle the text which means they don't let the grammar guide the rhythm and they don't reach into their soul to grasp the depth of meaning. A classic has not the same meaning as an in-depth interview on MTV. In fact many a video on MTV hints at the same issues as a classic play but does not give the public a chance to breathe and reach within. We are not meant to feel anything except the need to buy new grunge clothes. Humanity has always lost the plot. That is why a classic can always offend and challenge what is modern.

- 16 -
DIRECTION

You can do a directing course and learn a lot. This directing course no matter how long, intense, thorough, will not make you an interesting, gifted, nor an exciting director. You can learn directing as a craft.

There are all types of directors, and any type can be quite good. I would not say one way of directing is better than another.

A variety of theatre experience can help. Life experience though is probably the more important factor in good directing.

Directing for me implies that you face life and deal with problems. Problems. You can solve them or avoid them. If you are a director that means problems of human, technical and logistical nature must be encountered by you and your team. You do not have to have all the answers.

One director who was a mentor for me was Antoine Saleh. Antoine graduated in directing at the Sorbonne in Paris during the 1960's. The first year the directing students were never allowed to direct an actor. During the first year the directing students had to direct each other. Thus they could abuse, argue, enlighten, and terrorise amongst themselves. That is they could work out their own psychological problems. They also had to act and pull the projects together themselves. As a result Antoine says that directing is 95% psychology. I would say this means understanding fellow human beings and seeing clearly that an actor is a human being working in a very peculiar and vulnerable situation. I would further say that the psychology which a director uses should be strictly to help actors, technicians, and staff to work better and with harmony and individuality. In other words the director is a part of a moral and ethical matrix which defines the human community.

This is not airy fairy. Get the job done, do it well but treat the actors well. This requires not just honesty, candour and empathy but a decent businesslike approach. Director is a very special role to play. I have seen far too many people directing and calling themselves directors who should never be allowed near an actor. I have seen, met and worked with plenty of wonderful directors. How do you train a wonderful director? During Antoine's study there was a three month festival of companies playing Shakespeare, from around the world and appearing in Paris. As part of the training the directing students spent three months seeing each production in the festival. At this course also, the regular lecturer in the history of mime was Marcel Marceau, the Wednesday mime class was taught by Jean-Louis Barrault, regular lectures in philosophy were given by Jean-Paul Sartre. Directing requires that you open your eyes, your heart, your mind. Directing is very difficult. It is not about books though it requires an intelligent understanding of humanity. Each director must draw on their own interests, passions, insights, desires, dreams and experiences. This is the beginning of what enriches the theatre in the broadest sense. Even a director's weaknesses, vices, humour, wit, curiosity can add to a richer experience for the actor and audience. A few years after Antoine graduated, he returned to the Sorbonne for one year to study only light and lighting.

Some directors I worked with for only one day as in a TV commercial, some for only one project, some for one year, some for different projects. Some directors were friends and peers and we would see each others' projects and spend time discussing life and theatre.

Commercials on TV and Cinema ads provided me with money to produce my own theatre projects. Those commercials also provided me with different experiences as an actor. As an actor I got to watch how another director ran a working environment.

One of the best directing lessons I ever had was from a one-day commercial shoot. I'll call the director Mr. D. When I arrived at the studio Mr. D was there, at the door, to greet me. He owned the studio. On this day it was only he and I in the studio. He had designed the set. He built the set too though perhaps with help. I watched him set up the lights. Mr. D then proceeded to direct and operate the camera. What I learned from him was not to be a one-man band. He wasn't it's just that for him it was another work day. Simple. What I learned though was how simple and clear he was. Whether he told me what to do or asked me to try something he was clear, simple, polite, direct. I would try to do what he said. Each time we adjusted he corrected what he had said previously as he zeroed in on what he had to say to get me to do exactly what he wanted. According to Mr. D the actor never made a mistake. It was the director's job to try again and again to get the actor to do exactly what the director wanted. To him the job of the director was communication. As an actor my job is first to do exactly what the director says or asks, and to do it as best as I can. Then the director can adjust, change, or clarify to get me do what he or she wants.

Then there was the great commercial director who had a terrible stutter. I would stand there for several minutes while he tried to spit out the next direction. Or stand attentive for a long time while he tried to say "Thank you, that was very good, could you do that again?" He was an excellent director.

Another commercial director was a Mr. T who instead of the classic "lights, sound, camera, action" it was an elaborate improvisation which he uttered. "Okay, alright, okay here we go, everybody standing by okay sound are you ready, okay alright Ira are you ready now here we go, okay …" On and on it went until it was "action". Needless to say this annoyed me until I took it as a Zen experience and started to see that other aspects of this director were very good and very helpful. He drew out a special performance from me. He helped me. His way to help me was filled with absurdities but he helped. A few months later he helped me personally. He was a fine director.

The relation between director and actor is very special and can be very strange even in a very commercial situation.

During one period I played in a Neil Simon comedy in a small theatre. The director had about fifty years experience which included being a bit of a leading man. Owen Weingott. Owen gave me the co-lead in this play. Before the first day of rehearsal I found out a little about Owen. Yes he had played lead roles in many plays and worked on a great touring circuit. Owen had also been the fencing coach for an Olympic team, was an expert in judo, and had choreographed nearly 400 fights for theatre, film, and TV. So I was at least willing to try his method whatever that may be.

My co-lead had other ideas. This was JM. JM arrived with an armful of books, papers, maps. He knew everything about our characters. He had a map of NYC and could show me where our apartment was. He knew about the neighbourhood, the period, dates, current events. I thought, wow finally I will work with a real Method actor and learn this stuff from a practitioner. Owen the director explained the working process we would use, the schedule, etc. Everything was clear in advance. He would stick to the original stage directions except in a few cases. In 2 or 3 days we will have staged every entrance, exit, stage move and stage effect.

Well I never worked this way but okay. It's different and to me that is fun in itself. JM resisted all predetermined moves. Owen had to explain everything that involved JM and soon one of the other actors started to demand explanations. We finished phase one, all of the staging. After three days I was excited because Owen would openly teach me about acting in a comedy plus other classic stagecraft. I felt that I was in the hands of a theatre master of classical stagecraft. JM wanted to resolve things his own way. JM was an outstanding and gifted actor and a very kind person. But JM had some misunderstandings about theatre and acting. Owen tried to help him. In one instance Owen said "don't do it like that. If you do that you'll have trouble in performance."

Sure enough Owen was correct. I was thus in trouble too since JM and I were the co-leads. From JM I learned quickly the strong and weak points of Method Acting. I learned why basic stagecraft and common sense must be used always with any method. Owen also taught me how to see and trust that Neil Simon is a master craftsman. I learned about precise mechanics of text and action.

Just before working with Owen, I had been teaching at a state acting school called WAAPA. WAAPA had a real period of greatness for five years. The overall director was Dr. Geoff Gibbs. He was a rollicking, fun loving, bear of a man who still worked as an actor. The WAAPA theatre department was lead by Aarne Neeme. Aarne was a happy and light hearted workaholic. Aarne was a classic director who could rather easily tackle any play. He gave the actors tremendous leeway to resolve the character and action, but also insisted on their responsibility. When necessary Aarne would sweep and mop the theatre or rig and run lights. Until the age of 21 he had been a ballet dancer. After Geoff and Aarne came the Head of Acting, Lisle Jones. Geoff was the clown, Aarne was the busy bee and great facilitator, and Lisle was the walking encyclopaedia of theatre. Lisle was of the "old school". His knowledge was profound and precise when it came to Western classic playwrights yet equal also with the playful-prodigious-pucks of print such as Ionesco, Beckett, Pirandello, Pinter, Ayckbourn, Miller, Coward. When Lisle directed he focused on style. Not his style but the playwright's. He made distinction between any two playwrights and between two plays of a single writer. Distinctions in language, action, intention were noted. Different classes and types of characters in a play had to be approached with distinct solutions from the actor. He did not tell the actor exactly what to do. Lisle taught and told them whatever they didn't know. He explained history, techniques, choices. He focused on the work at hand

and the context of the play's reality. Lisle was still an actor. Still studying and open minded.

A clown, a busy bee, an encyclopaedia,... next was the artist. The Head of Directing was Caesare Ross Coli. Directing for him combined clown, hard work, knowledge but all moving towards a vision of light and love. Ross was totally impossible to control or comprehend. He was thoroughly embraced by the other three chiefs. Ross was an immensely gifted artist. His art was directing and his directing was always a work of art. He could drive actors right up the wall. Yet every time they went up the wall they found the light. Ross bordered on madness and often went over the border without a passport. When need be Aarne held Ross like a baby. Part of Ross' madness was that when it came to directing, he was in the light. Aarne and Lisle though had the wisdom to stay grounded and Geoff always had humour. Do not emulate Ross' tragedy but learn from that young master to work for the delicate balance of light, sound, action. Directing is sensuous. It is not the act of a bully, a know-it-all, a psychiatrist, nor an intellectual. You are dealing with delicate matter just like a surgeon. A surgeon must also have strong arms and know where when to cut. A surgeon must also have assistants and assistance.

On different projects I assisted Aarne, Lisle, and Ross. Always I was brought in as choreographer and always I was allowed and encouraged to give acting notes and to coach the actors. Many of the actors at WAAPA were already hitting a high professional standard. After seeing them act, coaching them, studying them and teaching them, I decided to jump back into acting more again myself.

My relation to directing, acting, teaching and studying is ever flowing. By the time I was at WAAPA I had directed for 10 years without giving a thought to directing as a separate career for myself. Aarne, Lisle and Ross took me into the directors fold and gave me a rebirth. It was they who insisted that I should be a director.

Before a rebirth at WAAPA I had created and directed and performed constantly. Directing happened to me simply because my fellow actors or creators always asked me to direct. I always said yes and things always worked out and were usually fun and challenging.

From my experience one thing I would like to explain about directing, I learned by directing.

I directed short sketches which I co-created. These pieces were solo, duet, trio, quartet, quintet sketches, dances, mimes etc which often evolved into a full length work. This is much the way a choreographer would go about learning their craft, that is from solo then to duet then to ensemble.

This is retrospective knowledge and a recommendation. Direction is very much about action and spatial relation between actors/characters on stage. Simple? Not really. What those few or several or many bodies do on stage is the responsibility of the director. Also how, why and in what balance or displacement, is, the craft of directing. I love full scale productions, but a director should be able to craft a show or play with three things. One actor, one light bulb, one floor. Maybe you can do without the bulb or the floor. A director needs an actor or actors. Contrary to popular myth, an actor does not always need a director. Usually an actor needs a job. Guess who does the hiring and firing.

I'll write more about directing later in relation to specific projects.

- 17 -
MULTI-CULTURAL THEATRE

The first 27 years of my life were in a multi-cultural society. I don't know if I believe in multiculturalism. In fact I don't seem to believe in any "ism".

My parents insisted on a few things in my youth. I was a rather wild and uncontrollable creature. My parents taught that I should learn how other people pray and to understand that I was Jewish. I was taught that all people are equal, that I should never hate anyone, and never hurt anyone physically, nor with words, nor with thoughts.

My experience of multiculturalism was if I wandered into the wrong neighbourhood there was a good chance I would have to flee or fight.

There are major problems with multiculturalism in society as well as in theatre.

However we have to face facts...the human race is a multi-cultural fact. There were numerous of distinct Indigenous tribes in what is now called North America. This is not going to be a history lesson but there are some interesting facts to have in the back of the mind when we discuss multi-cultural theatre. Africa had hundreds of different tribes. So too did the Aboriginals in what is now called Australia. Distinct languages, myths, terrain, physical features. The Maoris of Aotearoa - New Zealand had 12 distinct tribes. However there were others there before the Maoris invaded. The Sami of Norway-Sweden-Finland-Russia have nine distinct language groups. The English are a mixed breed of Romans, Saxons, Vikings, Normans, and Celts. Who are the original people of the land? In Japan there are still aboriginal people but very few. There are many Koreans who were brought to Japan but they will never really be Japanese. The oldest royal family is in Japan. There are 6,000 languages currently on Earth. The Earth is a multi-cultural experience.

So too is the theatre. In Western theatre can we separate the influences which we inherit from ancient Greece, ancient Rome, Italy, Russia, England?

What is now accepted as multi-cultural theatre is often nothing more these days than an act and fact of survival.

Governments throughout the Western world do not know what to do to combat problems of unemployment, refugees, racism etc. So they are currently trying to quell future riots, disturbances, trouble, protests... by funding multi-cultural projects.

Everybody with any sense is jumping on that bandwagon and creating projects which governments are willing to fund.

The irony of course is that usually who gets the money and credit is the dominant group in any culture.

Now lets get down to business, to theatre in a multi-cultural society.

First a brief look at my "homeland". The USA. I am not a big fan of the USA's military/industrial/Congressional complex as Dwight Eisenhower labeled it. That complex is "in bed with" the industrial Lobbies to Congress.

I am Jewish and know full well that America provided a safe haven from the pogroms and prejudice of other lands. I also know that the USA failed to receive enough people in the early 1940s. However the USA was built on the back of slavery. Slavery included blacks and whites. The Founding Fathers owned slaves. In the 1960's there were race riots throughout the USA and deservedly so. Four university students were murdered by soldiers for protesting a war in which mostly the poor would serve, be maimed, or die.

So do you think that the theatre in the USA would be so liberated and multi-cultural? The USA today is perhaps not a segregated society but it is certainly racist. Paradoxically it is racist at the same time as it is filled with opportunity for anyone. Yet the Vaudeville tradition allowed people of any background to survive and prosper in the performing arts. Whereas the traditional theatre had to paint a lily white picture. A black American could play a maid, or butler and on the rarest occasion an Othello. In the liberated world maybe today in a special production about racism a black could play Romeo or Juliet.

Then you have visionaries who always were seeing right through the myth of the USA as a land of the free. They challenged their own prejudices, bias', career security and did what was in their hearts. Martha Graham hired anyone. Two of her stars were black and Japanese, or from other cultures than her own. Leonard Bernstein co-created West Side Story which gloriously de-anglicised Romeo and Juliet. The Bard, Shakespeare, by the way seemed well aware of multiculturalism and racism, as it was a regular theme in his work. Why? His father was a Catholic at a time when it was quite un-kosher. Shakespeare's mistress was from a non-Anglo background. Back to the bad ol' USA...in the 1950's TV was trying to fight the racist tide. The Amos 'n Andy show was an all Black American cast. Later, Bill Cosby arrived with more mature comedy and was for decades the most prosperous entertainer. He understood well the healing property of humour. He had a great head start since his father was a teacher of Shakespeare in a leading acting school. There were many Black comedians who were actively trying to transition a racist reality via the theatre arts. One of the most gifted was Richard Pryor. Then came Eddie Murphy and a great breakthrough was the director Spike Lee. Finally the USA and the world is starting to accept the talent and intelligence of the Black Americans equal to their full capacity. At the same time it is quite difficult to accept the full Italian source of Robert De Niro and Al Pacino; or the Jewish source of Barbara Streisand, Woody Allen, Steven Spielberg, or the Coen Brothers. In other words no matter what your culture background in the USA there is really an arch conservative level to which you are limited to express your cultural self. Anything more and it is a threat to the dominant culture.

There are parameters determined by producers, by government funding bodies, by teachers, directors, publicists, peers, friends which determine how much of ourself we reveal. On the other hand sometimes the theatre limits your range to only performing as what you physically appear to be.

Why couldn't Sylvester Stallone play Othello? Why couldn't Bill Cosby play Shylock? In the theatre anything is possible and can work. The conservative forces in every country limit our creativity by promising success.

The theatre community fails over and over again to accept the full power of multicultural theatre to give us unlimited creative potential. Even in the USA, Canada, England, France. Places where they love to sing their own multicultural praises.

Again in the USA there were many successes and tests such as Jesus Christ Superstar, Hair, Oh Calcutta. One of the greatest projects though was from Orson Welles producing Macbeth in Harlem, he was leading us over fifty years ago. Numerous Jewish performers were actual activists consciously fought to assist Black Americans to have equal rights and opportunities. Even while the Jewish comedians inherited the blackface art the more famous ones at the same time were activists and that included Eddie Cantor, Al Jolson, Milton Berle and numerous others including often the producers.

These wonder projects were decapitated by the overwhelming sense that in the USA we're all just Americans and we speak English. This left no room for a theatre run for and by Native Americans, no room for a funded Estonian language theatre. Or Italian theatre etc. Even today when Spanish is the official second language it is hard to justify supporting a dozen Spanish language theatres. For many years the Jewish community supported a Yiddish theatre. This circuit survived as a regular business. When the community lost interest the business died and the investment and experience went elsewhere. This same creative and business force built many American industries such as Vaudeville, Hollywood, performance unions, jazz, and musicals. From the Jewish creative freedom in a safe homeland artists from Irish, Black, Italian backgrounds flourished. In vaudeville people from any culture who had an act could survive and flourish. Without Italians, Irish, Blacks, Jews, the American theatre would have little development. Some of the English immigrants who flourished in a multicultural society were Bob Hope, Stan Laurel, and Charlie Chaplin.

We must learn from history though. See the opposition between Chaplin and Hope. Bob Hope backed the USA all the way but Chaplin expressed his own views which happened to differ from the accepted policies and thus he had to leave a home he had for forty years. That is Charlie Chaplin ...in the USA ...the land of the free.

What do you think is going on with talents of lesser note in lands of lesser mythological freedom?

How many Russian artists would be welcomed and supported in the Czech Republic today? in France... or in, or ...

Yes France accepted Nureyev. Yes the USA accepted Balanchine. In these rare acceptances though it is to create or enhance a National institution .

However, if we look at the ballet world it is frequently harbouring a multi cultural climate. Ballet is historically passed on through the great masters from Italy, Russia, France, Denmark and England. Modern Dance is generated from the Germans and Americans. Jazz is the domain driven by Blacks and Hispanics. So there is a multi-cultural network on going. Where there is no limit in teaching there is a great limit in creative freedom and financial support.

Here we see the Wall in the multi-cultural myth. It is acceptable only if you directly and obviously benefit the host company or nation. It is pure business it is not enlightenment.

As Jews we know we must assimilate and this is the tragedy.

Once you assimilate whether you are English or Sami, you lose the multi and become cultur-ised or pasteurised. Like a very poor quality bread you lose all the vitamins, minerals, fibre, and flavour. We all lose. Even the new home country. This is the tragedy. The more support and freedom given to the many cultures the more beauty we will see in the host culture. What happens is people are scared of loss. Loss of support, of security, of prestige. Just like in a village we are scared not of one person but scared of an invasion and a loss of our way of living.

Assimilation robs the Jew of everything. It does the same to the melody and gift of language to the Black Americans. Assimilation denies Hispanics their own rich poetry. What about the poetry of Arabic culture? What about the loss of heritage from abundantly diverse Asian cultures? The loss of wisdom from indigenous cultures. The Jew can be secular without assimilating. As a Gershwin song says "it ain't necessarily so". Until the recent past such a paradox of secular without assimilation seemed possible. Now it is unlikely to be achievable. Cultures can adapt and still survive, but assimilation tends to dominate every traditional culture. In part that is due to the regression of what is now, in 2020 called "Progressive".

Assimilation is less than survival. Assimilation is a loss of life force and loss of beauty. Assimilation is a denial of our past. Multi-cultural policies are often driven by prejudices about other people's past.

At the same time George Balanchine is a great example, he didn't create another Bolshoi or Kirov. He created a genuinely new, fresh, visionary

American ballet. He grew as an artist. He challenged himself to find new inspiration in a new land. However, Balanchine's genius was totally supported, for four decades, by the American visionary Lincoln Kirstein.

Then part of the goal of multicultural theatre, is to enrich our theatre experience. But the artist can do this thousands of ways. Can the governments and funding bodies support possibilities which challenge their (the bureaucrats and politicians) personal belief systems.

The range is vast. The policies are limited. These policies are executed not just by bureaucrats but also by directors, artistic directors, critics, teachers and everyone who controls the doorway in and out of the theatre. They are referred to as gatekeepers.

- 18 -
MULTI-CULTURAL II. AN EXAMPLE

Australia is a multicultural society. A very successful one. Most of the population derives from other lands. Less than 1% Aboriginal. There are more Greeks than in Athens. There is a nearly equal number of Italians. People from over 140 nations live in Australia this includes 80,000 Jews, a larger number of Muslims, very large groups of English, Irish, Scottish, and Lebanese. There are also immigrants from other multicultural societies such as the USA, Canada, Israel who have found a safe and fresh haven in Australia. Hundreds of thousands of New Zealanders and Maoris now call Australia home.

One of the biggest industries is around the backpackers who visit and work throughout Australia. The majority come from Sweden, Denmark, Germany. But many other young people from Brazil, South Korea, Europe, USA come on one-year work visas. The Chinese may have visited a thousand years ago. However the First Fleet came from England only ten generations ago to colonise. On the first ships there were at least a few who were Irish, Jewish, Greek. The Chinese have been resident citizens for well over 100 years. Now there are major investors from Hong Kong, Japan, China. There are also strong mafias from Japan, Russia, and Cambodia. In the theatre there was said to be a Gay mafia in the past who helped to create a more open theatre scene for all. There are refugees from every war zone and every side of conflict. That includes Koreans, Vietnamese, Iranians, Iraqis, ex-Yugoslavs, Latin Americans, Africans. One Australian Prime Minister's wife was from Holland. And some Prime Minister's have been born in England.

From every angle, Australia is multi-cultural. The restaurants are unlimited in range. The theatre is not. Yet the first Australian pantomime was a multicultural saga. Until the 1950's, theatre in Australia really meant English accents, English texts, English flavour. Then Ray Lawler created the play "The Summer Of The Seventeenth Doll" with a uniquely Australian flavour and voice.

Earlier, the American musicals arrived on tour and two profound people stayed. An actor named Hayes Gordon and a dancer named Beth Dean. Dean was already married with a singer in that production, the Australian Victor Carell. The Sydney opera house was commissioned and the chosen architect was the great Dane, Utzon. A play, an actor, a dancer, and an Opera House opened a world of self discovery. When the Sydney Opera House opened after 14 years of construction, Beth Dean's ballet "Corroboree" was one of the early works performed there. My teacher Clete Ball performed in that. The musical score was composed by John Antill. The first performer at the Sydney Opera House was the American Paul Robeson who gave a concert on the construction site for the workers.

Beth and Victor had lived briefly with Indigenous communities and researched the Australian Aboriginal dances. From that period she created a number of related ballets. The nation has yet to catch up to her vision. But one stream supersedes her wedge into the society and that stream is led by the Page family who founded Bangarra Dance Theatre. Beth Dean founded the Opera House Folkloric Festival to celebrate Australia's multicultural heritage. For nearly 20 years Guillermo Keys-Arenas was the director.

"The Summer of the Seventeenth Doll" toured England, and the play was adapted and Americanised for film. The Negro Ensemble Company in NYC did an All-Black production of "the Doll". After the London season, a young Australian arrived and worked as an actor and formidable teacher of acting and theatre, he was Lisle Jones.

Hayes Gordon founded an acting school in Sydney and a still flourishing company, The Ensemble. Not to be outdone by Gordon's school, the National Institute of Dramatic Arts gained momentum by competing with Gordon.

Yes even the conservative Australia of the 1950's was a multi-cultural society. Victims of the Holocaust were rescued as were the executioners of the Holocaust. They had to work together side by side to create a new society. At this time Aboriginals were not citizens and were often taken from their own mothers, others were hunted like kangaroos. The wisdom of the writer Patrick White was starting to flow on the printed page. Xavier Herbert had already written *Capricornia*. David Malouf, of immigrant parents, became one of the greatest philosophical writers who encountered the myths and mystique of Australia. Oodgeroo Noonuccal (Kath Walker), Alexis Wright, Judith Wright, May Gibbs are a few of the women writers who worked to encounter the 'myths and mystique' and mistakes. Pamela Travers born in Queensland created one of the most successful and profound female characters - Mary Poppins.

The 60's and 70's brought the social upheavals of Paris and Berkeley directly to Sydney and Melbourne. The Irish blood of Australia protested in every possible way with its over protective mother England. This was the time of the British Empire's gradual global defeat. Australia was not only giving a rebirth to itself it was a welcomed voice of free spirit along with New Zealand.

It was very heady times in the theatre. Besides the Ensemble Theatre which was founded by a foreigner, two other profound theatre projects were starting. In the viscous rivalry a tale of two cities began. Sydney and Melbourne or should I say Melbourne and Sydney? Each had their own pot-a-brewing. In Melbourne the Pram Factory (APG) grew to 100 theatre workers, actors who had never acted, writers who hadn't written, designers with equal experience, and directors with even less. These became absolute first class artists. However a quick overview reveals that the "White Australia Policy" ruled the waves. Those '100' still rule, maybe not an all-white policy but a very Anglo 'entitled' approach to reality.

Meanwhile in sister city Sydney perhaps there were not 100 anointed ones but no less profound a voice for a new spirit in a new land was screaming to be born. This birthing was at the Stables, the manger for the Nimrod company of soon to be actors, writers, designers, directors. Again without any doubt they too became utterly excellent artists who also now rule with smiling clenched teeth and arm's length policies that take with one hand and hold with the other.

Theatre is a tough business and at the end of the day only the tough will survive.

In the world of multi-cultural theatre though, 100 ethnic actors cannot possibly survive. Before they are allowed to survive they are forced through social interaction to assimilate. They are robbed of their blood, the language, their manna. Foreigners are accepted only to fulfil the task of betterment in the eyes of the dominant group. Once this is done the foreigners are quickly edged out. However this always comes back on the dominant culture as they often succeed in killing their own artists. For example one absurd case in Australia where one of their most gifted and dedicated artists could not get funding to produce what he has dedicated a lifetime to, the works of William Shakespeare. WHY? Shakespeare of course wasn't an Australian!

Arts, governments, multicultural policies are really no more enlightened now than in the dark ages.

Policies and their execution and exceptions leave one bewildered at humanity's stupidity.

For a brief period Australia had a flourishing flow of multicultural theatre. All types and views and a lot. But what I observed was an unwritten slaughter of ethnic artists careers. As the ethnic workers were always supervised, administered, directed, scripted, or funded by White Anglo Celt Australians, the moment this support was taken the ethnic theatre worker had almost no chance to survive. There was an in-built limit to the control, freedom, and support the New Australian artist could have. In other words the growth industry was for Real Aussies, or the very white washed artists who could sing all day every day "I love Australia, Australia has the greatest theatre, ...". Well those who sing it everyday in every-way and agree on cue and disagree on cue have survived and flourished. Oddly enough almost no ethnic survives, if they do they are

a. married to an Australian, or
b. effervescently gay, or
c. a good party animal, or
d. commercially valuable...temporarily.

Many will argue. Most will agree. But the saddest thing is to watch the wings of creative spirit get clipped.

One success story is the French director Jean Pierre Mignon. He did well with others and created the Anthill Theatre and received a top honour. He was however married to an Australian and of course mostly hired real Aussies. There is nothing wrong with being married to a Real Citizen of the new Homeland nor to hiring the Real Thing. It is known though to work too much with people of your own background...even occasionally can be success suicide.

Survival. It is driving our artistic choices much more than we realise. Even in a liberal, democratic, open society our choices as artists are part of being pawns in an elaborate game of social protocol.

Individuals can create policy changes which allow for change to begin. In Australia Gough Whitlam and Don Dunstan brought in policies which directly allowed such changes. Chris Westwood was a person who understood the opportunities for everyone in new policies and administered accordingly in every position she held. The English festival director Anthony Steele kept an ongoing flow of performing artists from every global region coming to Australia. This was a secret warrior for creative growth in Australian theatre. He was a very rare bird. He recognised worth through all cultural boundaries and instigated challenges which the Real Australian audiences always accepted with pleasure and delight. He knew the intelligence and openness of the audience. Anthony created challenges and inspiration for local growth. This director always took not only the great Western theatres but also indigenous troupes, dance troupes, choirs, musicians. He understood the profound need to cross fertilise the arts. This was a great visionary of a multi-cultural theatre in Australia.

- 19 -
MULTI-CULT III

Initially I spent twelve years between Aotearoa (NZ) and Australia 1981-1993. In NZ the chieftains of the theatre were two Maoris. Actor George Henare had acted in something like 200 stage productions and about 200 radio plays by the time he was only in his early 50's. Don Selwyn was a TV regular who decided to take his name and create an arts project. I acted with him in "The Merchant of Venice" and taught with him at his then new Maori performing arts school. That led to him casting the film, "Once Were Warriors". In 2002 he directed the first Maori language film, "The Merchant of Venice". Henare had once explained to me that in the all Maori community he grew up in they "did Shakespeare our own way".

At Selwyn's school it was not just an acting school. It was a school to learn about the self, rediscover Maori culture and language. There were always Elders on site who the young people could talk with at any time. It was a genuine school in the Socratic tradition. Out of this and other changes ushered in by the Prime Minister David Lange a cultural shift occurred. A Maori cultural revival started. Films such as "Other Halves", "Utu", "The Piano", "Once Were Warriors", were creative releases.

Through many steps and experiences I began to see patterns and changes in theatre that had a multi cultural significance. Beforehand though I never thought about these things and never gave much focused thought to my Jewish heritage.

Now we must all face drastic changes in the world. We must find out who we are and what we are meant to be doing.

There are messages coming from the Maoris, the Aboriginals, the Tibetans, the Jews, the Black Americans, the Muslims and from many other sources and religions.

The theatre should be at the vanguard but it is not only behind, it is initiating entrenched politically correct bureaucratic policies and projects which are backward.

We are in this together.

In Australia I saw perhaps 500 theatre projects including dance. Many of the projects were visiting troupes. Many projects could be called multi-cultural.

One project was the "Mahabharata" directed by Peter Brook. I took a 1000 mile bus ride with my friend and gifted director Kerry Dwyer. We chose to see the whole event. All three parts 6pm thru to sunrise the following morning, with several meal breaks. It was an adventure and as the show lasted all through the night and climaxed at sunrise.... I found it at times difficult to stay awake.

Peter Brook is an English director. Now he lives in Paris where his company is based. He has an international company. He is the son of Russian immigrants. His parents according to rumour were Jewish. Peter does not freely give interviews about any private matters. But he discusses artistic matters rather candidly. He took his great reputation and has made a great statement to the world of theatre. His actors are from many different cultures and do excellent theatre in English or French. When he came to Australia there was an artistic statement about doing multi-cultural theatre only Peter is already way ahead of the game and is doing International theatre.

The multi-cultural theatre policies are already out of date and backwards thinking. They already reinforce the power structure in the hands of those in power. Multi-cultural theatre is not really about freedom it is about control. Peter Brook is ahead of the times as an artist.

As crazy ol' life would have it.... two years ago (1993) I went to Israel for the first time. This was at the invitation of my friend, the Israeli born Arab-Christian Antoine Saleh who was visiting his birth-land. The first night two of the "Mahabharata" actors were giving a lecture demonstration. Bruce Meyers and his wife. Bruce was the teacher. Bruce has worked with Peter Brook for a very long time. The talk was on the "Dybbuk", a play with a Jewish theme and history. During the question and answer period, someone asked why did Bruce choose to do the "Dybbuk". He briefly told how he was asked to do it in NYC many years ago. It was a play, he was an actor, simple. Not quite. NOTHING in MULTI-CULTURAL, NATIONAL, INTERNATIONAL, JEWISH, BLACK, ARAB, HISPANIC theatre is simple. He was asked again about his choice to continue working with the "Dybbuk" for twenty years. He answered directly. Yet all of us innocent 'secular' lambs in the audience, in Israel, in Jerusalem, in love with theatre and with the artistry of Brook, Bruce, his wife wanted a straight discussion on the question. What does the greatest Jewish play have to do with one of the greatest Jewish actors? That's all. But in the multi-cultural theatre and even in the international theatre it is not kosher to discuss who you really are nor what you really think or believe. I understand his anger. It was the sense of survival and assimilation. But if Bruce and Brook cannot discuss what everyone can see then they might as well be doing English Panto next Christmas. We need to know that Jews are <u>very happy</u> working with Muslims with Christians with atheists, agnostics, maybe even with Pagans, as well as with fellow Jews. As Brook has done for a span of 70 years. We need to know as my parents observed, "how other people pray". We need to observe and talk. We need to share our differences.

Peter Brook is indeed the greatest visionary in the theatre but needs to take a final step backwards and tell of his early family journey.

Ten months later I was in Prague for the first time. It was Jewish New Year, so what the hell I went to the house of the Golem, Rabbi Loew's old synagogue (Judah Loew ben Bezalel known also as the Maharal of Prague). I sit down. Lo and behold in walks Bruce Meyers. He sits next to me. We talk. For two such assimilated, secular, nonreligious Jews to meet in Jerusalem at a lecture on the "Dybbuk" and next at the "Golem" house on Rosh Hashanah (Jewish New Year) is that such a surprise? No. That is what multi-cultural policies are scared of. That we ethnic people might magically get together and do very exciting theatre in our own (God-forbid) sacred languages. Our own way, for our own people and then we may not assimilate in the ways deemed acceptable by the dominant culture.

I'm only telling stories but I wonder how you are interpreting.

I'm only telling stories because I think not only do policies have to change... artists have to change. Ethnic, White, Black, English, Jew, Muslim, Christian it doesn't matter but we do have to change. It's not enough just to do the best theatre in the world, the artists have to change.

In Australia a director was in his friend's garage and saw some old manuscripts. He asked if he could read some. Out of this chance reading came a show which sold out every single night for six months throughout the country. Nine nights out of ten it received a spontaneous standing ovation. There is an art and technique to getting a standing ovation. This was a spontaneous ovation.

The show was "Bran Nue Dae". A great rollicking musical about aboriginal life in the town of Broome. Most of the actors, dancers and musicians were aboriginal. There were three white actors who played a German priest and two German backpackers.

This musical played mostly to all white audiences. "Real Australians". They cried, laughed and jumped to their feet in thanks to these glorious actors and story and music.

If ever theatre had the chance in two hours to heal a tragedy of two centuries this did it. No worries.

However the enlightened intellectuals set up an organisation to create Australian musicals.

"Bran Nue Dae" to the enlightened few was an aboriginal musical. True. But it was also an Australian musical. All Australian citizens, all Australian born. The Real Australians who saw it knew what they saw, the first genuine Australian musical and it was a ripper.

Our enlightened artists and intellectuals of the theatre often suffer from dyslexia of a lack of clear thinking.

How does this work? When I was in The Bell Shakespeare Company we were officially a multi-cultural theatre company. We had three plays, so there were three opening nights in each city. Accordingly in each city there were reviews for each play in a whole range of newspapers and magazines. All up I read about fifty reviews.

There was a pattern. Almost never did any of the ethnic actors get even a mention. Judging by first and last names every reviewer was a Real Aussie-Anglo/Celt species.

I talked to my friend Fred. He explained that for decades English painters came to Australia went out in the Bush and ended up painting quaint English countrysides. Many of the artists couldn't see what was right in front of them.

So when we have multi-cultural theatre who reviews the shows and who looks at the shows to decide what gets support?

Dyslexia in the theatre is more than a reading problem it is a form of myopia. If you write a new play who sees if it's worthy of national support? Pirandello, Ionesco, Beckett? Who approves at any level what theatre gets support, why, and under what conditions?

Believe me, the powers that be in any nation are scared of multi-cultural theatrical self-expression.

There may be nothing to fear except the ancient fear of the Fool who speaks the truth.

In good old liberal France, long ago, the French actors did everything possible to stop the Italian actors from establishing. True this was over three hundred years ago, but the battle has not changed one bit. Every time the Italians accepted the new policies, the French actors had new regulations and restrictions established. The battle is not different today if French actors decided to take up residence in Italy. The same prejudices and fears come up in Sweden or any country where even their own regional accents and social values are different in various parts of the nation. Thus prejudice also occurs within nations and cultures.

So the "Mahabharata" and "Bran Nue Dae" were examples of very fine theatre and theatre which heralded a growing vision of theatre.

Then there was a show called "Wogs Out Of Work". A wog is a foreigner in Australia. But it doesn't really apply to people from the British Isles, USA, or Canada. In spite of that I referred to myself as "an American Wog". The "Wogs" show started as one of the classic cabaret shows then common in Australia. Funny, fast, flirtatious. In a little room for a short season it was quite successful. With still no work in sight, the three actors continued to produce the show. The audiences kept coming. I saw the show four years later in a very large theatre. An old dysfunctional theatre was now sold-out every night for several months. A roadshow had to be created for a national tour. The first three actors had earned somewhat over one million dollars. A touring group was employed to play out of work actors. Money, money,

money and the show was very funny. Especially if you were part of the huge Greek, Italian, Lebanese or other ethnic groups who couldn't stand going to see the boring old Australian theatre. It's boring if no one on stage looks or talks like you. Well money talks. Jeez it must be time to really do some multi-cultural theatre 'cause we might get some multi-cultural "bums on seats" (paying customers) if we get some multi-cultural actors up on stage. Jeez I'm really concerned about where this country is headed. How much did you say they earned? Money, money, money. The three actors were excellent but one, Mary Coustas is on par with Barry Humphries or Lucille Ball. Soon the "Wogs Out Of Work" had a TV-show called "Acropolis Now" and Mary always hit the mark beautifully. The TV-show and the theatre show was not my cup of tea but they set a new competition level for Australia. TV in America was filled with multi-cultural comedy in the 50's, 60's, 70's but I can't say it ever did anything for the society. In the end TV is commercials, news and comic relief. It is not live theatre. Barry Humphries (creator of Dame Edna, and, Les Patterson) is quite clear about the difference and thankful to TV which helps him fill the theatre and sell books. Barry is a truly great artist. His whole career is a response to the mindset behind "Australia All-White Policy". That long dead policy is still the Big Brother controlling the coffers in theatre. The same story is in every country though.

Multi-cultural theatre policies are policies of money, funding, assimilation and control. It all has very little to do with artistry. Art is a huge industry. This is not wrong. But we still need genuinely innovative, creative expression. Only supporting the creative expression of foreigners new found on our soils will encourage new thoughts.

- 20 -
SHAKESPEARE II

1. Shakespeare is special because of the rhythm, beat, flying images, and overtones of text delivered out loud in a theatre.

2. Shakespeare also gives great plot, stories, sub-plots, humour, tragedy, characters, and general mechanics of theatre.

Part 1 cannot translate from English to another language nor can it be translated to modern English. The rhythm is in the language as is. There is a scholarly world which must piece together the plays for us laymen. The plays were printed after Shakespeare's death. Yet if you take even one speech and one scene from any play you see quickly a translation is actually quite unlikely to keep the richness of language. In the same way it is not really possible to translate Molière. Though perhaps Molière can readily be translated to other Romance languages? Even this translation would need to be of the same time period as the author's creation. The same is true of Strindberg. In that case translation could be close only in Norwegian and Danish. Perhaps Shakespeare can most accurately be translated into German or Dutch. For many decades the great scholars of Shakespeare were German and I think as early as the late 1500s the Dutch began to translate some of Shakespeare's plays.

Part 2 however can translate easily into any language and any culture.

When I work with Shakespeare there are two distinct worlds, the language or the theatre. In English these two worlds can be fully integrated, in translation they can partially be integrated. Yet if you want to see what can be expressed with Shakespeare then the English…i.e. British, American, Australian, New Zealand versions are easily outdone by the Russians, Georgians, Poles, Swedes, Danes, Germans, and probably many other cultures.

There of course can be versions from the English speaking world equal to the non-English versions, but the language gets in the way. The belief in the words themselves rather than the power of oratory is the single inhibiting factor. The next inhibiting factor is English language productions believe they must tell the story. No. The power of oratory, the rhythm, metre, flow of scenes will tell the story. That is Shakespeare at its finest.

You can play with Shakespeare as you like it. You can chop scenes, speeches, re-arrange, politicise, modernise, musicalise….do what you will. Though then there will be levels in the language which are very rarely reached. This requires an aural sensitive cast and director. Both must also be visually aware. In 2012 I saw two extraordinary Shakespeare productions. One of those 2012 productions was Macbeth by a Polish company. Their design was like a modern army, there was a huge live, actual, fire within the set. Directed by Maja Kleczewska. There also were excellent comic elements. The other 2012 production was from Moscow, "A Midsummer Night's Dream….as you like it" which was a devised theatre piece complete with actual clowns, acrobats, ballerinas, and one of the clowns had a small actual dog that was active throughout the whole production by Dmitry Krymov Laboratory.

Now I will give some hints, but I trust you have already tested on yourself my method expressed in the first article on Shakespeare. If you have tried that or have discovered for yourself point for point what I discussed in that article then what I am about to say will advance you or your students or your company. In other words there are mechanics in the spoken language and mechanics with the unique frame of each monologue which you must discover first.

We have lost the power of language. We have lost the power of spoken words. We live in the world of yuppies, CD Rom, MTV. That was 1996. Now 2020 there are many more un-natural distractions. As I said previously we must go back in our mind to the Time of Bards.

In the Maori culture the spoken language is completely empowered whether it is Maori or English. They speak from the soul. As do many Black Americans, as did the American Jews, as do many Irish.

The first idea which you must encounter is that in some cultures language reveals but in some it hides.

In Shakespeare the text reveals the inner truth of the character. The actor must literally vibrate with the language. Like a xylophone, your bones must rattle. The bones in your head, nasal region, your whole skeleton. Your vocal cords must vibrate. The muscles in your neck, back, diaphragm must be pumping extra blood. Your breathing bellows must maintain a steady fire. Your central nervous system, eyes, and flaring nostrils are active.

Good vocal technique and good acting is not enough to execute Shakespeare. I am filled with weaknesses as an actor but I can vibrate, pump blood at an even rate and act with inspiration and play. Shakespeare means play, vibrate, orate.

First you must find the Head and Heart in a play. Thus if King HenryV is the head, then Fluellan is the heart. Likewise,

Head - Heart:

OTHELLO - IAGO
CORIOLANUS - MENENIUS
TIMON - APEMANTUS
HAMLET - POLONIUS and GRAVEDIGGER
RICHARD III - BUCKINGHAM

The rest of the Anatomy of Shakespeare is more complex and is really only a play on words and image. In the play Othello the arms are perhaps Roderigo and Cassius. You see the whole play is an actual single being or character so to speak. In our age of plastic surgery, plastic cards, plastic food, plastic people we also have plastic theatre productions. The soul of Shakespeare is hidden in the complexity of the whole play. Even as scholars love to point out HE (W. Shakespeare) did not write certain passages. Fair enough. Apparently it was fairly common at that time that some writers worked collaboratively. But let us play Pretend and imagine somebody wrote a whole play called Othello. Yes we know HE stole the story, changed the plot, added characters but HE always stole a story. All art is a process of Steal - Change - Inspiration - Steal- Change - Inspiration etc. Until finally you are stealing, changing and inspired from your own creations. Let us now pretend and misbehave and have fun for a moment. We are all actors after all.

Othello - Head
Iago - Heart
Roderigo - Arm
Cassius - Arm
Desdemona - Penis
Emilia - Testicles
Desdemona's Papa - Rump, butt, ass, behind
Duke - Two feet
Clown - Testosterone
Soldiers - Eyes and Ears

If you are not the least amused by the language and images and humour … look again at the fulfilling filth in the play Romeo and Juliet. My God what comes out of Mercutio's mouth. Even the Padre-priest seems to enjoy an indulgence or two as he assists Cupid.

How is it that we can love Shakespeare and loath individual expression today?

What upsets us with a new or different or even a wrong yet funny idea?

When you look at a whole play by HE here are some steps to try.

First, read it as if it were a comic book. Read it quick in one sitting.

Second read it quickly again this time mouthing, whispering, reading aloud the whole play.

Third, figure out who is the heart and read it for humour.

If it is a tragedy that means the Heart character has a delightful, nasty wit, and loves to screw over other human beings. In a tragedy the Heart character is probably an atheist agnostic, godless person, who doesn't believe in karma, the only moral this character has is Thou shalt screw over thy neighbour.

Remember we are playing with words and images, and, thoughts no matter how feeble. This is theatre. Indulge yourself. This is theatre, be wicked and thou shalt finde delight.

Fourth reading. Read only a single act. Read it again, noting all the entrances and exits. Note the difference in each scene in this act. Now read this act again straight through. Repeat the whole process with each act.

In Shakespeare each scene has a completely different style and rhythm from the scene which precedes and the scene which follows. However, to find the connection and thread between scenes you must read and rehearse as if an Act were a single, fluid, chaotic scene.

Though as our scholars tell us, HE ...whom so ever HIM was, hmmmm, what we call Shakespeare may not have used any delineation betwixt scenes nor acts... it will help us to pretend that the punctuation, scene division, and, act sequences were intended. You cannot do Shakespeare without the aid of scholars. They explain to us what all those olde wordes mean. They explain the references of the time. They explain the Biblical and literary references. Thank God for scholars. However scholars lack humour when it comes to their own theories and interpretations. They survive like lawyers by proving themselves correct. They may prove it but it may not be the whole truth. In particular, the humour and very nasty and filthy wit of HE is frequently missed or ignored. As are the references to God, nature, sorcery. In addition the wit and humour of the officially labeled Shakespeare clowns and fools can be drawn out only through physical action. This action must be directly related to the text, grammar, punctuation, situation, character relation, and the sub-plot which is really what the clown presents in Shakespeare. In A Midsummer Night's Dream perhaps the mechanicals physicalise and verbalise the chinks in weddings. In Hamlet's Mousetrap we are shown how a play within a play is the thing to catch rats. To understand that parody, we must tie-in other references to the Players before they play their play and the beautiful monologue of Hamlet which follows the Players abrupt exit. We later see Hamlet take action and inspiration from the Mousetrap to go rat catching alone.

These are two examples though there is almost always a play within the play. Usually done with great humour and often with black humour. In Richard III there are scenes with the Mayor. The Mayor is a clown of a clown, a shadow or reflection of the soon to be king, Richard. To do Shakespeare justice in production these small scenes must have full, humorous life. Yet they cannot standout so much as to ruin the rhythm of the whole play.

Text in Shakespeare must be delivered rather rapidly. Not so much fast but more ever-flowing. A river with rapids is the metaphor in Nature which best reflects the natural structure of a Shakespeare play. The surface of the Earth is mostly water. Your body is mostly water. Shakespeare's natural consistency is also. The Earth element is the words and their meaning. The fire is the actor, the human being on stage. The air is the sound and overtones. The ether element is the whole production and interaction with a live audience. This ether element is what Stanislavsky called Prana. That was his final point after decades of trying to define what theatre is.

Prana in the yogic sense is not air, nor breathing. Prana is life force energy. It is something un-concrete, almost unphysical. This is the Quantum Point. This is the centre point in great theatre. The unknown and undefinable quality. No scholar and no critic can define this. It is more fine and etheric than the space between electron, proton, and neutron. It is this empty space which allows for Quantum interaction and Quantum leaps in the consciousness of theatre craft and audience.

It is your interaction with me through this text which is the technique you seek in what I call Quantum Theatre.

This is the starting point. Yes in the middle of the text. This is the beginning point to return to.

There are indeed mechanics and techniques but without your inspiration, agreement, disagreements, understanding, misunderstandings, interpretation then Quantum Theatre cannot exist.

It is the same idea as interactive video. The same as Socratic learning. It is how the learning of Torah and Talmud actually functions - total engagement soul-to-soul the writer to the reader and energised discussion and debate between readers face-to-face. This is what Shakespeare the Bard knew. It is the unfathomable way of learning and communicating which our world desperately requires: face-to-face discussion and debate. Technique and CD-Rom worlds can help us but of course they are mostly a distraction.

The techniques I occasionally expose in this book are to take away distractions. Yet like any technique they can become the distraction.

There is a Shakespeare industry. It is a distraction from the Quantum empty space inside the world of words.

The Maori culture carries some special seeds of enlightenment for the theatre. There are other such messages from the Japanese, Chinese, and Indian cultures. The Maoris were warriors and orators. In 1985 I foresaw that a Shakespeare War was about to begin. It is a culture war. The Maori culture is unique in this war because the culture still lives in oral levels and they have such command of the English language as well. The Jews and Blacks in America had this knowledge but lost it through assimilation. The Anglo culture could be rebirthed through Shakespeare but only by a complete and utter refraction through a prism such as Quantum. As many theatres fight and thrive in England, USA, Australia they are still scared of a quantum chaos and a Rediscovery of our Self and purpose. The rational use of words kills the deeper levels of theatre. Imperialism often removes and supersedes native languages and myths.

Shakespeare glorious Shakespeare. Henry V, like many of Shakespeare's plays, is a multicultural examination of the Self and the idea of Nationhood. The mix of cultures and classes and languages in the play is perfect for self examination. In some way in the Merchant of Venice the vociferous racism of Portia is greatly overlooked. Her incredible articulation also reveals the pain in the racists soul. She is the perfect nationalist...a yuppie and a snob.

Another concept with HE is the Lucille Ball - Vivian Vance Theory. Ms. Ball was the great comedienne on TV in the USA during the 50's, 60's, 70's. Her TV show I Love Lucy had four main characters. Lucy and her husband Desi, and Ethel and her husband Fred. Ethel's real name was Vivian Vance.

Lucy and Ethel were constantly getting into mayhem by plotting together. They were a team with utterly different characters. But, when the men, Desi and Fred left, the women did the real clowning and mischievous deeds.

If we can accept that there may be different ways that men relate together from how women relate together then we know that the I Love Lucy program imitated life. I wrote, co-created, one play which placed two men in a situation to express my feeling that in fact men will relate the same way as women and vice versa. My original play was "A Regular Couple Of Guys" that evolved into the co-creation "The Male Adored Bride" (see the chapter Co-Creating in *Clown Secret*). Neil Simon's play "The Odd Couple" has a related theme. Anyway's you think what you will. The theory will still hold water.

Again what concerns me in Shakespeare besides the overtone and Quantum points, is the humour. The many different humours in any given play. Again I will say much of the humour is quite wicked. Danny Di Vito humour, Fellini humour, Lucy's humour.

My theory - If in Shakespeare you have a scene with two female characters, you should, for a few minutes in rehearsal, change their names to Lucy and Ethel then the truth of the scene will reveal itself to you, via your changed perspective. This same idea can be transferred occasionally to two male characters. For example Richard III and Buckingham or Hamlet and the Player King.

There is a lot of plotting and scheming going on in Shakespeare. Theatre equals Life. So the essence of Lucy and Ethel was plotting in every episode.

Much of the humour of Shakespeare requires the actor to indulge to the fullest in the taboo of being anti Love Thy Neighbour. If the essence of Christianity is to Love Thy Neighbour then the essence of Shakespeare is to show humanity's true colour…yecch green. Love thy neighbour is actually the essence of all religions. Except the religion called Theatre. Nasty, nasty. Or Shakespeare humour. Black wicked humour. Maybe theatre directors should study more Drag shows.

What's this have to do with Shakespeare and Quantum? Everything. Go see a Christmas Panto would you? Lighten up. You're not a scholar are you? Whoops.

- 21 -
SHAKESPEARE III

Each scene in Shakespeare is so utterly different that it is almost a completely different style.

That sentence is a word to the wise director.

If you could really find the magic and complexity in any single scene of Shakespeare you will begin to understand the Quantum Point. Not my definition of Quantum, but your own realisation. That is Quantum Theatre. The Quantum Point is all about potential. The point of potential in any scene of Shakespeare is its creative interpretation.

In searching for overall meaning of a Shakespeare play you can take almost any scene from the play and begin to discuss its repercussions and threads throughout the play. That was the viewpoint taught to me by English professor Arnie Goldman. Using that scene as a philosophers stone. Let's look at this stone and say what we think.

You could easily take a scene from Shakespeare and do the play inside out. From middle to end to beginning to middle. Although I wrote that last sentence and most of this book in 1996, it was in 2012 when Leof Kingsford-Smith hired me to direct him and Japanese dancer-actor Shakti and to create my own adaptation of King Lear. In this case I did actually turn the play inside out. All of the words were Shakespeare's but I cut the play so that Lear's madness was that the voices and words of his daughters were like remembered conversations so that he was saying their texts and mimicking the daughters. Shakti played The Fool but also her character said some lines that King Lear or the daughters had spoken. As this was to be a Fringe show it had to play just under one hour. Shakti is also a choreographer and director of her own small unique dance company in Tokyo. When I accepted the offer to direct and create, I had not met Shakti. When I sought information about her I saw several videos and each of her performances eventually she is completely naked. So when I phoned to chat with her she said "Oh don't worry I will stay fully clothed for our production". I called the adaptation "The Madness of King Lear".

The first day of rehearsal I stopped for a moment and explained to Leof who was doing a very fine job as Lear, that we are not actually doing the play King Lear. We are doing our play "The Madness of King Lear". I explained that I was drastically more interested in him as a person than I was the imaginary character King Lear. So like Peter Brook said to his actors in his first production at the RSC - 'could you please all stop acting'. Leof as it happens has three children and a full experience of life, so I wanted Leof playing.

After our Adelaide and Avignon seasons Shakti was too busy to perform in Edinburgh, so I took over her role. The two actors were on stage together during the whole show. I was able to rehearse in Avignon and perform for a month in Edinburgh in between contracts when I was performing in Slava Polunin's "Snowshow". The following year when I had one more short contract in Snowshow, I also directed Shakespeare's whole, uncut "Antony & Cleopatra" for 18 actors. During its two week season in Sydney was also our two weeks season of Snowshow in Sydney. That double season marked my 40th year in theatre.

At this stage of my life i.e. so far, of the 140+ live production I've been involved with, more than 20 have been Shakespeare plays or adaptations.

The ten plays were either complete or standard shortened productions to about two and a half hours running time. The adaptations/inspired-by include my three-hander "A Girl's Guide to Hamlet". It has two main roles and one Vaudeville style character who is like a old fashioned Western Union delivery boy in uniform who delivers letters from Hamlet to his girlfriend.

Now continuing with what I had written in 1996.

With Shakespeare you can not only do what you damn well please, you can be irreverent, outrageous, irrelevant, flippant, frolicsome, and otherwise quite creative. A Shakespearean text can be inspiring for so many different impulses. It is just a pack of words, ideas, characters, and situations.

Thus we have two extremes. Do with the text as you wish. Do the whole text uncut and try to find the flow and rhythm. In between these extremes are endless possibilities. Much of what I have written about are ways to find the flow and rhythm which is very rarely possible in an ensemble - no matter how good the critics say a group or production is.

The words can be utterly clear, the actors actions well thought out, the director's concept executed precisely, the players can have a rollicking good time, the audience jump to their feet, the critics can articulate their best verbal gesticulations, and still chances are the work never comes close to the quantum point of overtone in language nor overtone in consciousness.

How to go further? How to find this mysterious Quantum Point? It's no mystery, it is almost scientific. Through science we know that there are sound waves. I suspect that even a single word, for example, "hello" may send four sound waves when clearly spoken. Perhaps a percussive sound on the two consonants and two longer sounds on the vowels. The audience hears all four waves. If we add, after a pause, "Harold" well spoken. The audience in their aural memory matches the four waves previously said. In the aural sense they will tie the waves of the memory with the waves of the present.

This is the same process as in the listening pleasure one experiences with music.

This is the musical level of Shakespeare. When we learn how it works with Shakespeare where it is implied by the sculpted words, then we will see that often when a playwright scribes they actually "hear" the words being spoken. A great playwright is actually quite sound conscious. This is one reason I consider Samuel Beckett on par with William Shakespeare. Their handling and sensitivity to the Question of Human Existence is equal to their sound sensitivity intended for the theatre.

Though I encourage actors working text to practise at a robust level vocally, the execution in performance requires the sensitivity of a concert musician. The best way for an actor to find this sensitivity is to be robust, playful, frolicsome. The craft of acting is distinct from music but we must see a relation and similar qualities.

So there is definitely a musicality in good text but there is also something else coming from the actor. The actor can have various levels of awareness happening simultaneously.

Likewise the audience is being stimulated on many different audial levels. The sound vibrations go not just to the ears, but to the hands, the hair, face and even parts of the body fully clothed. Sound is a physical matter and Shakespeare is rich in sound. It can be like the best of classical, jazz, or indigenous orchestration.

There are other writers who appear quite sound conscious such as Harold Pinter, August Strindberg, even Neil Simon. The Yiddish Theatre and the Polish Theatre are sound conscious. Probably Chico Marx was more sound conscious than Groucho. Groucho thought the opposite. W.C. Fields and Mae West were other sound conscious writers. Bette Midler, Barbara Streisand, and Ute Lemper are sound conscious.

In Quantum Theatre: Slapstick to Shakespeare sound consciousness starts with the body. Quantum implies perspectives from at least two angles (wave/particle; dot/circle; yin/yang;). Theatre implies the space where one sees (teatro) and hears (auditorium). Slapstick implies the body/physicality, and, by discussing The Bard, Shakespeare, we can cover a wide range of theatre subjects which inter-relate.

- 22 -
SLAPSTICK

Entrepreneur asks: Harlequin where's your mask?
Harlequin replies: What mask?
E What mask? The mask!
H The mask...oh, I see. (Harlequin makes a face like Harpo Marx)
E No you don't. Harlequin's supposed to have a mask.
H No.
E What do you mean no. Yes he is, Harlequin's supposed to have a mask.
H No, Arlecchino has a mask. Harlequin doesn't.
E Arlecchino. Harlequin. What's the difference?
H Big. (As Harlequin shows how big, he hits the entrepreneur in the stomach.)
E Ugh. How big?
H Little.

This is the beginning of a slapstick routine I made in 1993 with the actor Erick Mitsak. It is called "HARK. LARRIKINS.. or Harlequin and the Entrepreneur ".

A larrikin is an Australian term rich in cultural connotations. It harks back to a golden age of Australians outwitting the boss. Today it can be quite an endearing term.

The routine was authentic. It was funny, physical, fast, witty, with quick changes of psychology. It worked well, and in time it could naturally grow, improve, develop. The skill level in terms of mime, movement, and acrobatics was high. There were saltos, splits, tricks and schtick i.e. funny stage business.

However when you read those dozen lines you could easily judge them as cold, and unfunny. Perhaps though you read with slapstick lenses and see potential. That is what slapstick is: hidden comic potential anywhere. But in this case could you build a routine from those lines? How? It takes imagination. Maybe you don't have to think real hard. Maybe nothing comes. Maybe you have to memorise the lines first and play around with a fun-loving partner. Maybe you have to just keep saying the lines until your body starts to do something and your partner picks up on the action. Maybe you don't need the lines anymore 'cause you are just doing funny and physical things. Perhaps suddenly you start to say some of the lines in the wrong order and laughing yourself at your own stupid ideas coming out. This is where slapstick comes from. From nowhere, from out of nothing.

The routine continues.

The Entrepreneur is angry at Harlequin's stupid sense of humour. The Entrepreneur has other things on his mind like, Where the hell is Columbina? Things like all entrepreneurs have on their minds. Harlequin has almost no mind or Zen Mind. He's an empty vessel. A very mobile, active, empty vessel. He is a living dichotomy. He is absurd. It's catchy but the Entrepreneur wants to fight the disease, he is serious. That is his illness. That is his weak point that will defeat him every time.

It's all classic, Shakespeare; Commedia Dell'arte; Maccus, Baccus, Pappus; who preceded Commedia. It is all classic and natural. Slapstick is a very special world. It is the living world of the absurd. Not a happy place to be but it is funny. Come on in the water is fine. But you can't be a prude, you can't be ashamed, no regrets, just follow your impulses.

Be careful. Slapstick can hurt. But generally good slapstick, the best slapstick no one gets hurt. Careful you might have fun.

The Entrepreneur is always angry at Harlequin's fun. Harlequin imitates the angry gestures of the boss. Behind his back so's da boss can't see ya see? The Entrepreneur doesn't need eyes to see. Now the dialogue continues:

E What were you doing?
H Nothing
E Nothing huh? (H nods in agreement). You weren't doing nothing, you were doing something. (H nods in agreement) What were you doing?
H Something.
E Aha. (E says excitedly because he finally caught H doing something wrong). What something was that?
H Nothing.
E Aha. (E is not so sure now). What something is nothing?
H Nothing! (H says with delight because E still hasn't caught up. Silence as E mulls that over. E realises he's been duped AND EXPLODES).
E Get out of here. Stay, er, get out, stay here. Can you stay here? (H nods head and shrugs and squints eyes all at the same time to indicate 'maybe').
E Can we shake on that? (H nods a yes).
E Are you sure ? (H nods a bigger yes. E puts his hand out to shake in agreement E reaches, they shake hands but H shakes his whole body too).
E Would you stop that! (E pulls H's hand away and flings H's arm like a piece of rubber, the arm returns and takes E's hand so H's body shakes again).
E Stop that! (E fling's H arm again but now H's leg pops into E's hands).
E Harlequin would you stop that? (H's leg flung down but pops right back up).
E Stop it ! (leg flung down and pops up again E throws H immediately into a high back somersault. H lands exactly where he had been standing as if nothing happened).
E Now stay here. (As if nothing happened).

The Quantum Point is there was no somersault. Or was there? The audience was given no time nor invitation to applaud the salto. Done this way it hits a primal memory of what slapstick is all about. It's a surprise land of nothingness. It is not tricks. It is a place in the mind. The tricks take us there. They are not the goal, the tricks are the Jacob's Ladder of the theatre.

Just after E says Now stay here, E exits. H silently follows directly behind E. E stops short of the exit and senses H is behind and turns. H has suddenly jumped into a squat and is hiding behind his own hands like a mask.
E Harlequin I can see you. (Harlequin safely behind his mask shakes his head in disagreement). E Yes I can. I can see you, you're just there!

This whole routine is now on youtube within the whole show "Harlequin Dreams" uploaded in five parts listed as: Part 1, 2, 3, 4, and Final Part.

- 23 -
GENIUS OF THE THEATRE

The real genius of the theatre world is not a human being. The genius is Time. As we all know now, Time is Relative. Thank you Professor Einstein.

What we experience now as rebirth and genius in the theatre had very clear seeds one hundred years ago.

What were some of these seeds. The main seed was the change of the clock itself. Originally the clock was the Sun or the Moon. Various civilisations knew time by the 28 day cycle of the moon. There were of course other cultures which focused more on four seasons or even longer cycles of observing the Sun and Planets.

The device of the Sun dial gave us a 24 hour clock. Then at some point mechanical clocks were created giving precision to the hour clock. There was originally only an hour hand. Then at some point in Time the minute hand was added. Then the seconds. Now we have passed out of digital time and are into micro time.

The time of Theatre Genius for us modern, post-modern, post-post-modern beings began just before the dawning of the twentieth century. The 1890's started to yield a flood of geniuses who would change with the times. They were quite probably stimulated by muses, the Muse of War and the Muse of Technical Advancement.

Some of the scenery which set the stage for the march of geniuses were as follows:

Advancement of Transportation...steam locomotion, trains, cars, planes, speed.
Advancement of Photography.
Development of Cinema.
Advancement of Implements of War
Development of Industrial Technique
Advancement of Printing and Publishing
Advancement in Social Programs and Mass Education
Development of Psychoanalysis
Advancement of Ballet and Choreographic Concepts
Development of the Telephone
Advancement of Journalism via Telegraph and Telephone
There were developments in all branches of Science, Arts, Humanities.

There were major conflicts such as WW I, and the Sino-Japanese War, the Russian Revolution, the Women's Suffragette Movement, advancement of ideas and communication about liberation and emancipation of all humanity. Flotillas of Western navies began to arrive "peacefully" in Japan and China. That meant doorways opened between East and West and diplomats had more access to other cultures.

There were major centres for the Arts attracting not only artists but craftsmen, technicians, thinkers, philosophers. The main centres were Moscow, Berlin, Vienna, Paris, Hollywood, Beijing.

Two major players in regards to theatre at this time were Max Reinhardt and Serge Diaghilev. Reinhardt was an actor who specialised in character and comic parts. He was a vanguard thinker who transitioned from a very rich theatre tradition to become a director whose creativity burst the seams of creativity in the modern theatre. One document of Reinhardt's later work is a film of "A Midsummer Night's Dream". This was made in Hollywood in the 1930's. It included Mickey Rooney as Puck and the professional clown Joe E. Brown as Bottom.

Diaghilev was the great Russian impresario who delivered change and innovation from his stable of artists. Though his troupe was a dance company, ballet at that, what he delivered was the most advanced challenges to the idea of theatre. He released the artists such as Nijinsky, Stravinsky, Massine, and a large team who completely challenged the great centres of Russia, Germany, France, and England. There were riots in the theatre which were the intellectual seams bursting. About this same time in France the theatre critic Copeau decided to try to train a wave of new artists. In Moscow the directors Stanislavsky, Meyerhold, Tairov, Vahktangov, M. Chekhov were stretching their mental definitions of theatre. During this period Isadora Duncan was a source of inspiration for all. Then the great overtone of challenge arrived, the Chinese actor Mei Lanfang who embodied the profound wisdom which still today theatre practitioners are searching for.

Artists such as Chagall, Picasso, Kandinsky, Klee, and Miro were crossing into overtone or quantum awareness. They found a focal point which balanced senses of theatre, creativity, circus, clowns, colour, light and inspiration. They had theatre wisdom and were tied directly to the theatre changes.

In terms of literature for the theatre, people such as; Pirandello, Strindberg, Eugene O'Neill, Gertrude Stein, were reflecting changes in thought. Kafka drew directly from the inspiration of the theatre and eventually his creations feed back inspiration to the theatre.

At this time two odd look-a-likes appeared overwhelmingly on the world stage. They were born within days of each other. Both were astonishing actors, one with words and one in silence. Products of the time and destiny, Hitler and Chaplin.

This pool of technology, poverty, and war is the source of genius which today's theatre is directly created from.

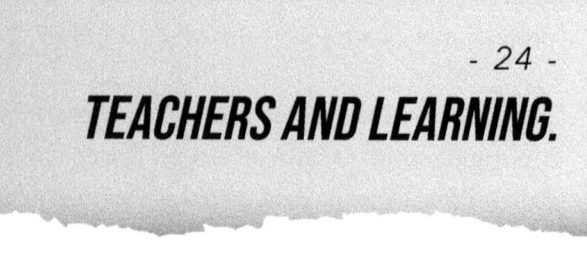

- 24 -
TEACHERS AND LEARNING.

Trudy Scott was the professor of drama at the Community College of Allegheny County (Boyce campus) in Pittsburgh. Trudy had been a dancer and then studied theatre at NYU.

I had just completed four years in the US Navy. One month later at the age of 21 I began to study Liberal Arts at Boyce. I got a job at school as a figure model. In spite of quite worldly experiences in the Navy, I had no idea that my job for the Art Department would be completely or even partially naked. I took to the job like a flash though. I mention this job because that is how I got taken into the theatre world. A student of Trudy's also studied Art. The student was directing a one act play and needed a male who could also act. I passed the obvious first test. During a break I read for the part in my dressing gown and I got the part.

We ran the student one act plays for four nights. Trudy sat in a spot where she saw me prepare to make my entrance and could also see the performance and could observe me backstage. On the last night as I exited she introduced herself, asked me what I was doing next semester. Then she informed me that I would act in the school project. I will? Yes you will. It was settled.

Trudy is the person who really took me fully into the theatre. She accepted me totally as the person I was and began to teach me not only theatre craft but also to trust one's instincts. Trudy created a classic nurturing environment where many eccentric creatures could fully live theatre.

I was with her two years while I studied English, Literature, Psychology, Sociology, Political Science, French, and civilian life. There was an excellent staff at this school which prepared people to then study at the top universities or to start a career choice.

I chose theatre "for a while". In the theatre we did a range of projects. I took two courses with Trudy outside of our projects. One was Modern Dance, the other was Scene Study and Stanislavsky. I did not have a clue what was going on in those classes nor with the concepts and craftsmanship which the other actors revealed. On stage though I was fine and in rehearsal I just listened and did what the director asked and when I had an idea I was always encouraged to try it. We worked continuously for two years. I became a top model in the city. The Boyce professor of Art began to teach me about Art history, the purpose of sketches, about line, light and dark, contour and other related concepts.

The first day I modelled though, something in my consciousness cracked the very first minute I began. I was hit with flashes about meditation, calmness, mime, creativity and imagination. Those are things I never gave any thought to so it was a stunning experience. My times modelling always fed my creative and intuitive insight.

All of my professors helped me in a profound way. Peter Dittrich taught Sociology and Political Science. He was 27 years old before he studied academically. He grew up in Germany and as a young lad he was constantly moved and marched from bombs. After the war he had been an actor, nurse, a construction supervisor. He had training as a dancer and as a jazz musician. Peter occasionally acted in Trudy's productions. He was the classic professor with whom you could either get drunk or have Russian tea and talk about philosophy and relationships and politics and laugh and laugh. In 1973: he explained to us that Ronald Reagan will be president in 1980, that there will be the re-unification of Germany; of the collapse of the USSR.

Peter and Trudy really double teamed me though to live with theatre. Trudy's theatre was life. Period. She had all the usual crises of a person and professor but she constantly directed towards self-empowerment of the individual. We had a wonderful zany, bright, lively group of actors.

Within the first month of starting college and starting modelling I started a relationship with a young wild intellectual named Laurel. I was 21 and she was a bit younger. What Peter, Trudy, and the Navy didn't teach me, Laurel did. She was immersed as an actress in the Pittsburgh Laboratory Theatre based on Grotowski's ideas. Before I met her the University of Pittsburgh presented Jerzy Grotowski with an award. He gave a public talk for theatre students and Trudy's actors said I should go with them. They all knew about Grotowski, I knew nothing. That was the first time I ever sat in a circle. I happened to sit one seat away from Grotowski, next to his translator. The Pittsburgh Laboratory Theater was connected to Laurel's school that was based on A.S.Neill's concepts. She reinforced the Life and Theatre deal which was a part of the zeitgeist that seemed to be a social revolution. Society was not only changing in many positive ways but was also planting seeds for future turmoil.

Art Jennings, Jr. was part of Trudy's ensemble. He was an English teacher, clown, comedian, juggler, and also a counsellor for disabled people. Art was the son of a clown, juggler and founder of the International Jugglers Association. Life and Theatre was Art.

Life stories happened to me in this period 1973-75 when I fell into the world of theatre. I landed 1500 miles away from Pittsburgh and into the backyard of an old clown in Sarasota. Danny Chapman had been Boss Clown for Ringling Brothers Circus. They had two troupes of the Greatest Show On

Earth. Danny headed one Ringling troupe's clown unit and Lou Jacobs was boss clown of the other.

When I met Danny he had been in the circus business for 55 years. He was the unofficial founder of the Ringling Clown College the year before it officially opened. Danny was every right thing for me at the right time. Sarasota, Florida where he lived is the circus capital of the USA. This is where most circus artists kept a home and then retired. So you had the absurd reality where people who worked in bookshops, restaurants, post office, etc had been often the most exceptional circus artists. Through Danny and life in Sarasota I got to meet some of these people. His circus apprentice Curtis Cainan went on to be a founder of Culpepper & Merriweather Circus. With his circus, Curtis mentored a nephew who became a master animal trainer, Casey McCoy Cainan.

Danny let me loose in his backyard where he had trapezes in the trees, a trampoline in the earth, a tight wire, unicycles, and a watchful eye and encouraging words everyday. After hanging around with Danny for a few months he initiated me finally into clowning. In this case I don't use the word 'initiate' lightly. When the right day came he gave me a costume, put my makeup on, then stood at a distance and told me "now put the nose on". I did and I had no idea what happened but it was like lightning went through the top of my head. My body felt cleansed, I understood something spiritual had just happened. Danny and his circus apprentice Curtis went into absolute fits of laughter. They couldn't look at me without literally falling with laughter and tears. Finally Danny told me to "take it off, take off the nose".

Danny took me thru a few different performance experiences and situations with him and his family who were all performers.

A few days after I first met Danny I met another actor who was also interested to learn about clowning. He was Ted Keyser from Holland and he just graduated from a state theatre university. This was his first time in the USA. He had hoped to train at Ringling's Clown College but was only allowed to observe for the first week. We met at the Clown College opening day ceremony. That was a Monday. The Thursday before though is when I arrived hoping to get into the Clown College but was informed they were full and had a waiting list of 13 people in case any of the accepted people canceled. I was told by the director Bill Ballentine that I was welcome to visit Monday to see the opening presentation. When I arrived at the circus rehearsal hall that sat a few thousand people, I walked straight thru the doorway and walked straight ahead and sat in the middle of the empty seats. However, when I sat down, I saw a smaller section of seating and there were a few dozen people. As I wondered if I was in the wrong section, another fellow walked thru the doorway and walked straight as I had and he sat right next to me. We said hello and then he saw there were many people sitting in the small section. While we discussed whether we should move, someone went into the arena which was set up with different circus skill locations set up for the welcoming demonstration. The person in the arena now took the microphone and announced "Could the two people sitting in the far section please come over to this side. So we got up and went to sit with everyone else.

After the introductions of Ballentine and a few senior clowns who would be teaching there were some talks. Then lunch. I had a car and invited Ted to go with me to find a nearby place to eat. As this was his first day or so on the USA, I took him to a classic roadside dinner. He ordered his meal but the waitress could not understand him so I helped. When she left he apologised for his poor English. I said his English was perfect but the waitress's English wasn't i.e. she was a real Southerner and just did not understand his accent.

After lunch I was told that I was only to see the pre-lunch opening talks. Ted had an agreement that he could observe the first week. So we arranged to meet at the end of the Friday at a circus themed bar that I had seen located nearby on the main road.

On the Friday before, I had rented an apartment on the beach. There was an extra space for someone else to stay, so I invited Ted to stay as long as he wanted. I introduced him to Danny. The two of us started to study together. We trained on the beach every morning starting about 6am before breakfast and before visiting and training at Danny's. Our training was doing the Chinese 4-minutes plan of eight different movements done as a choreography. I taught myself this routine many months before via the small book of instructions. I never had the music and that I heard years later and it is essentially 'fascistic' music. The movements themselves are simply excellent basics from martial arts. I still do the 4-minutes periodically and always teach it when I teach acrobatics and when I teach in cold weather as it brings blood circulation to the whole body and opens the cardiovascular system. After the 4 minutes exercises we would do a light run barefoot on the beach. The run was about 5 miles and took about 35 minutes. Then we would do some handstands and then swim. Then breakfast.

Ted had the postal address of Jango Edwards. I had met Jango about 5 months before. That was at the Experimental Theatre Festival in May 1975 at Ann Arbor. One afternoon I saw two clown troupes: Great Salt Lake Mime Troupe; and, right after was Friends Roadshow. Those shows made me see that I should be doing such work. I met Jango very briefly afterwards and asked if there was a place to study clown and he said Ringling had a clown college. I wrote to them and was a finalist out of 3000 applicants in 1975, but I was not in the final group selected. Now, in Sarasota I wrote a letter to him to see what he suggested. Two ideas were in the reply, one was to start performing on the street to learn about audiences and the other idea was to read the Fourth Way by P.D.Ouspensky.

Ted and I bought the book that same day. One copy. We would take turns reading it and immediately started daily discussions on the philosophy we read. This changed everything for me. I became conscious in a new way thru discussing ideas about self observation. Danny was profound so I was in good hands all around. I also bought a small book on self-hypnosis and worked with that every day. One basic practice was to keep a notepad near my bed and in the morning to record each dream.

One morning while practising handstands on the beach a little old man came up. He congratulated Ted and I on our efforts and said he used to do acrobatics. He told us to hold his legs and suddenly he jumped into a handstand and started to do pushups. This was Victor Drilea from Bucharest. He was 79. He had lived many lives in his 79 years. Once or twice a week he would give Ted and I voice lessons in the sea water up to our chest. When we would visit him at the trailer park where he lived, he would make us a cup of tea, play the violin, show his paintings and talk about philosophy.

Ted had plans to go to a theatre school soon in California. The name was The Dell'Arte School of Mime and Comedy. I asked what was dell'arte. He tried to explain but I couldn't understand why it had to be called commedia dell'arte if commedia meant comedy. Anyways we went around in circles. He told me of an article by the head teacher Carlo Mazzone-Clementi. Does that rhyme with commedia dell'arte? We got a copy of the article. The article had been in a theatre magazine. It was all about the foot. Well I had barely begun on the Fourth Way so these things still got nowhere for my way of thinking. However I had already in Pittsburgh found that I only would practise barefoot and preferably in the grass. That article was "Commedia and The Actor" in TDR (The Drama Review Edition 18) 1974.

Little did I know that with each step of my journey something was always right. Thank God because I had no idea about all these theatre ideas. I was just living life about ten days at a time. With my study of self-hypnosis at this time, things were fitting in.

Ted headed West on schedule. When he showed up about six weeks later at the Dell'Arte School, on the first day of the course, the first Monday of January 1976, I was waiting on the doorstep of the school and had a room for him in a house. A car pulled up right in front of the school. At the doorstep arrival with Ted was the car's driver a big burly bear. The bear said "AHA. DIS MUSTA BE IRA". I said "who are you?" The bear laughed out another "AHA!! A comedian. I am Carlo, at your service."

During the six weeks Ted was traveling West I wrote to him about each clown situation and performance I had with Danny. I didn't know on this first morning of school but Ted had stayed a few days with Carlo and had told Carlo all about my discoveries with Danny and clowning.

The students gathered in the studio with Carlo. Carlo told us first "You think this is a ten-week course. It is not. It is a ten-year course". I liked him a lot. He talked a bit of philosophy, jokes, ideas. He was friendly and funny. Carlo immediately has a bombastic, yet very warm approach to life. He asked some questions about people's theatre experience. In that group I could hear that I had the least experience. Then he asked if anyone had done any clowning. Several people had. I didn't say I had because I had done so little of course. Carlo asked again about clowning. Then he asked: Anybody else? Is there somebody else who's done some clowning? Nobody? Ira I understand that you have also done some clowning. I looked at Ted and he smiled. Carlo then asked: What were some of your experiences Ira? Oh, well, I've only done it a few times. Only a few times, I see. What about the first time? What happened the first time? What happened the first time you were a clown? Whoosh. Ol' Carlo got me to talk. I talked for well over an hour about clowning and discovering many things. Carlo kept nodding and smiling as if he were also meditating or something. During the hour when necessary he would prod me with another question?

Well I didn't know what that was all about until about ten years later. About then I met Cletus Ball. Right on schedule I guess.

What Carlo took pleasure in was in some way I had discovered many of the central things he would try to teach. It is not so easy to teach some things. That is the point of The Fourth Way. One of Carlo's main themes is the Art of Discovery and wonderment, amazement. Carlo's penultimate exercise is The Amazing Maze. I tell more about that and Carlo and Dell'Arte school in the book *Clown Secret*.

- 25 -
A SCHOOL OF DELL 'ARTE

The next 6 pages are a series of interconnected life/theatre personal anecdotes about trying to find one's way in the theatre/world.

I was at the Dell'Arte School in California at a particular time not only in my life but a particular time in Carlo's life and thus a particular time in the school's life.

To enrol in the school one had to provide two recommendation letters. My two letters must be the two shortest in the history of the world. Trudy Scott said, "Ira Seidenstein can learn anything." and Danny Chapman said, "I recommend Ira Seidenstein for your school".

I loved being at the school. Everything was good for me, improvising, training, listening to Carlo, and watching the other students. There was a wide range of theatre and life experiences in the group and the few teachers. Without any doubt what I learned about theatre at this school was equaled by what I learned about alternative lifestyles.

Carlo deserves a few books on his life and his influence on many theatre people. Carlo was very hard to get along with particularly the closer you got to him. I liked him at a distance like a bear, but I liked him very much. Carlo was temperamental and inspirational as he instructed. He was always philosophical and always a pain in the butt with organisation and communication. But he was always theatre. Carlo was theatre. He was always a complete dichotomy and paradox. So was every single day at the school. I loved the chaos. That was it, that is theatre. That Carlo knew. He said many beautiful things. Most will never be recorded because they were flashes at the moment, play on words, "a la improviso" which Carlo translates to "all of a sudden". He loved language though he said the way to learn comedy was through silence. Sometimes he would say "I am the wind". That could mean anything. Once when he was furious in the spiritual sense and he said with great force "You think I am talking about theatre, but I am not. I am talking about life."

There it is. Life and Theatre. That was what he wanted. But students, teachers, co-workers, and human beings do not do well with dichotomy and paradox. Dell'Arte was a paradox and a paradise for me. Carlo was at the right time for me. I worked very hard at the school. It gave me space and time to explore.

It did not give enough technique. This is a problem not just with Dell'Arte but with many theatre schools, i.e. especially the 'physical theatre' components (dogma), and schools considered 'physical theatre schools' which are usually dogmatic.

Carlo had wonderful exercises of his own for improvised mime. But his great strengths were not only language and philosophy but that he was an athlete. His father had been a calvary soldier and trained Carlo in fencing through very gruelling discipline. Carlo's strength as a mime and physical comic and as a wonderful actor was that he was an athlete and lived a wild youth.

He wanted the students to be athletic, but he talked too much. He did not talk too much for me. I loved what he said, what he had to say and how he expressed himself. I studied him as an actor. But, the more he talked the less we did in class. What he talked about and how was always inspiration. I made up for the sitting time first of all by training myself early in the morning before the school sessions began; I performed in pubs on weekends; I was always first to volunteer when Carlo asked for a volunteer for any of his exercises, until … one day after he described the intention and instructions for the next exercise he said something to the effect of: 'And in a moment, but not yet, I will be asking for a volunteer. And today when I ask for a volunteer, which I am NOT doing yet, but, when I do I would like someone OTHER than Ira to volunteer to be first'. From then I understood to wait as long as it took to have 2 or 3 volunteers then when a lull settled I'd look at Carlo like a forlorn puppy waiting for its owner to take off the leash so it could endlessly tire itself out running around the park.

My brief time with Danny Chapman gave me insight into the dichotomy of what is called, actor training.

Dell'Arte school was only a paradise if you were athletic, a bit zany and inclined to live in chaos. If you were like Carlo, temperamental and inspirational. Otherwise you could not possibly take advantage of the riches of Dell 'Arte. Carlo had worlds to offer but it was quite unavailable in reality. His wife Jane Hill was an extraordinary actress, comedian, and person. Jane had a tremendous literary and craft knowledge of theatre and acting. She was a great teacher. The school schedule had little space or time for her. She was a professor at a university and that took most of her time. Plus Jane was also a housewife and mother with three children, plus Carlo. She and Carlo supported my growth literally like parents. They would support anyone who was willing to stay and work but because of the paradoxes people flew away. Carlo's assistant was nearly a saint to him and thus to all of us students. This was Joan Schirle. She was a dancer and actress. She also was a teacher of the Alexander Technique. Joan was an excellent comic. She could also write and direct, and had lived several existences in her young life.

These three people Carlo, Jane, and Joan are who I consider my main teachers at Dell'Arte. The other staff teachers I certainly learned from but that was more to do with a paradox of them being part of a proposed package. Part of Carlo's concept was that to learn about theatre you should be close to nature so Dell'Arte is in a rural town (Blue Lake) but not far from other larger towns (Arcata, and, Eureka).

During my time at Dell'Arte, Carlo was the main teacher

There was a period with a guest teacher Jane Lapiner. She had a profound influence on me with connecting theatre and nature and also her physical technique was clear and precise. She had her own concepts with masks from animal skins. Rather masks that were not much more than animal skins. From her I learned about masks. That is, that masks are not a face or head covering, rather a mask is only complete when it involves the whole body - 360 degrees. Some years later she and her husband began Human Nature theatre company in Mendocino County.

Joan Schirle was also a real nature woman and a strong social activist and helped me to learn in those areas. Joan also gave me clear paradoxical feedback every week at presentation. In particular she gave harsh critique of my work at the same time always encouraging my ideas and individuality.

There was lots for me to learn from the other students. Several had already trained in mime, one was a professional mime. That was Bob Rosen who went on to co-found Theatre de la Jeune Lune. Other fellow students were what seemed at the time experienced dancers but in retrospect it's just that they had more experience then than I had. One man Peter Anderson was an excellent writer and creator. Doug Berky was on his way to being a great mime, clown, mask maker, teacher and by now I am sure he is also an excellent director. Gale McNeely was an excellent professional actor and tremendously funny. Another student, Cheryl, had studied voice mimicry. Jim Stephenson was another fine person and student from the Mid-West. After we each completed our times at the school we were in the clown theatre started by Gale. Hannah Edwards was in it when I joined and Paul Klusterman left which left the empty space for me to join. An important character for me was Peter Cuneen. He had just won national honours for his juggling. Peter and I had a personality clash and he handled it well. I learned a lot from dealing with him. In the end we became very good friends and we created a most exciting duet which we performed in pubs. I was the Wild Man and he was my Captor. It was classic Jerry Lewis - Dean Martin, with the wild clown doing absolutely outrageous things with the audience and the straight man delivering the funny apologies. It was "a la improviso" with clear structure. Cuneen became a first rate doctor of Chinese Medicine and now lives in Switzerland.

Another student with whom I have had a close friendship and exchange of ideas was Ole Brekke. He later ran his own school in Copenhagen. Ole was probably the oldest student, perhaps he was 34. He had become a merchant sea going officer by graduating from the merchant naval academy. After a few years at sea he decided to train as a teacher and as a dancer. He had been a wild little bunny in his early life but when he arrived at Dell 'Arte he was away from all vices. He had found his spiritual path and was devoted, in his own way, to spirituality and humanity. We made some wonderful clown acts together. A few years later we became teaching partners as a way for him to establish his school in Stockholm and later the school moved to Copenhagen. In Stockholm it had inherited the name "Clownskolan" and when it moved to Copenhagen it was renamed "The Commedia School". Prior to the Stockholm school there had been a growing interest in clown in Sweden as the great clown Manne began to emerge. At this time also the Americans of my genre began to tour extensively through Europe but also into Scandinavia. Those clown/mimes were from The Great Salt Lake Mime Troupe (including Georgio Peugot) and from Friends Roadshow was Michael "River the Mime" Lynch. River had taught many workshops and started a family with his Swedish wife Camilla. River and Jango Edward's troupe Friends Roadshow, and Katie Duck head of Great Salt Lake Mime all activated hundreds of clowns, mimes, jugglers throughout Scandinavia and Europe and the USA. River established a precedence for training clowns, mimes and alternative theatre in Stockholm as "Clownskolan" within Teater Huset. Ole arrived when River was preparing move to live and teach throughout New Zealand.

I joined Ole for a year as teaching partner. That was his first year to offer a long course. During that year I lived in the house of Ole, his wife Maria, and devotees of their yoga group. By the time I arrived in Stockholm I was teaching meditation and intuition development. Our time together was an exchange of ideas. I studied with mild fury everything their guru had written that I could get through in my spare time. Plus I learned about their practices and approach to community service first hand from everyone in the house. It was yet another crucial year for my poor soul.

Notably, I had not yet fully realised the depth of my own Jewish heritage's activism for Humanity's development. In 1976 I had read the book "9 and 1/2 Mystics", but it was not until about 1987 that I began the long, slow, gradual process of beginning to see the light within my own culture. In 1981 River brought me to New Zealand/Aotearoa to follow up and to further develop his teaching there. That journey kept this shaman's bones rattling for more growth. Later via meeting with the Maori, and, the Indigenous Australians and their cultures, served as lessons and reflections of my own culture.

Back to Dell'Arte. January, 1976, the school started on a Monday and by Wednesday something bizarre had happened to me. Before that Wednesday I was a regular meat and potatoes sort of guy. You couldn't fool me, I was streetwise.

Well, ha ha ha, life dealt me a big blow to reality in January 1976. Now, in 2020, theoretical physicist Lee Smolin explains that even Quantum physicists are divided between 'Realists' vs 'Anti-Realists' and that is a premise in his book, *Einstein's Unfinished Revolution: The Search for What Lies Beyond the Quantum*. Most spiritual paths refer to reality as an illusion. Whereas their mystical wisdom and experience is viewed as reality.

There was a small apartment in the school which was taken by three female students. Michelle was of Italian decent. She was a big voluptuous woman. She knew all about herbs, health food, yoga, massage, and life. She had a big passionate heart and filled that 'gap' at the school. Her roommate was Lenka who was of English decent on her father's side and Jewish on her mother's side. Her father was an acting prodigy of the great youth theatre/educator Peter Slade. Lenka had lived and studied with A.S.Neill at Summerhill. The next trio member in the apartment was Marlene, an AfroAmerican princess from Chicago. She was kind, sharp, precise and articulate with language, art, and classics knowledge.

On Wednesday of the first week of 1976, this trio asked me if I would like to have dinner with them. Well, okay, but I really must concentrate on my theatre studies. A feast was laid out. Vegetarian. Oh well. But they had even baked a cake for dessert. Okay I stay. At dinner they talked about all kinds of freaky (New Age) things. I listened. Then they started to talk about when this 10-weeks mime/theatre course was over maybe they could go study at The Berkeley Psychic Institute. Well even the word psychic set me off. What on Earth would you study there? Our past lives, came the multiplex reply. I was vociferous. You don't believe that stuff! Besides you have to live now. Okay says Michelle, I know an exercise to see past lives, we can do that before dessert. They got me there. I loved food. Michelle explained what to do. Fine, I can handle this. First I was to began to look at Michelle's face. Within one minute I saw something. A lot of something and vivid and clear. My eyes were wide open. No alcohol, no drugs, no heavy breathing. I saw flash after flash, a slide show of "masks" appearing on Michelle's face. Virtual reality. One after another I saw Michelle's past lives. Or the illusion of past lives. As Shakespeare's Macbeth states about the dagger appearing from his "heat oppressed mind". I closed my eyes to break the trance or phenomenon. And abruptly left saying I must go. Thanks for the dinner and keep the dessert. I did not believe what I saw, but I was deeply shaken since I obviously saw something. If there are past lives then I saw them. If there aren't then I still saw something that sure looked like a virtual reality of Michelle's past lives.

I went directly home anxious to hide in bed. I stopped to brush my teeth in the bathroom. Brush, brush, as I looked in the mirror. Oh shit. My face reflection started to alter. I tried not to stare because now even I knew what would happen. Then all around my face reflection appeared beautiful colours like a rainbow. Too much for me. Up to bed.

That was Wednesday. By Friday night Lenka and I were, maybe, in some type of relationship? The Shechinah of Kabbalist lore works in funny ways. A few days later Lenka told me things about myself which she could not have known. Before coming to Dell 'Arte, she had gone to see a Gypsy psychic. The psychic had told Lenka all about me.

Lenka being a rather shy person gave me five days leeway before fulfilling that Gypsy's prophecy.

Many things happened to me. The most important thing at Dell'Arte was not the theatre training though that was the excuse to gather.

I trained all the exercises of the school also on my own. I began to perform my own ideas and test concepts every Friday and Saturday in a variety of pubs. The main act was a Shakespearean act. But I also did my own improvisations in mime and movement. Peter Anderson and I made an act where I parodied a faith healer. The only problem was when I took "volunteers"... things happened. Something happened, like an electricity in my hands and forehead and the volunteers experienced a healing. Well I gave that act up quick enough.

Peter and I took up swimming instead. He taught me how to swim 'long' distance and improve technique. I swam only breaststroke. We were in the pool at 6:30 am. We swam for one hour. Buckwheat pancakes were in our stomach by 8 am. By 9 am we were in school, stomach, pancakes and all. In other periods even starting the first 10-weeks I was in the school usually by 7am. I lit the pot-belly stove with wood in the main hall and began my own training and physical research to learn whatever ever I could by combining exercises from the course with my own examination/research.

Because of Michelle I took up the study of Yoga. I saw how flexible she was while by the end of our first semester I had gotten stiffer and even had joint pain. For vacation one classmate had a large family house near San Francisco and several of us including Michelle stayed there. She was going to an acupuncturist she had been to, Dr. Naburo Muramoto author of the book "Healing Ourselves". In those days, one could hitchhike fairly easily if one was patient. So Michelle left me with Dr. Muramoto. He stood in front of me staring at my face for perhaps 1 or 2 minutes. Then he said "stomach no good" and we went into the treatment room. When that was over, I hitchhiked to a nearby 'new age' bookstore that Michelle told me about. I was going to get a book on yoga. I got a ride immediately and the older man driving told me he hadn't been on that road for 20 years and the last time was to go to the bookstore I was going to. As I walked in, the first bookshelf facing the doorway had some yoga books.

I bought a used paperback book. The first day I practised six simple postures for three hours. That book was by Richard Hittleman. The next day I started working with another book. That was *Hatha Yoga* by Goswami that was filled with great photos and information. I worked with that book for three years. But from the first day I practised yoga about 20 years. Occasionally I still do some yoga, sometimes I take only five minutes. Every day is a different story. I did yoga virtually every day from late March 1976 to about 1996 when this book was written. Sometime around 1996 I thought what would happen if I stopped doing yoga? Many good developments happened when I stopped doing regular yoga practice. Nature abhors a vacuum.

Also during the time at Dell'Arte I read about alternative lifestyles, healthy foods and diet, philosophy, and meditative concepts. Most important, popular at that time, were the writings of Herman Hesse and Ayn Rand. In retrospect I certainly left Rand, but still see much greater value in the ideas and art of Hesse's writings. Perhaps more important to me were the autobiography of Carl Gustav Jung, *Memories, Dreams, Reflections*; and, a book, *9 & 1/2 Mystics*, by Herbert Weiner that became particularly valuable in my journey's reboot from the mid-1980s.

Books were always balanced by practice and living.

There was a summer theatre festival run by Jane and Carlo. It was American summer stock theatre. Professional actors came from NYC, LA, and San Francisco. I acted in one company. There were two companies and each played two productions on a rotating schedule through Summer 1976.

Jane helped me tremendously during this summer. At this point in my career it was Jane's direct interventions that kept me on the path. Joan and Carlo supported this.

There was a beautiful university theatre we used. When it was free I would go on the darkened stage and improvise like a ghost. Only a working light was on. One day someone came in and sat in the theatre as I played. I could hear it was actually two people; a child and an adult. They were laughing so I played more.

When I was done the adult came up. It was the festival designer Alain Schons. This was the first time we talked. We spoke for about ten minutes but it was quite obvious he knew more about clowns than some of the Dell'Arte teachers.

I spoke to Carlo and Joan the next day about getting Alain to teach clowning at the school. They literally laughed at me. The designer? And they laughed again. I insisted, yes the designer. Laughter. I insisted. They knew me well after six months as my teachers. Okay we'll talk to him. About three years later Alain was the school director.

Alain was knowledgable about clown history, an exceptional teacher, designer, puppeteer, and theatre historian. He was also kind and generous. When I first presented my slapstick solo act of a newspaper and chair the two people I invited to show it to were Alain and Carlo. Alain was also an apiarist/beekeeper, and a chef. Finally he gave up theatre for life instead, for about 15 years as a chef in his own restaurant in southern France. But periodically theatre beckoned him away from the culinary world.

Unbeknownst to him, as he was in the kitchen cooking, his influential teacher Gerard Koch and family ate there each summer. I only discovered that in September 2001 after a few days with Alain and his wife Gail, and then stayed at the Paris home of my friend Isabelle Koch and told her of the restaurant and she said her family ate there at least once each Summer. Koch was the main art teacher and colleague who established the principle explorations in art in Jacques Lecoq's school. Alain studied there when Koch was the art teacher.

At the 1976 summer theatre festival I taught acrobatics for the actors. After a few lessons with Danny Chapman and his retired circus friends…lessons in acrobatics at Dell'Arte were a bad joke. Carlo himself knew partner acrobatics well and he was an ideal bottom/base man. He preferred to call himself an 'understander'. But Carlo really left acrobatics to two assistants.

It is through acrobatics that I saw the big gap between the authentic world of training as I witnessed amongst circus artists young and old, versus the theoretical theatre 'methods'. Even though I was a beginner, I could see that the so-called 'physical theatre' methods were very weak compared to the real circus. So, I went to the library and got three books on acrobatics and started to study and train myself. On weekends some of the students asked me to teach. In school however I did exactly as the teachers instructed. At Dell'Arte I also learned how not to teach.

This insight via acrobatics has now been applied by myself to other subjects such as: teaching, acting, voice, mime, dance, directing and other subjects. Even in conflict, I learned vital lessons at Dell'Arte.

Jane and Joan were excellent teachers. Carlo was always inspiring. Jane Lapiner was excellent. Later, she and her husband formed Human Nature Theater Company. There were two main teachers who lacked experience as teachers. Yet they were also my teachers and exposed me to new encounters. I took whatever they gave. Their problems seemed to be that they lacked the wisdom to understand the wealth of traditional artists' experience, insight and dedication. They had a lack of heart to understand the lineage which is unbroken in the theatre. A lineage which at the same time they laid claim to yet seemed not to honour. One of the teachers was a born clown and the other was a born intellectual. Their weaknesses as inexperienced or young teachers drove me directly to find better sources. Finding eventually Cletus Ball, finding Yoga and Meditation, finding the history of theatre, dance, and circus. Finding the seeds that Trudy Scott and Danny Chapman and Art Jennings had clearly planted. These seeds were watered by Carlo, Jane and Joan.

Now I feel in agreement with Jerzy Grotowski and say that theatre is a laboratory.

With Eugenio Barba I agree and say let us go to the purest sources and masters.

With Marcel Marceau and Martha Graham I agree about the responsibility which must balance our creative freedom.

With Jean Louis Barrault and Michel Saint-Denis I agree that the world of classic and modern plays give us strength and focus in the laboratory.

With the Chinese and Japanese classic opera and theatre I agree that the theatre should be filled harmoniously with sound and visual action, text and silence. Theatre requires apprenticeship to master practitioners. Practitioners who performed.

Carlo really believed that actors should train in Wushu. Carlo also believed religiously, faithfully, and philosophically in God. He also believed in study, practise, nature, and life.

Carlo's sources were his father's eccentricity, Carlo's priest to whom he confessed was a Saint. Carlo was a soldier for five years in the Italian hills during World War II. After the war he studied poetry, art, athletics and theatre for four years.

His source was himself. The source of the Dell'Arte School is pure Carlo. Carlo's wife Jane Hill was his equal visionary.

Carlo had humble gratitude to a theatre teacher. However, Carlo's real inspiration though is from his own powerful and undeniable life force. This was fed by opposing dynamics of his father and his confessional priest, war, and a love of poetry. Theatre teachers are often little more than catalysts. In Carlo's case as in thousands of others, the devastation of World War filled him, and other young people who experienced war, with a desire to seek creative life giving alternatives such as theatre. He had a passionate desire.

In the theatre, as Carlo told me, his spiritual mentor was Marcel Marceau with whom he toured about 1947 through war torn Italy. Carlo also said that Marceau was extremely funny and witty with language. Marceau is actually the angel or medium who redefined and released the desire for 'new' actors. His success was nearly instantaneous from the time he played Arlequin in the theatre and just a few years later his first appearances on USA TV burst open his international opportunities. Marceau was taught by Etienne Decroux who was inspired by Dullin and Copeau. Copeau like Decroux studied everyone and everything. Copeau had a great teaching colleague Suzanne Bing. Two of Copeau's strongest inspirations were religious contemplation and the Fratellini Brothers clown troupe.

Carlo's intellectual muse was his marriage partner Jane Hill. Some of Jane's inspiration was Carlo, but, also her own engagement with formal and classical theatre training at Carnegie Tech (name later changed to Carnegie Mellon University). While Jane did her four years of study there Carlo was the movement teacher. One of her classmates, Arne Zaslove, became Carlo's first prodigy. (Arne's book *UnMasking the Mask* was just published this week in November 2020 so I haven't had a chance to read it yet).

Quite coincidently I lived near the university Carnegie Tech, and its sports facilities were my main playground. During this time in Pittsburgh we had an Italian policeman named Vince who was a brilliant mime and clown. While directing downtown traffic Vince would clown, mime, dance and do pratfalls. Vince was a strong influence to me as a performer. We had other kinds of childhood heroes in Pittsburgh. Two athletes were extremely popular and benevolent souls. One was the Italian wrestler Bruno Samartino; and, the other was the Puerto Rican baseball star Roberto Clemente. Theatre must come from life. In that sense commedia dell'arte can never be taught. As Carlo said, no, rather shouted "You think I am talking about theatre. But, I am not! I am talking about life"!

I had lived with Danny and his family, been taught by Trudy, and inspired by Peter Dittrich. Carlo continued their inspiration thru all his temperaments. Unfortunately, Jane and Joan had to filter a lot of the temperament so the actors could get more of the inspiration. Ironically, when the inspiration came it fell upon too many students with deaf ears and lethargic bodies.

The first goal of Quantum Theatre is to open the ears, eyes, and bodies of novice or experienced actors. This is done by getting them into a Natural State. Once the natural state is reached, enthusiasm, desire, and rapid learning occur spontaneously.

Only then can one begin to teach theatre subjects. Then the word student is inappropriate. This means the teacher and the student simply become collaborators. Then we begin to live theatre and stop the nonsense called pedagogy.

Theatre teachers tend to become pendants. Boring, old fashioned farts, who mythologize their own part and romanticise theatre. Theatre is work. But the real work is on one's Self. This is the Fourth Way message, as explained by Gurdjieff and Ouspensky. Thanks to the advice of Jango Edwards I bought the book The Fourth Way and began to work immediately on my Self. One's self is a continual work-in-progress. Dell'arte School in California gave me space, time, support, and paradox to work on my Self while playing theatre. Although I read the book *Nine and a Half Mystics: The Kabbala Today* (1969) Rabbi Herbert Weiner, during this period, a book about authentic modern Kabbalist's. I read it in 1976. I was just starting my own experiments (conscious and subconsciously) with reality. It was about 15 years later that I began a slow meandering process of connecting deeply with the knowledge, wisdom, and understanding within my own heritage. My intended third book *Remnants* will reveal some of this ongoing journey and a lot about the value of that heritage.

- 26 -
TRY TO QUIT THEATRE

Finally I decided that theatre was not spiritual enough for me. That meant only that I needed something else. I went on a journey right out of Greek mythology. After six months of chaos. 12,000 miles of travel, bouncing from paradox to paradox, …I landed.

I returned to Dell'Arte. Mischa T Clown offered me a place to stay in San Francisco. I went the next day. Then with two other Dell'Arte students I went to a huge Renaissance Arts and Crafts Fair. There I got locked on to something strange. I stared at two people sitting in a tent. There was a healing going on. It was The Berkeley Psychic Institute's tent. I had completely forgotten about BPI from my first Wednesday at Dell'Arte. (Note: BPI now 2020 is drastically different than it was in the 1970s. In the 70s it was much more open while the actual Founder still ran it.)

One and a half years after this tent encounter I graduated from BPI's Advanced program.

The day after I graduated, I flew to start my second theatre tour with Gale McNeely and Jim Stephenson. This tour started in Pocatello, Idaho. Legendary town of song about Vaudeville "Born In A Trunk" sung by Judy Garland, "I was born in a trunk, in the Princess Theatre in Pocatella,

Idaho". In our show my main clown act was of a clown magician (Gale) trying to lock me in a theatre trunk to make me disappear.

The founder of BPI was Lewis Bostwick. Lewis and his staff provided me with a safe, light hearted, and clear environment for me to develop spiritual insight i.e. intuition. At Dell'Arte, Carlo said his school was to go back to first grade. Lewis said that BPI was like going back to kindergarten.

I was going backwards. The right direction to discover your deeper self.

My time in Berkeley and San Francisco was active day and night with BPI, Yoga, writing, theatre, and acrobatics. I studied also at this time with Joan Porter at the New College. She taught me mime, Tai Chi, and dance. I studied acrobatics with The Angels of Light Dance Theatre, and clown with Frankie Dailey, and acting with my stage partner David Pearce. Lenka taught me about art. San Francisco taught me cafe life.

I was creating my own blend of theatre, life, and spiritual focus.

- 27 -
PROFESSOR CLETUS

As I progressed in theatre studies and experiences over many years I still had in the back of my mind that I could find a teacher who had already lived in the world of physically crafting theatre.

I know now that Copeau had the same desire and hired the Fratellini Brothers to bring wisdom and technique to his Vieux-Colombier theatre. Meyerhold sought the same by bringing circus artists into the theatre world. Reinhardt sought the same with Joe E. Brown. Bert Lahr and Max Wall were likewise hired into productions of Waiting For Godot. Shakespeare's fellow players were professionals, the wisdom and technique was aided by people such as Richard Tarlton the most famous clown in that period. Although Tarlton didn't work directly with Shakespeare, other clowns did such as Robert Armin, William Kemp, and John Singer.

What was in the back of my mind was a teacher such as Cletus Ball.

I met Clete in 1985. The knowledge I was seeking was the living world of slapstick. The technique and craft. Nearly ten years before Clete and I met though, I had found a book on tumbling and stunts from the 1930's. It's curriculum was developed by L.L. McClow as he taught at the South Chicago Y.M.C.A. For many years in the USA the YMCA had a nationwide physical program that included teaching circus, clowning, acrobatics and slapstick. This book from the program was filled with stick figure drawings and routines. I worked with the book on my own and with partners. But I lacked a teacher with the pure knowledge equal to the book.

Cletus knew every trick in that book and much more. He had lived it.

One year before we met, before I had heard of Clete, I met two of his top students who were performing also outdoors near my stage in The Festival of Sydney 1984. They were Price and McCoy, an authentic, high-tech, pair of acrobatic actors. Terry Price was the bottom man and Tim McCoy was the flyer. I was performing a 35 minute slapstick show with Barbara Doherty. We used dance, mime and juggling.

Terry and Tim were doing many of the most advanced tricks in the book. Terry could throw Tim any which way and Tim could somersault, land like a cat and deliver the next joke. Terry could catch Tim or throw him no matter what.

The next year I moved to Sydney. Terry became my 'Australian guardian angel'. He took great care of this new immigrant acrobat and made sure I got work. Then one day he said "Look, there is someone very close to me who you should meet. He's my teacher Cletus and I think you guys would like each other." A few days later we drove to the outermost suburb of Sydney. That town Asquith was the beginning of the northern bush. There was an old sports field and sports hall. In we go. There are mats, a trampoline, mini-tramps, and other equipment. There are a few rowdy, small town teenagers practising and also mucking around. There's an older man who looks like Paul Hogan or Crocodile Dundee. He's the classic rugged, handsome Australian bush man of legend. It's Cletus, Price and McCoy's teacher. We are introduced and he starts talking and I listen. We want to see what each other can do. I go and change my clothes and come back and warm-up. Terry has a new partner now in 1985, Peter Dagger. Peter was also taught by Cletus. Peter could do everything Tim could but with faster rotation. For business purposes the team is still called Price and McCoy. The teenagers were trying to do the basic tricks but they obviously have no real technical training. Clete lets them play, explore, argue, laugh.

Then we start training with vaults over an old wooden gym horse. Shortly I can do all the basic dives, springs and front salto. That's over the narrow horse, oh shit now they turn it longways. Shit. It's a boys room now. It's definitely a trial by fire. Fear. First the dive. Okay. I did it. Now the salto. What already? Yeah. Blip. I smashed my hand because I got scared in mid air. It's broken. I broke my thumb. Tough luck. Terry comes over. Cletus comes over takes my hand. Holds it. Naw, you're okay. Just give it a rest. He doesn't let go of my hand. This big hunk of an acrobat just turns my hand over. He's staring at my hand like it's the Mona Lisa. "Geez you've got real beautiful hands. They're real artists hands you know that."

Cletus knew many things which exist in no book. Knowledge is in between the lines.

My thumb was sore but I was fine. I start to do some flips, saltos, splits etc. Cletus watches. Talks to me a lot now. He's very curious now. Then he started to teach me basic things of Price and McCoy. What he called doubles-work. Cletus was expert in doubles, trio, and quartet.

He performed with partners for over twenty-five years. His speciality which was as a lift act, designed specifically to lift the audience's energy, so that the star of a show came in on a cloud. He had performed many years also as a slapstick acrobat. He was part of a great tradition called Australian Knockabout. He was the "Real McCoy", that means he was authentic. Since he also had good dance training, he was eventually taken into a Polish dance-acrobatic team, The Ganjou Brothers & Juanita. Juanita was American born in Detroit. Clete created an act, "The Bal Caron Trio", and continued a successful career in NYC, Paris, London, and Las Vegas.

When last I saw him in Sydney he was performing all the standard doubles work with Peter Dagger. Clete was in his 60's and Peter was about 30. When Clete was about 57 he decided to try clowning for the first time. We did some performances together and Clete continued to teach me. Price and McCoy is now Terry and Henning who had worked non-stop for over 25 years. It is now 2020 and Clete is nearly 90 and long retired in his hometown of Albury. Henning teaches English in France and Terry coaches a few talented individuals and performs occasionally, but, he has developed a funny fun English language immersion course that uses song, dance, and comedy.

Terry and Henning have the Knockabout knowledge. They know precisely what they are doing and precisely how to teach. I never studied enough with Clete since I was always involved with writing, producing, and acting. But we maintained training time, we performed together, and Clete always taught even while I was directing him during our season of my play "The Male Adored Bride".

He survived for ten years by having a cleaning business from about the age of fifty. His alarm rang at 2:30 am. He was at work by 3:30 or 4 am. When he had an idea or an urge to talk he would drop by my house at 7 or 7:30am. His opening line was "Geez Ira, were you sleeping? I thought for sure you'd be up doing your yoga or swimming." My line was "Clete come on in I'll make some coffee." His next line, "Naw. I can come back later. You going to have a coffee?" Then the dialogue was improvised and soon breakfast was served.

The people who had knowledge were often the Punch and Judy men.

They were always called "Professor".

There is knowledge out there. Often we in the theatre are deaf to the idiosyncrasies of the very people who possess experience and wisdom well beyond our intellectual pursuits. It is the authentic traditional people of Show Business who posses this knowledge. Besides my own career as a theatre artist, which ebbs and flows of its own discretion, the work of Quantum Theatre is to open the heart, mind, and body of theatre practitioners to hear, see, and consider a fresh perspective on the traditional artists. Artists not only of circus, and vaudeville but also the vast knowledge which classical actors embody.

- 28 -
SHAKESPEARE'S SLAP SCHTIK

I will now focus on a single small role that I played in Shakespeare repertory. Earlier I had mentioned this role of Ol' Gobbo from The Merchant of Venice. The character appears in a single scene and normally there is no mention of the character in books about Shakespeare. It is called a minor comic role. This scene was the only scene which the actors in our company applauded during rehearsal. They applauded every single time the scene was rehearsed. It was the only scene which, except for one evening, was always applauded by the audience. To be quite pedantic, what I refer to as a scene in this case involved three connecting sections in Act 2 Scene 2.

Applause, though in the end, means only that people were generous and applauded, nothing necessarily more.

There was a single night when the scene was not applauded by an audience. This night was, to say the least, a jaded audience. On this night as I waited in the wings for my entrance, the artistic director exited from his first scene as Shylock. He said to me sharply, "Expect nothing from this audience. And I mean nothing". His stage sense was impeccable and he was right. Some nights are like that. This same invited audience was witnessing our three plays opening nights in a row. This was the third play in our repertoire. They were either tired of us or tired of Shakespeare or didn't like the production or rebelled against the racism of the play. This was our fourth city and this time we were in Melbourne for a six week season.

The previous year the company had also played *Merchant*. I saw that and it was a poor production. The Artistic Director, John Bell played Shylock. He was as great in the role as anyone could be. It was mainly because of his role as Shylock that I wanted to work and study with him. His wife Anna Volska played Nerissa, and she too is a special level of actor, of the finest quality. The Director of the play was normally excellent so I suspected and saw clear signs that something was amiss in the ensemble. The Director, Carol Woodrow also directed Merchant the next year with me as Ol' Gobbo. Carol is truly a great, intelligent and caring director. The problem if I may be so blunt was a woman director with uncompromising intelligence having to face God only knows what variety of subtle, underhanded resistance from that group of actors. I adored working with her. Carol helped me and educated me about the web of the play, and allowed me creative freedom not only as the clown, but in my two other minor acting roles in the play.

In Melbourne though, after our first matinee, a man came up introduced himself as John and congratulated me on my work. Then he said "Look I've already spoken to Carol and she said you really resolved the scene. I was the Dramaturg on Merchant last year and I could not resolve that scene. I'd love to take you to lunch and pick your brains". Like Harlequin, I am always hungry, so he got me.

John or Dr. John such-and-such as it turned out was wonderful to me. There was plenty to talk about and he was a world of knowledge. He was a Cambridge Ph.D with areas of expertise in Renaissance and Elizabethan history and theatre. Yeah, I guess that ain't bad for doin' Shakespeare.

The concept behind resolving this scene though can be applied to hundreds of scenes in Shakespeare, and each of his plays. The concepts can be applied then to any production of any playwright.

First to resolve any of Shakespeare's plays you must work from two opposite sides of your brain. You must work the text separately, its precise meaning, rhythms, and inter-woven dialogue between characters. The other work is improvising, clowning, having fun and being devilish. In comedy however you must attempt to make every movement in the scene 100 percent choreographed. The slapstick must be grammatically correct so to speak. "Suit the action to the word, the word to the action" - Hamlet.

You cannot find the depths of Shakespeare's vast repertoire of comic characters, and villainous characters who enjoy their villainy, without letting the actor try whatever their instincts says…and encouraging them to do so. At the same time the text must be perfect. Interpretation must come organically in rehearsal.

This all being said, there are worlds of interpretation available in Shakespeare's plays.

The partners in this scene are Launcelot Gobbo and his father Ol' Gobbo.

I will not go through the scene line by line but will focus on my own process as an actor.

We had a nine week rehearsal for three plays. Two plays were revival and revised productions. There was a new actor playing the role of Hamlet so before general rehearsal there was an extra week just for the new Hamlet and a few main characters. The 2nd, 3rd, 4th weeks of rehearsal was for Richard the Third. The 5th week began Merchant and again Hamlet. In the 7th week we were rehearsing all three plays. Soon enough we would open all three plays within one week with 16 actors.

Before rehearsals started we all had been given our characters and understudy roles. I was the understudy for Launcelot Gobbo. When we started Merchant rehearsals I was quite familiar with the scene and was asked on the first day if I would like to play Ol' Gobbo. Well okay. Launcelot played by James Wardlaw, and I, were given a few days to work out something and to tell Carol the director when we could show her the work.

James was an excellent comic actor. He played Launcelot the year before so he knew his character and which interpretation he was to keep. James had been a student at the National drama school when I taught there. Also I had just been coaching, choreographing, and directing him for three weeks as Buckingham in Richard III.

When we went into the studio as Launcelot and Gobbo he said "You direct." Fine. But this is different from my other relation with James when I was a teacher. We are now stage partners. He is the main clown since his character continues in the play. He knows his character, I have to find mine. Then through the work we will develop the relationship.

James is a few inches over six feet tall, I am four inches under six feet. Fact. Gobbo. The play takes place in Italy. In Italian the word gobbo means hunchback. Like Harlequin or Arlecchino, Launcelot likes to eat and sleep, and probably lance a lot i.e. indulge in sex. There is a folk joke that if one is too active with sex one will develop a hunched back (gobbo) or will go blind etc. What's in a name? Everything. Ol' Gobbo is old, hunchbacked, and probably lanced a lot. Maybe we are moving away from fact but that makes good fiction. Also in the text there is indication that Ol' Gobbo's eyesight isn't what it used to be. Maybe he lanced too much.

Now for me this lance-a-lot rationalisation will soon be quite boring for me as an actor. It's too much on one level a low level at that. But it lets the actors laugh and misbehave, thus releasing their inhibitions and creativity.

Well I start with the facts, James is considerably taller. With my ol' age ... "his shrunk shank" Pantaloon in Jacques speech of "All the world's a stage"...I'll shrink a bit. Add a bit of hunch in the back. Now James towers over a decrepit figure. Before, directly before, Ol' Gobbo enters the stage, Launcelot is arguing with his own conscience and weighing up moral values and mentions Shylock and his father. This speech is about running away from the devil, his self. Launce is about to run, but, out of his subconscience, the stage wings, there appears Ol' Gobbo.

Launcelot then tells us of his father's blindness. In our case Gobbo's voice appeared first, then an old baby pram, then the dancing, prancing pusher of the pram appeared singing an Italian song which goes back to Shakespeare's time .."Gobbo il padre, gobba la madre." (the father was a hunchback, the mother was a hunchback). I had learned the song 14 years before.

In the circus the clown's act is called an Entree. One reason is the moment the clown enters the arena we should know the character by his appearance, walk, mask, or voice. All or some of these factors should signal to the audience "Look out".

Exits and entrances are a great craft in the theatre. Shakespeare sets up perfectly exits and entrances. Launcelot is about to run. He is already an outrageous character, the father's interruption must be more so. Yet their first encounter must show the seeds of father-son.

Ol' Gobbo's mask was "with spectacles on nose"...again I refer to Jacques in the play As You Like It. Like Harlequin, Launcelot announces clearly that he will trick the "sand blind" Pantaloon. We followed Shakespeare's premise and saw that though the father entered singing in a world all his own, and true he was quite blind, and lost, he too could play tricks. After all who would have taught the son knavery?

The antagonism between Launcelot and Shylock must be equaled by the father and son clowns, so too must Shylock's conciliatory love for Launcelot be equaled by Launcelot's father.

My objective with the scene was to draw out every crevice holding another dimension of the text. James was rich with love and his father was a theologian. To find the depth of my character I have to draw on my vulnerable self. The director suggested I push a trolley or pram.

The last thing that I ever did with my own father who was known as "a clown" was to go grocery shopping in a super market. He was 72 and I was 27. My father was taking me to the airport for my flight back to California, but, he wanted to do his grocery shopping on the way to the airport. I frequently went shopping with my father when I was a child. Now at 72 and 27, he took a shopping trolley, pulled down the baby seat and said "get in". Being lean of shank I fit in. For the next twenty minutes my father pushed me around as he selected groceries. We got to the cashier and my father said "get out". We left and he drove me to catch my flight back to California. He died a few months later. The actor must draw on and transmute personal experience.

I also have a son who I have seen only twice. (In recent years we have written occasionally). At the time of rehearsal I would have just recently returned from overseas and seen my son for the first time. My emotional understanding of a "minor character" was hardly lacking in depth. James was a perfect partner. We laid out slaps, kicks, punches as father and son clowns trying to outwit each other. Where Shylock cannot dig a knife in, Ol' Gobbo can elbow discreetly his smart ass belligerent boy Launcelot. Where Portia, Bassanio, Antonio are reduced in the courtroom to verbal nastiness, here in the streets Launcelot can match blow for blow his streetwise father.

The first resolution comes when they are both, father and son, willing to recognise each other. This had to be a relief moment for the audience to experience the clear love of the 'other half". Then we topped it with a gag direct from Cletus Ball. From the tradition. The tradition of Australian Knockabout. I put it in as a test to see how does real physical slapstick fit with a straight Shakespeare production. It fits perfect. There was another gag a moment later also direct from Cletus and tradition. As a moment later the father-son love gives way to more competition as they vie for Bassanio's acceptance. Not unlike the three suitors seeking Portia's gold. James also played one of the suitors, with aplomb and relish.

The slapstick had to fit perfectly to the timing of the text. Yet we displayed how physical Shakespeare can be, and how it should be. The clowns should never be just witty or funny or melancholy. The clowns must be physical and visual. They must lift the audiences senses. They are not always meant to be funny. The clowns almost always parallel and parody the main action of the play.

As I stated in an earlier article about this scene, it was completely a team effort. As in real clowning though, the other actors must be drawn into the mayhem. In our case Ol' Gobbo fell into Bassanio's lap. The actor could have played the usual boring status rationale. Our Bassanio, John Adams didn't. He took delight at holding the ol' clown, which relieved Launcelot to know his new employer was a happy fellow. The two servants upstage had to respond watchfully and be surprised at Bassanio's acceptance. The Gobbos marked that servitude. As the Gobbos exited singing the "Gobbo il Padre" song and dancing, they laid a quick boot up the servants' bottoms. Launcelot was home safe to upset another household.

This is not how to do this scene. That is how our team under Carol's direction and John Bell's Artistic Direction, and my secret research, resolved it for the 1992 season. I was lucky to have a good partner.

As Carlo said "You cannot have a good Laurel without a good Hardy."

I have tried to indicate that Shakespeare's clown scenes are tied directly to the main plots of the plays. They are directly tied to the themes. The clown scenes are also vital in their timing of appearance. Often their abrupt appearance is like a jack-in-the-box. They show us the magic trap door of life.

Often. Very often. Usually. The clown scenes of Shakespeare are misunderstood for the depth and direct service to the play as a whole. It is usual also for the minor clowns such as Ol' Gobbo to be completely written off by scholars, actors, directors, producers. It indicates a loss of humour, wisdom and insight.

I would say that the minor and even silent characters in Shakespeare's scenes and plays are in fact vital to the total, consummate theatrical wisdom that Shakespeare provides throughout its collection of plays.

I admit it is very hard to see these possibilities purely through the text. Also the actors' execution no matter how enthusiastic has encouraged characters to be written off. The actors and the so called 'new' clowns or 'new' vaudevillians lack knowledge in the traditional acting and clowning.

Just today I read of family heirs to The Three Stooges settling the estate of their abundance of films. When it comes to slapstick, the real stuff, the Stooges were my first teachers via tv. They were the supreme rulers of Slapstick. Of course they were 'too' violent for some viewers. But the Three Stooges knew all levels of their craft. Particularly you must note their choreography. They were not just clowning about. Note too their looks, eyes, glances, takes, double takes, reactions, nods, agreement, disagreement.

With slapstick, sound though is also vitally important. "It's the clatter, the smash, the silence and the timing of all those rhythms that adds to the effectiveness of the assault on the audience's senses" (Ellen Osborn).

With regards to The Merchant of Venice as a play, I'd like to note some other things. I was asked by friends how I felt about being in the Merchant. At first I couldn't understand why several had asked. I had a great job and opportunity to work with John Bell and Anna Volska. After a few people said, "well isn't it an anti-Semitic play". My standard reply was "I'll know after the season of playing it."

It is a great play. An extraordinary comedy. It has given the theatre world one of it's most astonishing characters, Shylock. But it is not only anti-Semitic but quite racist. I cannot say that the intention of the play is to be either. But this raises the question of Hollywood's violence. Is it just showing us reality or is it reality the moment we see it. John Bell's portrayal was a living work of art. I had the luxury of playing the Gaoler in the court scene. Every night for twenty minutes I could watch and study John as Shylock. Yet as his body accepted the weight of the verdict John's Shylock exited more hunched… more gobbo than when he entered the courtroom. As this Shylock's pained eyes glanced upstage at the minor Gaoler I felt a growing sadness that I couldn't reach out to my fellow Semite. My job as Gaoler became painful. What if the Gaoler was Jewish? What if Ol' Gobbo was Jewish but never told his son?

John had asked me during rehearsals for Richard the Third if I could play the Scrivener as a Jew. My reply, "The question is can I play anything other than a Jew"? I was asked, allowed and encouraged to change the Scriveners text by adding some Yiddish. Then I was asked to cut back a bit on the Yiddish. In performance the short speech of the Scrivener had a bit of Yiddish added. That speech was a solo and lasted perhaps 2 minutes. It's a wonderful moment of absurd comedy. There is no reference (that I recall) to precede the Scrivener's scene nor any reference afterwards. Yet I held the audience enthralled, played to the whole house and helped to move the real magic of Shakespeare's spell and philosophy that every small human action in a day is parts of the Universe's continual expansion.

In the Scrivener's two minutes "Like a poor player to strut and fret his hour upon the stage" (Macbeth), I was able to mesmerise the audience. This was noted by the Company Patron. After we opened the touring season's three plays the company at a Green Room party to celebrate. This was John Bell's victory night. It was his dream to be a company-manager of a touring repertory Shakespeare ensemble. It was a long tradition that some considered to have ended, with the famous and infamous Sir Donald Wolfit. Our company had a brief ensemble toast led with congratulations spoken by the company manager of sponsors. She then came over to thank me "We could not have done this without you". But, she added that she doesn't know what I do, "But, every time you step on stage I can feel the audience breathe". I see my job as an electrician of the spirit. We are to light up the stage with our soul. As the clown Polonius is scripted to say about Hamlet 'There is method to his madness'. The secrets to that method of electrifying are in this book and in Chapter 2 of *Clown Secret*.

Back to Merchant, as far as that play goes, beautiful, articulate, intelligent Portia is not only a racist towards her suitors but also an outright snob. The worst racist though may be Gratiano. Gratiano is a clown equal to Mercutio in Romeo and Juliet. Our Gratiano, Marco Chiappi was absolutely glorious and therefore loathsome. God was he funny. Perfected delivery. Then as the role demanded he would be vicious. His tongue was painful for this Gaoler. How could I play the Gaoler? I thought of the capo in Auschwitz or a jailer at the Nuremberg Trials. That's not how I played it but I thought yes even I too could be a gaoler for Shylock. Even I.

I learned from two people how to make a minor non-speaking or hardly speaking role come alive. One was John and Anna's daughter Lucy whom I saw in a student production. The production was awful but she was extraordinary and not only didn't she speak but she made the stage alive. The other teacher of the thankless task was the opera singer Chris Doig who is usually in a leading role but his presence on stage is always alive. Chris and Lucy simply looked, listened, and followed the action of the scene. Simple? Maybe. It's easy to overdo it. I was happy playing the Gaoler. There was a lot to do, to listen to the arguments, and watch for potential trouble as the courtroom drama intensified.

Soon enough everyone exited. I had to re-enter soon from one wing to take out a prop. From the other wing two actors had to enter to remove another prop. While waiting ever so briefly in the wings those boys provided me with live entertainment. They were busy a la improviso, kneeling, bending over, unzipping, and God only knows what. I couldn't always look because how would it seem if even the Gaoler entered laughing? But I think at the best moments they were doing some form of erotic slapstick from ancient Greek routines.

That was Dimitri Psiropoulus and Grant Bowler. They were also Bassanio's servants. What they couldn't do (wouldn't do out of good taste) to me on stage in my big scene as the minor clown; they did to me across the wings. They were very funny! Two devils really. After we saw the great Maori actor George Henare as Othello, I began to call Dimitri and Grant "the Iago Brothers".

I had just mentioned good taste, and two actors choosing not to use bad taste, on stage. We had one actor who had such bad taste that every scene, he thought, was his big scene. No one in the company had any trouble taking the stage. This "actor" who we can refer to as &%¤#!? was an average actor, but was loud. The &%¤#!? had exactly five habits which were used in every scene in every play to steal and pull focus and "act". The &%¤#!? loves to use words like harmony, ensemble, suggestion which to my naive eyes were his obvious screens for a manipulative manner. Yeech! The art of upstaging has not been wiped out by New Age rhetoric. Several years before I had studied upstaging, and how to balance a scene when a &%¤#!? starts creeping around on the boards. I like a challenge. In the company no one could figure out why certain scenes would not work in rehearsal. I'd be called into have a look. Almost always the &%¤#!? was in the scene. I'd watch once just seeing his moves. The second time I'd watch to see how the other actors were pulled into his upstage focus. Easy, then I'd direct or choreograph a better balance and explain to the humane actors where or what to focus on during the scene. I had fun. It was a game we could now call "Creep Chess".

One such scene was more complex. Hamlet, Chris Stollery, came up one day and said "look there's just one scene I'm having trouble with, could you have a look at it"? Of course. Chris was outstanding. He was quite special to work with in several ways. He had an old fashioned classic education which I think included Greek and Latin. This gave him a great edge with understanding grammar and language, and to play different characters distinctly with great ease based on their written words. At the same time he had equally accurate intuition. He was easy to work with on stage and could roll with me or whoever was willing. Guess who wasn't willing? &%¤#!?.

So Chris brought me in to see the gravedigger scene. John Bell was directing, Adrian Keirnander was in the room too as dramaturg and assistant. John's direction of Hamlet was rich, vivid, and vital. This scene was dead. Oh the lines were there, clear and Loud. &%¤#!? was always loud.

John normally sat with the actors before beginning a scene just to let them talk out any ideas, creative blocks, or questions. He was great at those sessions and listened mostly but then he was a walking resource book on Shakespeare so he could always point the way gently. I sat in on those scene readings specifically to learn from John. I was the minor gravedigger and exited before Hamlet and Horatio enter. I spoke a lot about Yorick and lo and behold the father-son theme returned. We tried to conjure images of what Yorick would have been like and of singular importance the relation of Yorick and Hamlet.

Now in rehearsal I talked of the discussion, and also the beauty in the scene because as we can see Hamlet's love (yes, love) for Yorick then we see a fascination with this new Yorick, the Gravedigger. Yes this is one of the greatest scenes in the world of theatre. From the setup with the two diggers, to Hamlet and Horatio's contemplating, to the comedy, to the terrible farce with Laertes. Well of course the &%¤#!? tries to override all balance. Well the scene does not work. You know why! But I can't say why because I am supposed to help. I am only meant to fix it, go away, and have the world think I am a minor actor and a movement teacher. Okay. I'll fix it gladly. I'd love to see this scene work to its fullest.

I talked about Yorick, the skull, resurrection, puppetry, ventriloquism. Chris got it all. No problem. What an actor. The &%¤#!? now has a resurrected Yorick to contend with. Chris now has a prop which can counter balance the huge, unnecessary, untimely movements of the &%¤#!?. Okay so now the scene works. Horatio (played by Simon) is now aglow from Hamlet's charm. Chris was great, the &%¤#!? said what Shakespeare wrote. As Noel Coward said about the art of acting: "Say your lines and don't bump into the furniture". There was no furniture and the &%¤#!? was as always Loud!

John Bell played the Ghost of Hamlet's father. I was asked to help with that scene.

Well, okay. Yum yum they were great. John wasn't loud but he roared with power and fury. He simply circled Hamlet. But the words lingered in the air. Overtones. At the right moment the psychic transference of father's angst flowed visibly to Chris as the mantle of murder and revenge was passed on. Chris played that transference as if a fever was beginning to overtake him. Ellen Osborn explains what is believed about Shakespeare's own son: "Coincidentally, fever/plague (before Hamlet play was written) is what Shakespeare's actual son died of while Shakespeare was away on tour in London, his son's name was Hamnet, which is the same as Hamlet (the l/n were interchangeable in those times) - so the ghost etc could've been written in a cathartic or spiritual way of dealing with his personal loss".

After that scene, a little later John would enter from the wings with Grant or someone and I to carry on a large prop, a circular platform. Thank God that Dimitri wasn't there with Grant, what the two of them would have done in front of my eyes?

John and Anna were onstage totally giving to each other player. Minor roles and all were involved in John and Anna's execution of total theatre. They took the stage with valour and warmth and shared the energy flow completely. They were an example for any ensemble. Offstage also they were completely down to earth.

Some of the choices made in the company I didn't agree with but mostly those were choices of political necessity. The running of a theatre company reeks of impossibility. John and Anna had done the impossible for a long time.

Anna played Gertrude, Nerissa, Queen Margaret in our plays and like John she also filled in with minor and chorus parts. In workshops and talks she had the most articulate expression about the acting craft that I have ever heard. She no doubt would make a first rate teacher.

When I taught, choreographed, or directed John and Anna jumped in like giggling children ready to try anything in the theatre 100%. They set the example every day.

One great scene I was asked to look at was Hamlet, Rosencrantz and Guilderstern. I didn't touch it. It was perfect as was.

In Hamlet I was the choreographer. I played various roles. I started to coach three actors in text delivery though I'm sure they will deny it. One had several years tutelage specialising in Shakespeare. God help us. A play such as Hamlet is usually chopped and changed. So we did one version but I loved it. I experienced the ritual of Hamlet's journey.

Ophelia was played by Suzy Dougherty. She made the great counter journey. I was doing my gaoler/solider bit when she wailed in Laertes' arms, then he'd start wailing. I was next, I didn't do it, but I could've. Some soldier!

Later when I waited back stage to step out and warm up the laughing muscles of the grieving audience, Anna would be sulking in a motionless meditation. She had to step onstage in a deep grief to announce Ophelia's final fate. I never asked Anna what she meditated on but it worked whatever it was. Then according to Shakespeare's amazingly creative 'Will' power, it's bring on the clowns.

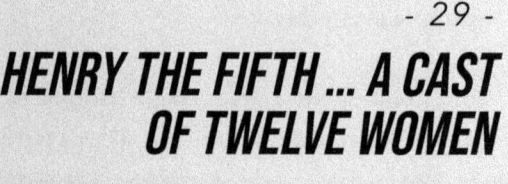

- 29 -
HENRY THE FIFTH ... A CAST OF TWELVE WOMEN

This project of Henry V with a cast of women came about because of a dream I had. The dream was preceded by some very logical and conscious thoughts. The rehearsal and workshop process lasted nearly two months. Although ten days before the performance, the project was dissolved, it remains a profound experience which yields fresh insights into playing Shakespeare. 11 days before the scheduled public performance the 12 actors performed the entire, uncut, Henry V as a straight run-through with two invited witnesses besides myself.

The dream occurred on a sensitive day and period for me.

My 1992 year with the Shakespeare company was complete. I had been invited to create a piece for the Independent Dance Collection. I created an autobiographical story which included a rich woven text mixing social satire and a monologue from Shakespeare.

I had an afternoon meeting with the Artistic Director of the Shakespeare company. The two of us spoke for three hours. It was positive but I would only continue with an official contract stating that I was the director's assistant rather than or in addition to stating the previously agreed terms as "Resident Teacher and Choreographer", and actor which I also fulfilled. More about that later.

After the meeting, I proceeded to the theatre to perform for the opening of the "Dance Collection" in which I was to premiere my new solo piece "Harlequin Suits Me...or Can A Wog Be A Larrikin". The piece was very risky but was obviously a hit with the audience. I was happy, and relieved, and ready to start life again.

That night I had a vivid and delightful dream of Sir John Gielgud acting in Henry the Fifth. I tell the details of that dream in a show on youtube "Harlequin Dreams". At the end of the dream Gielgud performed only for me and then nodded his head to me. At the dream's conclusion I asked what does this dream mean? The answer was that I should direct Henry the Fifth with a cast of women.

The next day I had a fax, from John Bell, which said that, for the time being, I should not continue with the Shakespeare company. I had a truly life changing year with the opportunity to work in a classic Shakespeare repertory company. I conducted my own secret research, within the given circumstances, as Stanislavsky had done throughout his career. However, my experiments were better able to naturally and serendipitously evolve outside of a formal, conservative and commercial company. In that next year, starting with my dream of Henry V, my subconscious had immediately begun to guide me. It was one year later I came across the book *Quantum Gods* and thus named my method Quantum Theatre: Slapstick to Shakespeare.

I went to my agent to have a general catch up chat and to say that I will not be working with the Shakespeare company. I was asked what would I like to do. I said I am thinking of opening a studio and starting a company. I left the office and walked up the nearby Glebe Point Road that had plenty of cafes and restaurants for me to choose for lunch. As I had many times before I walked by a hall with a studio. I knew the manager of the hall. He saw me across the street and in the hall's storefront window he waved to me excitedly to come over. He welcomed me. Asked what I was doing. I said I was on my way to find a place for lunch. He said "How would you like to teach in the studio and start a school and company"?

"Well I could try". I said I had this idea to direct Henry the Fifth with all women. He said maybe I could meet a woman who had been training in the studio until recently. That was Ellen Osborn. A day or so later we met. I was given the studio nearly gratis to start with Henry the Fifth.

But, on that first day after talking with the studio manager and after having lunch, I ran into an actress who I had taught at the National school. She was Mary Ann Henshaw. I began to say I had a project I was hoping to do, but, before I could tell her what the project was she said yes she would be in it. She was to be Henry.

The next day while warming up at the dance theatre while I was in the splits I was practicing the Shakespearean monologue I used in "Harlequin Suits Me". As the stage manager, Jo, leaped in a grand jeté over my bones, she also completed the rest of the monologue! Hmm, she should be the Archbishop of Canterbury I presume.

Each day for the next few days I would have a chance meeting with one more actress. As I tried to describe the project, each said "yes" before I could say anything except "I've got this project in mind...".

Preceding all this was almost twenty years in the theatre, the last year of which was full of the Bard. Three key things preceded the dream of John Gielgud's nod to me.

I had been recently studying the plays Henry V, King Lear, and Macbeth. I thought I would love to do a whole play of Shakespeare un-cut. Every word. Many of his larger works are of course chip-chopped always since they would be 3 or 4 hours playing time.

Secondly, during the Bell Shakespeare Company workshops there were always girls schools who presented pieces of whatever play they were studying. I realised that every year in Australia there might be one or two hundred girls schools doing all female productions of Shakespeare. Some schools combine with boys schools and some boys schools did all male versions.

During our Bell Shakespeare company Melbourne season one actress Tara Morice had her world premiere in the film Strictly Ballroom. She had the female lead. Tara played Portia and Lady Anne in two of the BSC plays. In Hamlet she played a minor role and danced and mimed in the Players scenes. On her premiere night of Strictly Ballroom our scheduled production would be Hamlet. She asked our company director John a few weeks in advance if the understudy could play her bits in Hamlet the night of her film premiere. It was a bit taboo but it was no problem, so John readily agreed. Years later she became the tough teacher in the TV show "Dance Academy".

We had plenty of time to rehearse. On the first day the two actresses, Tara and Carla, immediately went to work. The understudy was Carla Aquilla and the Player King was Marion Dwarakowski, and I played the Murderer in the Mousetrap. As choreographer I just watched the two actresses take care of everything they needed. Carla knew the scene very well, and Tara coached with delight. When they were ready to run the scene I stepped in.

Tara knew all the text in the scene and much of Hamlet's other text as it turned out. Easily, she could have played Hamlet and obviously with great aplomb.

So I had mental preparation to accept the message of my subconscious about Henry V.

It was to be a bare bones production. The cast was an extraordinary group of people. I saw two runs of the whole play. The second run-through was already breathtaking if on no other level than the language. The text flowed with melody, and image. The delivery of the language alone exceeded most productions of Shakespeare in English that I have ever seen. The women, a diverse group of people acted every line and scene with an emotional charge combined with cool and focused physicality and verbal and vocal dexterity.

I was able to freely coach the actresses in my method. Mary Ann needed no coaching nor coaxing. She is a great actress. Some of the "actresses" had never spoken a word of Shakespeare. Some had spoken much but gradually started to make whole new discoveries about the whole game of Shakespeare.

The first day we happy few gathered, the biographies left one bewildered by the potential of this group. But the first sharp challenge was immediately to follow.

Were we to play women, or men, or women playing men.

A famous directorial reply came out "Well let's see how it develops and evolves."

That was the first deflection but that wasn't enough of course. Then the director has to expose himself in more detail with more vision.

There are over forty male characters so one can't just play a male. One has to play the character, and for me always the actor or actress must discover their own relation to portraying a particular character. Plus some of the women were to play five different men. Only Mary Ann played a single character. In addition I said of course we all have masculine and feminine sides so perhaps there was no need at all to play a man, only to let the male energy come out. Also some actresses may choose to work with their energy and acting resources in quite a different way from another actress. So I didn't feel we had to have a company agreement as someone suggested. There was also the complication that twelve people is too few to play the whole play without some very free form character changing.

In one situation an actress had the impossible task of the last line in one scene as one character and the first line in the next scene as another character. It was resolved simply by a semi-circle walk up stage. On the walk the "exit" line was delivered, as the walk curved another actress entered in step and handed over a waistcoat, as the garment was going on the character changed and delivered the next scene's opening lines. I am always happy to support any excuse for meta-theatre, that is, showing that what we in the theatre present is the reality of actors presenting characters.

There were the most simple garments, mainly matching overalls. There were only three props in 3½ hours of playing. There was one chair, one hairbrush, and one vegetable, which was a leek as mentioned in the play. There was a single lightbulb over the centre stage. There was a unified flow of action, text, movement and playing which is normal only in a dream of seeing Shakespeare. There was a constant physicality even in exceedingly long winded characters. Only the great "stage manager" Jo could have the charisma to carry off the Archbishop of Canterbury. Jo literally danced that whole character; improvised dances always brought fresh, daily clarity to excruciating long winded passages. Where Mary Ann was seated her presence was always tied directly to the text's flourishes. Like Jo, Mary Ann had over twelve years of classical ballet training.

There were no swords nor knives even though there is direct reference in the text. Gesture was used instead. Not mime, but gesture. In this production a raised hand was enough to convey clearly and effectively the threat of a sword or dagger which the text implies.

Jo, who spoke fluent French, also played Katherine. Samantha played her hand maiden and had never uttered a word of French other than "baguette". Nor had Sam (as she was actually called) ever understood a word of Shakespeare and had never acted. The French in Henry V is as archaic as is Shakespeare's English. Sam handled it all like the superstar she was. Sam was the youngest of the group and during each crisis meeting she could floor us all with words direct from the soul. Later, she became the Head of Movement at the Sydney Actors Centre, and, then at WAAPA in Perth.

Mary Ann pounded away at her 1000 lines, constantly adding to her research of Henry and every word in the text. After the first week she was talking way over my head. Fortunately she never stopped explaining new discoveries to me on a daily basis.

With an actress such as her the director need not tell her anything except spacial choices. Also the director must bring the whole group to match her strengths.

Jo, in her case, could easily match her although Jo worked the opposite way. Jo relied on realisations. In her case as with myself realisations come every day quite naturally. Jo also was the company eccentric, within our quite eccentric collective. She arrived late every single day, so she was dependable. When she burst through the door she was in an extremely different mode of dress every day. She was the physical expression of female energy. During this time it was a personal crisis as her boyfriend had taken off with the star singer with whom he worked. Then finally one day Jo burst in. In new colours of course, and some regular loud words as the front door slammed behind her. Today it was "I did it "! What Jo? ...came the obligatory reply from a fellow thespian. Jo gave us the gruesome details of how she had just thrown her boyfriend (ex) over the hood of his car and slammed his girlfriend (new) up against the garage door.

Jo was not the only lethal warrior in this cast. There was Kathy McMorrow. Kath had never really "acted" but had studied some play of Shakespeare in high school. However she liked a challenge. Kath had been on the Canadian Olympic team as a gymnast. For several years she played an acrobatic pirate at Wonderland which included diving into frigid water from 90 feet. She then became a fully fledged stunt woman... car crashes, explosives, falling with horses and all that her job required. She soon became Hapkido Woman of the Year. In her spare time she was studying at university in liberal arts. Geez, do you think I should give her a chance. You know Shakespeare is pretty tough Kath. Well, okay.

I can assure you that no director would have given Kath a chance after her first reading of Shakespeare nor after her tenth.

But Kath is Wonder-woman personified. She did exactly as I asked her with the text. What happened was right out of Pygmalion. The flashes went off in her brain, she studied and always complemented the other actresses. She played the Prologue as her main character. How's that for an intro to Shakespeare. I videoed her speeches (which were complete with mime, gesture, the most expressive eyes and face, perfect diction, natural rhythm, and back flips and saltos). An actor friend who had thirty years as a professional and was an expert on British dialects and voice in general asked me about my method for teaching Shakespeare. I showed him Kath's video. Those speeches were part of his audition repertoire and he confirmed that Quantum works. Kath was the embodiment of mutual trust leading each person further to develop.

Another martial artist was Ellen. She was not your average warrior. She was an ideal. Ellen was proficient with a form of Tae Kwan Do and also Tai Chi. Along with that she was a scholar in theatre, literature, and teaching. She was in a permanent state of Chi though she had just spent two years in a black hole with a very misguided theatre person. Henry V was very much a project for her to get full recognition of her worthiness. After about ten days in the group, clouds lifted from around her. She was also the company expert on the English language. Since that time she became an established independent yoga teacher.

Another actress said that our way of working was "getting a second chance" in life and theatre. That was Imelda and she had been a secretary to the Prime Minister of Ireland. Recently she graduated from the state theatre school in Perth, Australia. Imelda played Fluellen. Through studying her and Fluellen as we allowed it to be, a new theory arose. It seems clear to me, that the reason much of, and many of Shakespeare productions are dreaded is because often the heart is cut out.

For example in Henry V, if Henry is the Brain of the play then Fluellen is very much the Heart pumping blood to the Brain. If you have a tragic hero in Shakespeare then you can bet there is a central clown. That is the primary structure in the play which gives it an inherent Yin-Yang flow and balance. In the same way the play Othello has the cursive wit of Iago. Fluellen is not just a soldier but a source of regular comic relief.

Thank God for women. This project showed me that most productions stink like a filthy men's gym. A stink of hundreds of years of precedence of male dominated studies and execution of Shakespeare. Hundreds of years of willy wagglin'.

Woman warriors. In this project the femaleness was pure vital energy. I don't know if I could ever stomach seeing a male hero on stage again. Too often it stinks of men who should have marched off to war instead of playing dandy-lions up on stage. That was written in 1996 and still holds true. Here though are a few exceptions; Macbeth done as a military coup by a Polish theatre in 2012 that I saw in Edinburgh; and, Tadashi Suzuki's King Lear.

Maybe I've said too much now. But you are an artist, surely you can handle a bit of controversy, a bit of another view point. It is only words, ideas, images, thoughts. But oh if you could have seen what these women did.

Yes I directed. Yes, as they all told me, it helped to have a male balance in the work. But that is precisely what I am saying. Too many productions of Shakespeare are lopsided from the start, from precedence and bias.

Another woman warrior was Dahlia. In our first few days the company was discussing the violence in the play and many thoughts and viewpoints were expressed. For the first time Dahlia spoke. She simply told about the mother lioness protecting her babes from anything. Dahlia had been in the Israeli army for two years. Currently she was a masseuse exclusively for Holocaust Survivors. Daily, over years she hears stories of war which no one else has ever heard. As she massages, the stories come out in their own time. Dahlia was the elder in the group. Her daughter Lily was also in the project. Dahlia had worlds of life experience, patience, humour. One day Dahlia and Lily said they couldn't come to rehearsal the following day. Dahlia's first husband, Lily's father, had just died.

Dahlia, our oldest actor, played the Boy. She hadn't gone near Shakespeare in over twenty years. She had a good teacher though, Laurence Olivier. He gave her lessons at RADA in London. Dahlia only finished the first year since she had no more money and got taken into a theatre troupe touring England. Eventually she settled on singing. For nine years she had her own act touring the Hilton Hotels throughout Asia. She sings in twelve languages and is fluent in eight. She taught us a mock French soldiers drinking song created in1866 for a comic opera about the Arthurian legend of the Knights of The Round Table. She arranged the song and that song was to be the beginning and end of our production.

Lily had her own band, wrote her own songs, had studied ballet and gymnastics. She was a classic and natural clown. Lily Dior is herself now established as a jazz singer in London.

Linda was a yoga teacher with the demure of a Siamese cat. She worked for Greenpeace and was a writer and journalist. She was very shy and soft spoken. However once scenes were set and focus was clear she radiated pure power equal to her beauty. She was aware of energy and scene flow. She is now a long established yoga teacher in Sydney.

Sabrina was a Muslim woman from Yugoslavia. She was the essence of unleashed fire while Linda was the tension of fire held. Sabrina was also a writer. She had been studying directing for several years. But her biggest passion was Flamenco dance which she studied and performed. She played the French king. As the king she simply embodied stately power and seethed at her council.

Mistress Quickly was played by a classic buxom English actress who studied with Imelda in Perth. She also played two other roles.

An actress named Julie grew up in England and was from Poland. She was a clothes designer to survive when she wasn't acting.

This then was the group. It was a fantastic situation. Mary Ann worked full time answering phones for a wine ordering business. Like many other under-employed, at the wine business hotline she worked alongside some of Australia's most talented theatre people. Theatre is a very strange business.

I thoroughly loved working with Mary Ann. What a talent and intellect! She embodied the young King Henry without ever a loss of femininity. Apparently she got rid of her lovers in the middle of the night or early morning by starting her daily work on text and research for Henry V.

Once she was going to pull out of the production because she felt it was too short a time for the less experienced actors. I asked her to wait until she experienced the first run through of the first three acts. That was the next day and as I expected the inexperienced ones were way ahead when it came to hitting the stage and playing. There were plenty of weaknesses at this point. But she could see clearly they were fine players.

A little while later after a day of rehearsal the three "actresses" (those who completed a state training) asked if I would meet with them. Oh boy, the male director is in big trouble this time, something's wrong. They took me to a pub. I do not have theatre meetings in pubs. Parks, cafes, restaurants, beaches, even offices but to pubs *niet*. This was an exception, the three actresses were English, Irish, and Scottish. I was ish too so what the heck. Gulp. What is this all about. Same ol' story they're a wonderful group of people but they won't be ready. Okay, okay wait let's compromise. So instead of doing the short season, let's do one performance and invite friends and call it a workshop. Deal. Pubs are great. Day to day and the show is not just good but excellent because the actors grew layer by layer.

Another theory is proving true. With Shakespeare actually there should be musical overtones from the text. Not every scene yields easily to this. I found the ideal scene to push the test. Sabrina's council scene with her and the Dauphin. The Dauphin was Ellen, who also played the Duke of Gloucester, and a hilarious Pistol. It's working. Yippee. I'm very excited. Now I start to take stock of the decibel levels in all scenes. It's working. I feel like I'm at NASA in Houston or cyberspace at the Globe. I invite the composer. He's meant to do whatever may be required and to play live. Philip Griffith, he had worked with the Royal Shakespeare Company. Heck do you think I should give him a chance? He sat motionless for the three hours-plus of our second run thru. If we had a break it was probably only so Jo could fix her make-up. Phil was astonished. The language filled the time and space. You don't need music. That's right, this is Shakespeare, overtones and all. For musical input there was one other guest to see this complete run-through of the whole of Henry V, uncut, played by 12 women, with only three props and the most minimal/simple costume of overalls (plus one dress for Jo when she played her other character of Katherine). The other guest was the great folkloric singer Mara Kiek, of Mara's Band, and director of the Martenitsa Choir of Bulgarian song. She agreed totally with Phil, that the voices and language clarity was such that no extra music was needed. Our run-through started with the collective song Dahlia taught "Chevalier de la Table Ronde" a classic learned by all French youths.

Mary Ann rode the waves and paced herself like a heavyweight boxer. Oh God her speeches. She is a great actor!! Crispin, tennis balls...balls? Hell she was full of force. Glory! Her passion with Williams. Her fury. Her romance with Katherine/Jo. Passion, peaceful eroticism. The air they breathed. Two great actresses playing this scene with overtones, timing, calm, and energy. It was something to behold. I saw it with my own eyes. Mara and Phil saw it with ten days to go. Ha! Ten days and they were flying on a steady course of improvement and confidence. Each day provided new levels of discovery. This is not only good acting, it is great theatre. Discovery as a daily course for actors. Real discoveries the way Jo, and Sam, and Kath, and Linda ... and all did it. Row, row, row your boat gently down the stream. The action, the stillness, the earthiness...Bardolph, Nym, Pistol, Boy, Quickly...the clowns. Fluellan. Revelations come naturally.

The next day doom.

We had to start the day with a meeting. Not a good sign. The actresses who graduated from state theatre schools knew how to handle things. It was that trio that called this meeting before rehearsal was to start. We sat in a circle. Mary Ann was crystal clear, articulate. She clearly said she stops here. She was upset that we didn't train in dance or mime or slapstick or anything from my background like we had discussed. Of course the show was filled with action, dance, mime, gesture, and physical comedy. It's just that in rehearsal I don't call it a class even though people are learning everyday when on the floor and I direct intentionally for that purpose i.e. so that each actor learns. Another point was that Dahlia didn't really teach us singing. Phil and Mara heard the singing. Teach a group of women like this a musical arrangement and it's a snap. Done. Overtones isn't something worthwhile? An empowered ensemble? Are you kidding? Physical?....sorry, but how could an actress playing Henry V(all of it, the whole play un-cut) how could this actress not see the perpetual flow of action and hear the glory of the language lingering in the air?

She was clear. She quit. She had her reasons. I said "I stopped you twice. I will not even try to stop you now". Her two accomplices backed her according to their plan and agreed views. There were words, people expressed themselves. This was no place for a male director. Oh shit. Jo laid it on real clear. No punches pulled; words and feelings. Sabrina's eyes were fierce. Hapkido - woman is ready to demonstrate some stunts. Let me out of here. Ellen's controlling the exit with her Chi. Shit it's hot in here. Who took out the air. Queen Henrietta reigns ever so calm. It's the Irish to exit first. For the first time I see Imelda is the real McCoy, full blooded Irish. Out she goes. There goes Sabrina. I can't look. Gulp what would Peter Brook do? Sabrina the Muslim Flamenco dancer from Yugoslavia negotiates a temporary truce with the Belle O' Eire. My God she's coming back. Words. The three actresses are released from their bonds. The remaining actresses are not just angry. They are very hurt. They're very sad they only wanted to work. They were finding their strength. They knew the rhythm and pace of the whole show. They knew. They knew what the three from the state schools didn't. In a few short weeks they knew how powerful theatre is for change. Personal change. And they knew they were good. Maybe not as good as Mary Ann, so they all said. They said she was great, but they said she was also wrong.

Mary Ann made a personal choice. In that she was not wrong. She was very wrong about the quality of the production and the high level of the acting. The text was nearly impeccable already.

QUANTUM THEATRE

In Australia, over and over in co-operatives actors quit. They think they know when they do not. Even a lousy production is better completed than abandoned. Generally speaking of course. We all need experiences.

The last ten days or so before a premiere is not a pretty sight inside a lead actor.

What could I have done. I knew Mary Ann, the first two times I convinced her was because she allowed me to. She did so out of friendship and respect. I would happily work with Mary Ann again any day. She's a great person and great actor.

We unhappy few decided to meet on the eve of the proposed performance and to have a wake. Mary Ann and accomplices were invited to the wake.

The first day after the blow-up meeting though…at about 8am I got a phone call. Whoever it was, they were crying and said "Ira I'm sorry, I'm sorry. We were wrong we were wrong. I never met a group of people like that in my life. What can we do? I'm sorry. I'm so sad". It was Mistress Quickly. She was too late. The damage was done. If it had been one actress leaving I would have coached someone to read the text which was certainly too massive to learn in so short a time. But it was three actors playing Henry, Fluellan and a range of other characters.

I have no regrets. It was well worth leaving an established company for seeing this group grow, seeing Mary Ann in glory, to see revelations in my theories of theatre and Shakespeare. The next day I was asked to direct The Suicide by Nikolai Erdman, for twelve actors. No regrets. Move on. Four weeks later The Suicide was playing. My dearest friend Fred played the lead and produced.

At the wake of Henrietta the Fifth I asked Ellen to play the bearded priest in the Suicide. Sure. But, with one proviso that she wear a fake beard. Either she or I also said she should use her own Greek head of thick Medusa like hair placed also as a beard. Mary Ann joined us for dinner at the wake. I asked Julie also to take a role in the Suicide and that was a fun and wild project. An actor pulled out with ten days to go. I took the part. I met with Fred, Eva, Tim and said they each had scenes they were not in so each could be an outside eye for my scenes as I direct myself. By this time I had more ten years experience directing myself in my clown theatre projects. All of the actors were terrific including those who were more eccentric and it all was just another adventure.

My studio was opened for a three hour daily class Monday through Friday. Other productions followed, four more in fact and two of those I directed and acted in.

It was a great year. My last performance in Sydney was November 6, 1993. That was the single performance of "Harlequin Dreams" that is on youtube. On the 7th I flew out of Australia and a few days later work began in Copenhagen, Denmark. There I was to teach Shakespeare and direct a King Lear project, and teach acrobatics.

Henry the Fifth with women still is a dream. If you do it I hope you ask Mary Ann Henshaw, she deserves another crack at it.

- 29a -
KING LEAR

I have worked on three King Lear projects, but, not the play as a whole. Very often long plays of Shakespeare's such as; King Lear, Antony & Cleopatra, Henry V, Hamlet are edited to be 2 to 2 1/2 hours instead of their full running time that would be over 3 hours.

One of the shortest projects was within my three-weeks Summer workshop "Quantum Clown Residency". The focus that year was on Shakespeare as a topic. I was asked by two of the Co-Editors of The Shakespeare Annual Yearbook if I would take the 'trial scene' of King Lear and do one of my creative experiments with that scene. Those two professors were: Tom Bishop, and, Peter Holbrook. I, along with the actors, did our best to tell the story of that scene but to stretch the creative elasticity of Shakespeare's meta-theatre. Amongst the actors was a veteran of Shakespeare study and performance, Flloyd Kennedy. As director, I took poetic licence but still fully honoured the text.

Another project was "Nuncle: A Fool's Tale" that was an adaptation and highly condensed version of the play King Lear. This was produced by an actor, Ian who I had worked with in a clown theatre project "Cleavers Family Wreckers" for the Woodford Folk Festival 2002. Ian was to play the Fool in "Nuncle" and the play was primarily Lear and the Fool. One day when Ian was working on one of his monologues that I was directing, I stopped him at some point. Rather I tried to stop him but he kept going. Finally I got him to stop so I could help work on an early part of the speech. He said "You're interrupting me". I said "I thought I was directing you". He said "No. You've interrupted me.". I tried to briefly explain that there was a section I wanted to work on. He was furious. I said "Look, I think I'll go have a little walk around the block. And I feel like I will take my stuff because I think I will just keep walking to the train station. Then we can talk tonight if you want". I left. We spoke on the phone and I had no desire to continue and I didn't. Like in any and every business some arrangements work out and some don't. "Nothing new under the Sun".

I had a short contract to teach Shakespeare for a semester at a two-year half-days theatre course. I chose to work on a one hour section of King Lear. The section itself was uncut and involved mainly 8 characters. There were 15 actors. We made two groups and one actor played the same role in each group. The actors were from several different countries.

Although we were going to work in English I had them forewarned to get a copy of King Lear in their own language. We worked as a whole group working line by line, clarifying the meaning of every word. I also taught them the basics of my methods for integrating Shakespeare's language with the actor's body. That work was always on the floor working, whereas the clarification of meaning was done seated. I wanted to ensure that each actor understood the whole hour's text because the project was for each group of 8 to improvise freely while at the same time saying every word clearly and with meaning. For one group I cast a short woman from Finland as a Lear and a man a little taller who was from Brazil to be the Fool. For the other group I cast a very tall slim man from Norway as Lear and a tall athletic woman from Sweden as the Fool.

The school had a lot of costumes and props at one end of the large studio. After about four weeks of work we had one group do the hour section then we'd take a short break and the other group would do the same section. There was no rule except to say the text, every word of it, in a meaningful way. They did a studio performance then once a week for about 3 or 4 weeks. Each actor was completely free to wear whatever costume they felt like and was free to interpret their character any way they felt like. Those were individual choices and they rarely discussed their intention beforehand with anybody.

I wanted to experiment with how far we could trust the actor's intuition and freedom while holding true to the writer's words. I also wanted to see how elastic was the work of Shakespeare. The text and each hour and every actor was totally exciting every moment. There was no choreographed action so every action was real and true and creative. One time, for some reason the first actor sang their lines and the second actor sang back, and it happened that all of the actors in that hour only sang their lines and naturally made the presentation both operatic and opera buffo/comic.

The final King Lear project I had mentioned in another of the Shakespeare essays in this book. That was "The Madness of King Lear" for which I was also to create a performance of 55 minutes as it was for the Fringe and quick changes have to happen between productions. One often has only 5 minutes to clear after a performance and only about 15 minutes to set up a performance.

I turned the text inside out with the idea that when someone is upset they tell another person 'Do you know what Regan said to me today?'. And then they tell the listener not only the words but they will also act out the way and manner of how Regan said whatever it was. So our show was two actors Lear and the Fool with Lear saying text from his daughters' as well as Lear's own text and the Fool sometimes saying text from Lear or his daughters, as well as the Fool's own text. The words spoken were only from Shakespeare and various sections were intact but I had rearranged the order in various musings. I was only familiar with the whole play, but, really I selected and ordered the text in an intuitive way rather than an academic way.

Naturally some viewers and critics would think this was nonsensical sacrilege. I had told Leof Kingsford-Smith, the producer who was playing Lear, that I won't look at reviews during the one-month season when I acted The Fool for our Edinburgh Fringe season 2012. His colleague Shakti, a Japanese avant-garde dancer and actor was The Fool for Adelaide and Avignon short seasons but she had work with her Japanese troupe so she could not be in the Edinburgh season. Shakti is the daughter of: a Japanese Mother who is an official National Treasure of Japan for her career as a dance teacher; and, an Indian Father who was a Professor of English. Shakti studied Modern Dance in NYC. For many years she was artistic director of Fringe venues in Edinburgh, Tokyo, Adelaide, Avignon under her company name Garage International.

Many people who knew the whole play very well found that our production provided numerous fresh insights into the actual complete play King Lear. One reviewer seemed to understand completely what we were doing artistically. Others not only 'didn't get it' but they seemed to not want to 'get it'.

Here is the favourable review by Chloe Stopa-Hunt for the Edinburgh Fringe, August 2012: "To explain the quality that elevates The Madness of King Lear into the sphere of superlative interdisciplinary theatre, we must look to Federico García Lorca: this transformed Lear burns and shimmers with duende, a Spanish concept that Lorca defined better in the 1930s than anyone has since. Duende is "a power, not a work" – the fusion of expressivity, intense feeling, and a realness that cannot be counterfeited. "Everything that has black sounds in it, has duende", Lorca wrote, and The Madness of King Lear tears up its black sounds from the depths of the heart, translating them into a performance artwork that begins with visual beauty and then unfolds, flower-like, into a masterpiece of wit and grief, tears and music.

Leofric Kingsford-Smith and Ira Seidenstein play Lear and the Fool respectively. Kingsford-Smith more than equals many full-length Lears, delivering a performance so well-sustained and emotive that it can fairly be described as flawless. Seidenstein is a joy to watch: in addition to wonderful verse-speaking, his background in clowning comes to the fore in several sequences of contemporary dance and mime. These interludes are beautiful to the point of being almost frightening, distinguished by a rich visual purity more usually associated with Japanese woodblock printing. Seidenstein's physical acting is more communicative than many actors' words, and its adaptable muscular grace underlines his shamanic role in the piece, as like a loving vates, he leads Lear through the close-crowded forests of the mind.

Lear's troubled mind is a dynamic prism, presenting Shakespeare's Lear in a refracted form: the events of the original play begin, halt, and alter before our eyes. Both actors fluidly ventriloquize other roles. This practice is often a stumbling-block in small-cast Shakespeare adaptations, but here this is no hint of making do: what we see before us is not a grown man doing his best to voice a young girl's part, but a tormented Lear who repeats Cordelia's words in an attempt to annul them, control them – or, perhaps, to understand them. The play's wrenching finish, unhampered by reverence for the characters' original fates, includes Lear's blinding of his own Fool – who in turn becomes Cordelia, lying dead and blind on the ground as Lear tickles her with a leaf. This moment, which replaces the feather held before Cordelia's lips in Shakespeare's Lear, epitomises the interpretation's dramatic power. There is something appalling about its tenderness, as for long seconds Lear becomes the image of a parent playing with a very young child – only his child is dead, and, more than dead, a chimera played by the Fool. What theatre conjures, we must always lose: that is the shadow-meaning of this ending, alive in its duende, reminding us that the price of all our pleasures is their departure.

It is impossible to overpraise this production: a hugely eclectic and well-chosen soundtrack complements astounding performances and cements The Madness of King Lear's status as an interdisciplinary masterpiece. Lorca's duende is "the subtle bridge that unites the five senses with the raw wound, that living cloud, the stormy ocean of timeless Love" – Shakespeare's Lear lays out a whole economy of love, and in this adaptation it is brought to life with such shining tempestuousness that to watch is to be swept away. ***** – 5/5 Stars".

- 30 -
CRITICS

Critics rule, o.k.? My first eleven years in the theatre I never thought about critics. The few critic reviews I read were of my own work and the articles were brought to me. Then one day I popped in a shop and bought a foreign paper which previously I had never read. Inside was a review of a show which a friend was in. The review was deadly against the production and direction. Yet I had the feeling it was a director whom I should work with. A few years later I did two projects with that director. I began to wonder about critics.

When I first moved to Australia to live there a minor incident happened. The first morning, my host prepared breakfast and asked me to get some milk and the morning paper at a shop. I came back with the "wrong" paper. I had bought The Australian. I was told that it's not a good paper and that I should read the Sydney Morning Herald. For the next eight years, nearly every day, I read both papers. I began to read and study the reviews and reviewers. And to see what was written that I was not supposed to read.

On my previous tour in Australia I was guest artist with partner Barbara Doherty. We were guest artists of Limbs Dance Company for the Festival of Sydney. Limbs was at its peak at that time and played a large theatre. Barbara and I did two comic pieces, one was a dance and the other was a mime. There was very little doubt that our two pieces were a clear hit with the audience.

The review from the national dance critic chose not only to ignore us totally, 100%, no mention of guest artists, but the reviewer also revealed herself. The review's language showed a probable lack of humour when it came to her field of expertise.

In eight years in Australia I would have read around one hundred of her reviews! I studied her. There was an absolute lack of humour and even a disdain for daring to mix humour and dance. The great humour of many dances went unmarked but the choice of costume or one overbalance in an evening was noteworthy. This reviewer was also an extreme nationalist. This was quite positive in her case since she helped to force dance on the public. Of course if there was no vital dance scene then she would have no job. Never the less she was drastically supportive to local products, to a fault. Then of course she did have her favourites. Yet when foreign troupes, or duets or soloists arrived they didn't know what hit them. No matter how faultless, she succeeded in colouring the presentation with her own night blindness.

Once in Sydney there was a small modern dance festival. As usual I tried to see all I could. One soloist was royally insulted by the words of the local queen of criticism. The dancer was a foreigner. The critic was a nationalist. I had never heard of the dancer but I went to see some of this festival. This was a modern festival. In this show the modern dancer proved not only could she choreograph impeccably, she created pieces with content and integrity. She could, and did also dance en pointe, sang opera, was an excellent mime, and a hilarious first class clown. Well we don't want to encourage her now do we? Her next main contract was choreography for Nureyev's Paris Opera Ballet. No she's not our type of modern dancer. This was Janis Brenner. The performance I attended had a near empty house, so I sat in the front row so that this soloist knew someone was there. We met afterwards and chatted. I was rehearsing a solo show at the time and had to go to my scheduled studio time slot. I invited her to watch rehearsal. She liked what she saw, and, in following days she choreographed my two main clown dances. Those pieces are now on youtube in excerpts from that show "Reflexions".

Back to the critic. It took me nine years but I got her to notice me, laugh at me, and give me a quite positive review. Nine years. Some critics are a little slow to catch on.

This critic like many others loved free food. Others focused on the free cheap champagne, others the other freebies like being the real stars of the opening nights.

I studied all the main critics. Each giving me the opportunity to marvel at their own patterns, some had extreme biases, personal weaknesses. They were naked before my watchful eye. In several cases I was a voyeur to their intellectual perversity over 100 times for some individuals. I met them, knew them, several helped me. Several just liked my work, but occasionally let me know who really knew more about the theatre. Who does know more, the artists who live it or the critics who ever so want to be a part of the party?

The real problem with critics is the lopsided relationship. The role of the critic is actually a moral position or situation. In Sydney we had one great critic that was an old man who was prone to patronise pretty young actresses. If a show had one such actress, and, particularly if a bit of skin was shown well there was a lovely light frolicsomeness in the review. This grand ol' man was good though he had other weaknesses. Hype. If a group, foreign or out of town came in on the horse of hype he then had no vision of his own as he regurgitated the hype. He would also write from the director's program notes verbatim.

He retired to be replaced by a seemingly dispirited soul who felt he was "turning over tables in the temple". Vicious? Well this was Sydney after all. A cosmopolitan place. He was often good, often honest and often lacked a sense of balance and purpose. Yet he sincerely fought for better theatre.

His dispirit was valid, in part, from seeing a demise in the theatre. His animosity helped to imbue the theatre in Sydney with the threat of a harsh critique. I know he made a genuine challenge to Australian theatre's own natural tendency to maintain an inner circle status quo.

There was another critic with 40 years experience who had a policy "If you can't say something kind then say nothing hurtful". That was the Catholic Weekly so that's disregarded huh? Imagine that as the motto of Critic School.

Now mind you I generally received very positive reviews and criticism. But that is often the problem with us artists. If the crits are good to us we think they are quite well educated, if they are not good to us our little minds go "they don't know what they're talking about".

When the negative crits occur I take them to heart and weigh it up, and take it as a reflection of some weakness on my part. I do this with great caution and care! On several occasions a critic has helped me to grow. But, that was their intention.

There is a big problem when a critic who is a frustrated director looks at direction! Or a frustrated writer looks at and comments on the writing. Same is true with acting and dance.

Often the critic believes in their own quality education. Danger warning.

There are also critics I have known who are genuine theatre activists and are committed to seek growing perspective and communication. But if you are on the opposite side of their views, it becomes the wrath of God from this same angel. If you as an artist are growing and changing look out. You are either falling in favour or out. It actually takes a moral base to be a critic and in that sense the Catholic Weekly was a guiding light.

Here is the single review for the November 2005 production "Chaplin's Eye" in Brisbane:

"Brisbane's new clown ensemble, Chaplin's Eye, fittingly made its debut as the first production in the recently dedicated Sue Benner Theatre, a well-deserved homage to Benner's advocacy and support for independent theatre as CEO of Metro Arts since 1998. This was 'pure' clown, joyful, energetic, and wise. Brokered by Red Spoon's Andrew Cory, it arrived fully fledged due to the sophisticated, mythopoeic vision of veteran clown and director, Ira Seidenstein, who beautifully choreographed the work in terms of colour and line. Seidenstein is passionate about communicating clown craft, and it showed. Traditionally, to study a craft is to study one's own nature. Amongst his own "obscure complexity of influences", Seidenstein alludes to working with Frank Theatre and, unusually, to his spiritual mentor, local Rabbi Levi Jaffe. Given the 'centres of excellence' or 'centres of innovation' set up for limited, short term goals, it was salutary to be reminded by the overarching metaphor of the piece that the stages through which a work must pass to achieve completion parallel human development where 'ripeness is all', and so sheds light on our own needs and possibilities. In this regard, Seidenstein's program notes state that "Chaplin's Eye in an ultra naïve guise is a parable about sharing existential and material space and personal objects."

Beamingly clutching a small brown suitcase, Femmla (Kristen Duffus) innocently enters the bright sunlight of the sensual world and ingenuously invites the audience to participate in her attempts at positioning this sole prop on a bare stage. The action resembles changing household furniture, but Duffus finely indicates that, beneath Femmla's emulation of the questionable 'good taste' of a home-decorator, an effervescent re-assembly and adjustment of self is in constant motion in relation to the changing sites of the object of desire. Femmla's tentative coquettishness is the first flowering of a genuinely tender heart. After she departs, leaving the suitcase, the ultra feminine is troped by the attention-grabbing, determinedly lumpen and kleptomaniacal Zophtie (Jane Barber in thrall to a toe-tapping, banjo-plucking version of The Hills of Connemara). More crony than Crone, Barber wickedly succeeds in convulsively embodying uncontrollable natural forces, and celebrating wild desire.

Zophtie is no softy either—or is she? She has no qualms about stealing the suitcase.

Femmla returns with a bigger green suitcase denoting different, burgeoning qualities. From this Zophtie appropriates stockings and stole by sleight of hand, and, in a scene reminiscent of a classic confrontation between Lucille Ball and Vivian Vance, Femmla joyously discovers her aggression and bumps Zophtie off the case. Zophtie cries and cries. Innocence and Experience converge when Femmla consoles Zophtie with a rainbow umbrella. Cue for the entrance of Lanky (Andrew Cory). If Femmla is heart and Zophtie libido, Lanky crankily depicts the vagaries of the mind by adopting the Commedia fly lazzi as his stock in trade (the fly does not exist). In fact, he is a walking compendium of traditional Commedia character traits: Pantalone's paranoia; Dottore's illusions about himself; and Harlequin's imagining objects that aren't there. Cory blends these elements of his performance masterfully. By contrast to the women, Lanky is always suspicious and controlling in relationship to objects, but is easily controlled in turn by Zophtie who literally mesmerises him with her umbrella.

Clever lighting design, recalling the opening sequence of Les Enfants du Paradis, signals the appearance of Pirouette (Kayt Douglas). The shift is from the quotidian sensual realm to the sensuous, sublunar regions ruled by Dionysus and the imagination. As if blown about in high atmospherics, Douglas introduces a delectably light tone which helps reconfigure the overall spatial composition and brightens the pace. Everything becomes possible, and the descent of Charlie Chaplin (Ira Seidenstein) from the gods is just such an epiphany. This advent is a bitter-sweet return of the proletarian Everyman that Chaplin once represented in the iconography of the arts. In Seidenstein's hands, it is uncanny. After a life time of clowning, he provides a meticulous metronome to the ensuing slapstick choreography which becomes more intricate and labyrinthine, more democratic than antagonistic, as the clown characters (who somehow maintain their individual poise and rhythm) dissolve into shamanic 'bags of bones' and reconstitute themselves in a continuous recycling of the death and resurrection game. Charlie presents Femmla with a flower, and the mechanism begins to wind down. There is a moment of psychic (or social) integration when the rest of the cast proffer flowers from offstage, then a series of dissolving group snapshots with the double photographic message: 'I am/was here.'

It is not disparaging to call this work light. It is full of light.

Chaplin's Eye, producer/performer Andrew Cory, devisor/director/performer Ira Seidenstein, performers Jane Barber, Kayt Douglas, Kristen Duffus, lighting David Lee, costume design Tiffany Beckwith Skinner; Sue Benner Theatre, Metro Arts, Nov 24-Dec 3, 2005

*Chaplin's Eye will appear in the 2006 Adelaide Fringe Festival

RealTime issue #71 Feb-March 2006 pg. 31." Review By Doug Leonard.

For the Adelaide 2006 season Kayt and Andrew did not perform. Their replacements were Amanda-Lyn Pearson and Annette Schonenberger. Although the troupe idea of Chaplin's Eye did not occur, Jane became a successful hospital and elder care clown, and a Mother. Amanda-Lyn created The Crackup Sisters which I have mentored since its inception. 2006 also began my overseas work, initially within Frank Theatre to London, Wales, Switzerland, Chicago. From our short London season including a few performances at Hoxton Hall, I was hired to be in Tanushka Marah's UK tour of her production "Nothing Left to Lose". My next short contract was in Cirque du Soleil's Corteo for its two back to back seasons in Los Angeles. 2008 I gave a single 3 hours workshop arranged by Caspar Schjelbred in Paris. That evolved to me teaching more than 100 workshops in dozens of cities internationally between 2008 through to November 2019. Generally speaking, with only a few exceptions, critics were not part of that work period. Critics are a valuable part of the performing arts industry.

- 31 -
THEATRE AS RELIGION

Do you believe in Theatre? Do you believe it has value? High worth, much value? There are, in the Theatre, people who actually believe deeply that something is of so much worth that there is a reason to hold a passionate commitment to that something they believe is so very special which they call Theatre. In the Theatre I consider such believers to be hidden religionists. You may even have a religion and not know it. You may be strongly making choices also because of your religious upbringing or lack of or prejudice of or hate of or intellectual sense of superiority over others who believe in anything.

The need to believe is strong in the human being.

Belief and Religion may be a natural inclination perhaps in our existence as a human? A sense of belief is often strong in theatre workers.

Some of our gods in the theatre are:
The God, Belief and Religion of Intellectualism
The God of Funding Bodies
The God of Freedom. Sex, Drugs, House Parties
The God of State Approved Institutions
The God of Scientific Logic

The God of Out-witting All of Our Peers
The God of Good Theatre
The God of Environmental, Physical, New, Avant Garde, Original Theatres
The God of The National Theatre
The God of The Royal Theatre
The God of The Local Theatre
The God of Our Theatre
The God of My Hidden Spiritual Truth

Theatre can often be so special because it is like A New Religion. It is a metaphor for the way humans can interact and accomplish a worthwhile goal regardless of religious beliefs. However there is protocol and reverence and ceremony in the theatre. There is a suspension of disbelief. Or there is its opposite, the intellectual and clear understanding of the purpose of the gathering and meaning of the words and ritual presented.

The history of Theatre is actually a history of attempts to create and sanctify a new religion.

Our dominant theatre religion today would be The Religion of I Don't Believe in Religion Because I Have Seen The Damage Religion Has Done.

My Confession:

I believe that we humans desperately need to believe. The word believe is usually related to religion, but, to believe is a human instinct. The next step of that instinct is to formalise it, and that naturally leads to religions even of one's own design. Or, as some do, they only believe in science. Thus even that takes on a fundamentalist approach to its own dogma.

It seems we are prejudiced against religions or other religions because we know of the worst habits of the fanatics, extremists, fundamentalists.

The sad thing in throwing out religions from our lives is that we miss a depth of wisdom which comes from almost no other place in the human experience. We long for a deeper, profound experience in the theatre. As artists we know that religions want to either destroy us or control us. The religious also misunderstand, and that is really the main problem with religion. The religious people may be the problem, not the religion.

On one level, that of human psychology, many religions carry a far deeper, richer, more varied, more profound, more intelligent understanding of the human condition than any theatre.

Shakespeare has become a religion. Actually he has also been placed in the role of spiritual ambassador for the Glory of Anglodom. "Shakespeare Says" has replaced "The Bible Tells Me So".

What I am seeing is the religious wars which are behind much of what appears to be creativity in a neutral form. It is not neutral.

We in the theatre are part of a religious war. Western Society is battling the East. It battles culturally, politically, and economically.

But the real battle is an unresolved religious battle. It is the Current Crusades. It is quite confusing too, because often when people talk of God or Spirituality the hidden agenda is power and money. No religion has proved angelic. Nor has any spiritual group. Nor has any political belief system.

The term Middle East is interesting. The place is a destined disaster. Yet if we resolve that mythological minefield perhaps we in the theatre could actually experience the profoundness we long for. Perhaps.

Our Western hubris is so deep though that we actually believe Easterners who tell us how wonderful our theatre is. It can be, it could be but we lack a profound purpose. We lack some depth of wisdom. Shakespeare is not the source but he is a prophetic gateway. His inspiration came from life and literature. One great piece of literature being the Bible.

The Bible I will refer to as a great source of literature. It is great because it is the richest record of human paradoxes. Conflict is central to theatre. Paradox is the point. For me again, what I call the Quantum Point which can release endless creativity. I do not look at the Bible as the word of God unless we mean that God is within, and The Whole of the Human Experience, and that God is one's highest calling that manifests as profound intuition and creative inspiration. Historically and scientifically we know much (not all) where and when different sections of the Bible were created, that is written with encoded wisdom stories. Just as Indigenous stories must have a beginning: place, date, person.

Wisdom stories are each an act of creative inspiration. Inspiration leads us to advances in science, technology, and theology. Those are not meant to lead us into temptation and that is the great perplexing paradox. That is the historical lesson of the myth of the worship of the Golden Calf. That is our mistake in the Western Theatre. We still worship golden calves of our own design. My culture's Bible is the continuum of literature of the Torah, Tanach, Talmud, Mishnah, and the Zohar.

There are lessons from the Mahabharata and other Vedic literature which tell us much about the human condition and paradox. There is literature from the Tibetans too. There is the Koran and explanations from the Sufis. There is Mythology from the Aboriginals, Native Americans, and others which carries wisdom of the many levels of human experience.

In the Theatre we have literature such as: Bartholomew Fair, Don Juan, Faust, Waiting For Godot, and other plays which point out central human paradoxes. They teach us in some way moral parables which humans must constantly remind themselves of lest they go back to the Golden Calf - that is worshipping some material object of their own creation.

All religions have the seeds of wisdom. All have failed at times repeatedly from within, by pointing the finger and blaming. We on the outside must also put down our weapons, our pointing fingers of blame, and must begin again to move towards the light. No golden calves this time. No holy word, no sacrament, no ark, is greater than nothing. Nothingness. That is the lesson of Zen, some think. Koan and Cohen. But then your meditation pillow, and incense, your own temple becomes the golden calf. Your own theatre dogma becomes your golden calf.

The idea of the Chosen People is a grave, deadly misunderstanding by all humanity, even some of us who are Jewish. Yet people in the theatre constantly look in the dressing room mirror and see the New Chosen One. The idea of the Chosen People is a moral responsibility, burden, and yoke and it has an inspirational and psychological insight. Each race and tribe of people is chosen so to speak. Each human is a Chosen Person. Just as Abraham left Ur for Canaan, The People of Abraham left Canaan only to return to The Promised Land; just as farmers decide under inspiration to go to NYC to study theatre. Or from London to LA, or Sydney to Amsterdam. You do not knock on the City Gate of Paradise and ask to come in. You prepare your monologue, or play, or repertoire and go to conquer because you see that as your divinity to follow your star. You will step on toes. You will see your foes fall down and not stoop to help. You will today follow the Commandments of the New Age: It is not my problem.

It is your responsibility.
It must be their karma.

All so that you can conquer the Canaan of your dreams.

It is not easy to study the Five Books of Moses, the New Testament, the Koran, or Scriptures from the Far East. It is very easy though to misinterpret. Yet it is so beautiful if you start to understand any parable. Often it can even be painful to realise perhaps we have done something wrong. Perhaps we have transgressed. Perhaps we are in the habit of transgressions.

Perhaps we in the theatre today are so busy empowering ourself and sense of destiny that we have forgotten to practice forgiveness for those who have transgressed against us. It takes practice.

I cannot say that there is a God. I cannot say that there isn't a God. I cannot say anything is the word of God, unless we have the maturity to understand that God is all-inclusive and the word comes via the human's highest inspiration. I am a man of the theatre. I question God's existence. Yet I don't doubt God's existence. I live by faith. I can understand and experience literature, inspiration, co-operation, conflict, the body, subtle energies, ideas, concepts, thoughts, synchronicity, intuition, coincidence. When I embrace and comprehend those twelve concepts I can begin to contemplate that it would take years to fly to the nearby star which we call the Sun. But it would take 100,000 years to fly to the next nearest star. I can then contemplate that there are 400,000,000 stars in our galaxy. God only knows how many galaxies there are. I can then wonder how can this all come about? I can simply say this is beyond human comprehension. This is another level of existence which in English is called God. Then I can go back home to the studio or theatre and begin from a humble place to find my own place in the universe right here in Mother Earth.

Now it is 2020. In recent years, I have finally come to grasp, to begin to grasp, the abundance of theatrical and human drama encoded in the Torah/Tanach. My main editions are bonafide, authentic. Primarily I have "The Torah" published by Kehot Publication Service. The Torah is five books, so there are five Kehot volumes. Each with excellent explanations on different levels. I also have the whole Tanach which is 24 books as a single volume but with almost no explanation. That is The Stone Edition "Torah/prophets/Writings" from Mesorah Publications Ltd.

Like other Indigenous cultures, the Jewish culture is totally based around a yearly cycle that includes seasons of the Sun, cycles of the Moon, weekly passages referred to as Parsha readings, and we have several calendars which guide those and other cycles. Those cycles are encased in sagas as in all Indigenous cultures. Notably, our sagas have specifically four levels of understanding called *Pardes*. Pardes means orchard and in a sense a saga is like a tree. First we see oh, that's an almond tree. Then we learn about its leaves, roots, then the vitamin and mineral rich kernel hidden from our sight by the hard protective shell. In our culture it is well known that the story is a mere snapshot of the tree. The treasure is in the hidden kernel. In our culture, to get the Torah's nourishment it is well known to require some daily study, for a lifetime. In the theatre we have some works which are so profound that one can go back to them repeatedly and can receive fresh illumination endlessly. Many of Shakespeare's works are like that, as is Waiting For Godot. Notably, one of Beckett's longest friendships was with his publisher John Calder who wrote The Philosophy Of Samuel Beckett, and, The Theology Of Samuel Beckett. Calder wrote "Like all the greatest writers, Samuel Beckett was primarily interested in discovering the meaning and purpose of life and the world into which we are born. Knowledgeable about the religion of his family and education instilled in him, which as an adult he could neither accept nor reject, he used it extensively in his novels, plays, and poetry".

- 32 -
COMMON SENSE, CLAIRVOYANCE, AND CAREER

I would advise you to listen to your common sense first rather than clairvoyance or intuition.

If you get stuck in common sense though it will indeed stop your career in most cases. A career is created by taking advantage of coincidental circumstances. To do this however, you must listen to your intuition and you must often take a risk.

However to decide between common sense and intuition is not so easy. Often the theatre artist will attempt some sort of scan, weighing up the different possibilities.

Repeatedly I see actors, directors, and producers listening to fear above all else. I am not talking about good business sense. But good business people, police, criminals, doctors, all people in all walks of life use intuition.

Common sense limits discovery. Even a scientist is intuitively pursuing the outer realms of their common sense. A scientist follows a hunch, an intuitive hit or hint. Then they pursue it; test, challenge, research, and investigate.

In the theatre we must draw on thought processes of science, religion, law, art, psychology, and philosophy.

Generally our intuition works in the theatre by scanning which of these areas to focus on at any given moment. In other words if science or psychology or art is our religion then we will have very lopsided interpretations of a play. There must be flexibility in our mind. The mind and functioning of the brain is quite fantastic. Intellectualism is really a perversion and a limited use of the mind.

The Quantum Point sees no conflict between religion, science, psychology or art.

The mind of the director can often be the exact opposite of the function which an actor requires. Likewise the mental focus of the agent can be in opposition to the director or actor. In the theatre we are seeking harmony so all goals can be achieved and each individual can flourish.

Actors, directors, agents, and producers all learn to play each other. It is the gross manipulation and lack of ethics which has perverted the theatre.

One of the most delightful theatre minds I ever witnessed was an agent. Kevin Palmer was an absolutely delightful witch of a man. He had extensive experience as a stage manager, some as a director. His mind and intuition was ever pursuing a business vision.

In Australia all of the Casting Agents, in the 1980s and 1990s, were women and they all function at the mental, intuitive and business level of Kevin. As an actor you must skim along on the mental waves of the agent, casting agent, and director in an audition. Thoughts are flashing extremely rapidly. It is an intuitive process of a super mind or cooperative mind. This process though is frequently completely ruined by logic, fear, and common sense. As an actor it is my job to get the job. I am a bit of a quirk or quark as an actor. Repeatedly I have watched directors override their logic and common sense and take a risk in hiring me. Once hired it is my job to fulfil the directors artistic needs and including artistic whims or trials.

Auditioning is a highly intuitive art form! It all happens too quick. The actor cannot know what the director has in mind. The director often cannot possibly tell an actors potential. The actor must reveal potential, flexibility and stability.

How do intuition or clairvoyance work? Does it work? Is it real?

There is scientific logic in religion and there is a religious goal in science. Both are pursuing altruistic goals of understanding existence and bettering the human experience. There is a practical and scientific side to what we call intuition and clairvoyance and all that we refer to as ESP or psychic phenomenon.

Science tells us that all is energy. All matter can be reduced to energy. When we look at the body we see a physical form. This form can be dissected, then we can examine the composition of tissue, then the composition of cells. Then we start to examine elements of energy.

Energy takes physical form. One form is sound and sound waves. Another is light and light waves. Science is also busy trying to see where or how thought exists as a form of energy. Some people also try to prove that spirit takes a form of energy.

I cannot say that spirit exists as matter. I can talk about spirituality as a philosophical concept of living.

Nobody can prove how intuition, clairvoyance, ESP, or psychic abilities work. Nobody can prove scientifically that God exists nor prove that God does not exist. God as I understand it is a word for the total universe including whatever was 'The Nothing' before The Big Bang; and, during the $.0015^{th}$ of a second that some propose as the duration of The Big Bang; and, Everything that followed after which includes the understanding that the Universe is both expanding and evolving. The Kabbalah 4-letter word for 'God' means that; all and everything i.e. what was, is, and will be. As Shakespeare put it, we are made of stardust.

There is a logic to the psychic realm that can be reduced to energy.

When I look "clairvoyantly" I "look" at energy. I get a concept of the energy that the conscious mind can hold. This concept can be a colour, shape, symbol, picture, image, or word. Other psychic abilities engage concepts of feelings, sounds, or smells. In other words psychic abilities must go through conscious, or physical senses. In science data must be perceived through equipment, registered mentally through concepts, and interpreted.

In science and psychic realms there is the exact same logic. Data is received either in equipment or the body (five senses) and registered mentally as a concept and then interpreted.

Seeing with your eyes or your third eye is a complex act of optics and refraction. To see with my third eye is a sense different than seeing with visual sense through my normal or physical eyes. Yet your physical sight is actually just a sense and is a concept of perception. That is why ESP Extra Sensory Perception is a wonderful term, as it just says it is an 'extra' sense.

It is not extra that some people have it and some don't. It is extra because it is outside or different than the five basic senses. Likewise everyone can run. Some people may have to run in a wheelchair. People do have such wheelchair races, we now have the fully developed Paralympic. When it comes to ESP though, scientists are running in wheelchairs when in fact they could just stand up and walk. Some people like crutches to lean on. Something concrete and real.

Science is now proving via quantum physics that what we perceive as concrete and real ain't necessarily so.

Energy and perception is quite interesting and real.

In science, ESP, and theatre, the problem is often the interpretation.

I would say a good scientist is probably happy, healthy, funny, curious and has a sense of wonderment. I would say the same generally about a psychic or a theatre worker.

The psychic world cannot yet be proven scientifically however it is quite real. It is a realm of energy just as real to me as sound or light. The CIA, the KGB, and various universities and businesses know that the psychic realm is very real. More and more police know to use psychics. You must also use logic. You must learn to interpret the data that comes through a psychic.

What comes out of a psychic's mouth is not gospel.

When it comes to one's mind, what comes out, depends on what goes in. Same in science what data you choose to program in determines what comes out. What is discovered is already present.

Clairvoyance in the theatre is not such a good idea. Intuition is quite normal yet can be developed. Clairvoyance is a wonderful ability and tool.

Clairvoyance is regulated by interpretation.

To learn clairvoyance is very easy, logical, straight forward.

To learn to interpret well is almost impossible.

I was and am an able clairvoyant. That does not mean that I predict the future it means I have an ability to 'see' energy with my mind's eye or imagination.

There is a mass of information about people, places, situations which sits in space or the confines of the mind. As a psychic I know how to go into the original cyberspace, have a look around and pull out or attract the data I am searching for. Before I interpret I simply describe what I see. Maybe I can interpret at that point maybe I must wait. Clairvoyance is not a power, it is an ability to see energy. It does not mean you can predict the future though you may be able to see some possibilities. Life is much more complex than simple predictions.

I cannot say whether past lives exist nor whether the future exists. Science is now helping us to understand that the present does not exist as we perceive it or believe it to be.

I can say a lot about a person if I check my "CD-ROM" called "Past Lives". But I program to seek only the information which will help a person at that moment. It is called a present time reading. If you help a person with the present problem you probably help them with the future and the past.

Just like a good doctor though the clairvoyant knows what to report and what not to, what tests to take and what questions to ask.

A Doctor of Chinese medicine can read your face, you do not have to come in and complain nor kvetch. A Doctor can say "you are healthy", so too can a clairvoyant.

There is a place where Oriental Doctors, Western Doctors, Priests, Rabbis, The Happy Sinners of the Theatre, Psychics, and others meet. That place is the Quantum Point. A place where we are clear, knowledgeable, filled with light, and undeniable truth.

There is a point in consciousness where we all want to be and exist. We all know where that place is and how to get there.

Too often our common sense kills our creativity, it kills mutual success, it kills a growing harmony.

We kill ourselves and we kill each other. Religion has been a killer at times. Science and technology have killed. Education has killed often the mind and the spirit. Theatre has to do the same cleansing of corruption and breaking through its own proscribed and indoctrinated dogmas, as do the religions, politicians, sciences, higher education.

There is a moral dilemma in the world. We do not have to be angels nor saints, yet. We do not have to give up common sense, clairvoyance, nor careers.

We do have to understand that there is wisdom to guide us, whose guidance we need.

The most basic tenets can provide the anchor we need. In the Western theatre we do not understand many basic concepts. Metaphorically, much that science knows was already recorded mythologically by sages in all cultures. Religion, greed, covetousness often took us on a wrong turn.

When it comes to common sense you cannot beat Patanjali's yoga sutras, or the Ten Commandments. Even if we are only hitting seven out of ten, ...even five is a good start.

Clairvoyance requires wisdom and neutrality neither of which comes easily. Science can help to understand that all is energy.

Careers require common sense and clairvoyance. It is common sense that an actor's training is based on intelligent training of the body. Yoga is actually common sense of the highest order.

It trains you in the body and scientific intelligence. It is not a religion and should not become one, but it usually does.

If you are in the theatre chances are your religion is either common sense, clairvoyance, or career. Perhaps it is time for your own self reformation.

- 33 -
CCC 2

My intuition no matter how good, must work with the intuition, common sense, and career motives of others. Some of these others are fellow actors, directors, choreographers, technicians, publicists, agents, casting agents, producers.

My intuition has been excellent to help other people. In terms of my own success, my intuition may have helped me or hindered me, I cannot say. Success in terms of fame and fortune has been quite fickle. My own success has been to stay in the game, so far, nearly 50 years. Another success has been to have the chance to try many fields within the broadest sense of theatre. Other successes may come or go, I am only human. Perhaps I should have been a cook, I cannot say.

During a period of my life when I was employed as a Clairvoyant, Healer, and Teacher of meditation and intuition I saw many things. It was an interesting experience and helped many people.

In my own life I saw that I had to temporarily leave an active psychic career and pursue just plain living. No big deal, just a little refocus in life.

Another thing I saw was that creativity was more necessary for most people than meditation. Nothing earth shattering there either but it's quite interesting seeing how powerful creative energy is and how people do everything to avoid the full force and responsibility of this energy.

In time I gave the whole New Age movement quite a miss. No matter how much it helped me and no matter how much I was able to help other people, there was something quite corrupt in the so called new age. It was not more corrupt than medicine, science, religion, politics, education, spiritual groups, nor theatre.

Theatre was, though, equally corrupt because like other fields its focus was money, power, and control. For myself, clairvoyance and psychic abilities are nothing to do with power nor control and one must also be clear of avoiding some aspects of the money which detract from the spiritual essence. Farmers, teachers, doctors, lawyers, librarians, meditation and theatre teachers must all eat and pay rent and deal with material aspects of modern life so it is not to take a pure view of money. But power and control are definitely out and so too is manipulation when it comes to any of the fields I just mentioned.

I was not against the business of the New Age but I was against its lack of business ethics.

It was no different than doctors who abuse social medical systems or doctors who uphold the righteousness of drugs without knowing equal, better, safer, healthier alternatives. I don't really want to single out the New Age nor the medical world they are just two opposing fields that can serve as an example.

But much of my world at the time was the New Age and therefore its opposite force, that of modern medicine and science.

I didn't like the salesmanship pushing New Age products. I thought it was great that people could start to pursue alternative businesses but I suppose I am quite anti-commercial generally. I'm not anti-business, but I am against the selling of materialism as a way of life. We are bad enough as it is, so who needs encouragement. So I preferred the corrupt theatre as a way to serve society, humanity, and to develop my self.

All along though my journey is nothing more than an objective mix of spirituality, theatre and life.

- 34 -
CONCEPTS INSIDE QUANTUM THEATRE: SLAPSTICK TO SHAKESPEARE

In Quantum Theatre a primary idea is the concept of The Dot and The Circle.

When we first see a Dot, we can see nothing more. Yet, if we imagine the Dot expanding we can create a Circle. Inside this Circle is either empty space or infinite Dots of possibilities.

This thought is essential to create a ready, aware, alert state of mind.

The Dot/Circle idea I learned from the book *Quantum Gods* (1976) by Jeff Love. Jeff Love was inspired by Samuel Bousky "a research physicist specialising in the application of laser technology to high density data recording systems". Bousky was inspired by the writer Neville Goddard. All three were inspired by the Torah and Kabbalah simply as symbols and a conceptual template for human creativity and potential; and the relation of the conscious and subconscious.

In creative and practical ways the concept of The Dot and The Circle begins to release mental blocks which hold the artist, student, teacher or director back from their own potential.

In the theatre it is not the problem which creates the difficulty it is our way of thinking and of processing thought.

It has been expressed another way. We must take the "UGH" out of tho-ugh-t. That is to take out unnecessary anguish and create pure Thot. Thought minus "ugh" equals Thot.

>   Thought
>   -- ugh
>   --------
>   Thot

I must emphasise though that in Quantum Theatre all work must be professional, efficient, proficient, practical.

You must guard against light headed philosophies which stop you from being goal or task oriented.

To be professional means to resolve problems quickly and creatively. Speed and accuracy. Speed and accuracy was our motto as Radarmen in the US Navy.

Charles Chaplin was and is an example of professionalism. Occasionally he was stuck creatively for weeks on end. Chaplin stated, "You can never be professional enough".

Peter Brook learned in his first major directing job that his intimate and detailed two weeks preparation for the play's first scene was completely useless when faced with his creative partners called actors.

Whereas Ingmar Bergman plans and executes every detail and in the first days of rehearsal and the actors must do what is precisely planned. Then after that first phase a new creative partnership begins as all people involved in a production begin to discover the Circle of Possibilities in each moment of the play. Woody Allen when directing does not preplan his shots in detail. He does know where, when and whom and also which scene will be filmed the next day. Many details are left out. When he arrives the next day on location the real creation takes place or is born.

To be professional can mean many different things. As an actor you must be mentally flexible to work with any director's method, or lack of, and their moods. The good director is simply the one who draws out the best from each actor. That is not so simple.

The concepts I will now express are the often hidden Thots inside creative solutions of professionals. Each Thot/thought is a philosophical idea which is not conscious in the artist, yet, such thoughts are how the correct creative buttons get stimulated in the brain. The practical side of professionalism is one thing, the hidden thoughts or concepts are another.

In Quantum Theatre: Slapstick to Shakespeare, here are some thoughts about how to expand a Dot into a Circle. How to create thoughts which expand your potential.

As an example, I have an idea named The Principle of Three. That idea has a few definitions which each comprise of three elements.

One primary definition of The Principle of Three is a unity of: Time-Timing-Timelessness.

Time. On the practical level one must be on Time for work, for class, for rehearsal. Basically if you are not early then you are late. To be "on time" is very misleading. Is it "on time" to be where you are meant to meet or is it on time to start the work at the agreed time. There is simply never enough time in the theatre. Often to allow more time without changing our mental ways means a further abuse of time. Time is the essence of professionalism in the theatre. How you use time is the professional's first art.

Timing. The way we achieve or attempt to achieve Timelessness is through Timing. Timing is the creative steps we take and how we piece together our choices. Time is the stable ground which keeps our choices focused on the method Timing and the goal Timelessness.

Timelessness. In the theatre our undiscussed or unconscious goal is Timelessness. Timelessness in the theatre means lifting the audience from low thoughts to high thoughts, from negative feelings to positive feelings, from sleeping to awareness, from apathy to action.

Time is relative. For example it is very normal that a dancer warms up before a dance class. Yet a dance class must begin with a thorough warm-up taught by the teacher. What is the warm-up which a dancer does on their own? It is a meeting with their own Self, body, attitudes, pains, anxiety, excitement, determination, relaxation. They must meet their self before they meet the teacher. The dancer like the actor must prepare mentally, physically and by implication also spiritually to flow with the teacher or director or choreographer's personal and daily rhythms. One prepares also to deal with co-operative agreement to compete to achieve one's highest potential. The competition is to stay aware and alert and to give out your fullest being.

Competition has some negative connotations. Yet competition is the only way to arrive at one's potential. Za-zen is a competition to clear out competition against oneself. Christianity is a competition to clear out evil and find redemption. In the Tibetan and Judaic ways to create pure spiritual leaders the student must not only memorise scripture they must team up with a 'chevrusha' - a study partner, to argue and reason in what seems superficially a shouting match. It is a type of competition which not only purifies the soul, brings a flying healing energy into all of the complex systems of the body, but also flushes out all unnecessary thoughts. It is a warm-up and training for the higher practices.

Not until I began classical ballet classes did I know that actually it is a great mental discipline when properly taught. There are higher levels to the theatre, but one will never realise them without dealing well with

Time. Time is of the essence to our brief moment on Earth. Theatre is at all moments a reflection on human existence. Time, competition, mental discipline run parallel to each other.

As a teacher I teach Time first by starting my class exactly on time. Exact though is relative, I start within the minute of the appointment. I do not scold those who come late. In fact I make a point of welcoming people who are late by acknowledging them with 'Hello. Come on in as soon as you are ready'. But, I don't stop what the class is doing. Sometimes I simply wave 'hello' to the latecomer. Within days those people who tend to come late have to begin to confront themselves since they see I start on time and that the class is moving ahead without them.

Soon enough the process will shift and they will learn to come into the studio and begin their own work without a leader. I will then begin the class different ways on different days depending on the feeling, energy, or activity in the studio. This is the same for class or rehearsal when I direct.

Then there will be another phase where I can and will come into the studio late. I will not be late for work but I know I can start to deal with production or creative ideas outside of the actual studio room. The group by this point will have already developed a spontaneous sense of discipline and creativity. Sometimes it happens if I make myself late enough the artists will be involved in a full scale rehearsal, or improvisation, or an improvised dance or dance class or a discussion while warming up. When these things begin to occur then the experience of Time-Timing-Timelessness has begun and the group has evolved to a troupe. I would not have discussed any of those ideas beforehand. And I rarely mention them afterwards. Here I am writing and throughout this book, more than anything, I am simply sharing some thoughts.

During class and rehearsal though I would have already taught a few classes in Timing. Usually I teach a few classes in Slapstick in the beginning of a process. Through this method I can study each actor's communication tendencies, I then apply Slapstick as a way of discovering partner timing and communication. This is applied sporadically and spontaneously in rehearsals. Over time the actors learn not a rigid, formal slapstick technique. They learn rather how to adjust and adapt to each different person they work with.

Learning by adjusting to partners is central to learning Aikido. In my brief two years intensive training in Yoshinkan Aikido there was a daily class with around 30 participants. The primary training is with partners and one rotates during the class and works with a variety of partners during each class. Our teacher in Brisbane was Sensei Mori, a 7th Dan (7th level Black Belt), he is now 8th Dan. In any class there may be one or more 5th, 4th, 3rd, 2nd, 1st Dan students as well as a large selection of us as Brown Belts, and there are White Belts. Before the school's annual public demonstration there would be a few minutes per class where a single person had to practice a technique against a relentless tide of about ten other students 'attacking'. That is for the soloist to learn the particular defence technique and to instantly, spontaneously adapt to each different 'attacker' who varied from 5th Dan thru novice White Belt.

I create different slapstick rhythms or routines which are very simple but absolutely precise. The main slapstick exercise is one of the duets in The Four Articulations for Performance. First this involves clapping and slapping. Then "takes" (use of the head, neck, eyes) and reactions. Acting is reacting. So this is not about absurd comedy, it is about classical acting and how to make the rehearsed look spontaneous and the improvised look rehearsed. It is how to get genuine communication between two actors through focus and relaxation. The slapstick can evolve to be usable stagecraft and skill. Eventually evolving to an art form known as "Knockabout" for those who have acrobatic skills. There are many plays written which can accept this high skill level. For example many of Shakespeare's plays have fights and implied physical slapstick.

The best work of Charles Chaplin, Buster Keaton, Lucille Ball, Norman Wisdom, Nils Poppe, combined slapstick with well thought out drama.

Audiences absolutely love slapstick but the real thing is extremely rare in theatre. The techniques of slapstick are still in the authentic traditional circus clown teams. One of the best resources are films that show such physical skills are those like; The Three Stooges, Laurel and Hardy, Keystone Kops, Harold Lloyd. In the 1970s and 1980s, the Russian State Circus had created several acts which involve the real, authentic slapstick. I don't know the names of the acts or troupes but there is one which was of old fashioned firemen with a hand pump & hose and teeterboard. Another troupe played basketball on two trampolines. There is one act, a duet in a mock hot air balloon. In the circus or night clubs there are the traditional acrobatic chair and table routines which combine slapstick and acting. That form using such props, is called "Knockabout".

Every theatre production is trying to perfect Timing to create illusion or drama and to carry the message of the playwright or show. The playwright is also trying to achieve the best Timing.

I am saying that Slapstick is a key to training. Presumably when Copeau had his studio Vieux-Colombier in the early 1900's in France he had slapstick taught by the circus clown trio Les Fratellini Brothers. The skills employed in slapstick timing express the essence or can be a metaphor of human communication, and miscommunication.

In Quantum Theatre: Slapstick to Shakespeare, we realise quickly that Shakespeare has numerous slapstick moments. Even the play Othello begins so with Iago's counterfeit to stir up Desdemona's father. In terms of Quantum Theatre, Shakespeare is the Circle but the hidden or unseen Dot in between Slapstick and Shakespeare is Samuel Beckett. The central piece of theatre for me is "Waiting For Godot". It is the Philosophers' Stone of Theatre from which we theatre practitioners might learn the stagecraft alchemy that turns a base metal into gold. I mean besides the story, the theatre craft imbedded into the play's action by Beckett there is also the depth of his personal knowledge of art and music. Waiting For Godot is a complete work of art, at the same time it is a musical composition, as well as being a play, and an essay on the futility as a human on the Earth yet floating in a complex Universe.

I saw "Godot" directed by Beckett on the San Quentin Drama Workshop. The perfect play, perfect director, perfect players, perfect production. It was perfect, great and perhaps sterile or surgical? Some might call it boring. As did some of the well educated young high school audience at that 1984 performance in Adelaide who periodically actually screamed "Boring".

They had fully studied the play and sometimes called out, on cue, at the same time as the actors spoke lines such as "Let's don't do anything it's safer". As Beckett has said, "If I did theatre the way I really want it would empty the place." I've seen the perfect production. Now what? I am relieved of the burden and illusion that a piece of theatre can be perfect. There the only Timelessness was for the Players and the Producer. A great way to take an audience into Timelessness is via slapstick. Still "Godot" is the perfect vehicle. Samuel Beckett already did it the way it was intended now we are free to find its Timelessness.

I'll let this imagery of Time-Timing-Timelessness trail off to another concept that I work with: Something From Nothing.

Even if I work with a play or a script I imagine I am not. I go into the room usually with no props and see what happens. See how I feel, what I feel like discovering or playing with or trying. Usually I start with some movement. For example if I wanted to begin work on "A Midsummer Night's Dream" I could say to the actors "Imagine that you are stars in the sky on a Midsummer's night". When you go into the studio there is nothing but the empty space. What happens is your impulse, your impulse to create something from nothing. Follow your impulse and do anything. But for God sake don't be too formal. It's like a wedding night. The Bride and Groom shut the door and what happens? Do they laugh, cry, hug, do it, shower first, what? Do what comes naturally...nothing...something will come. Everybody is tired, okay lay down and go to sleep. It's a play you have plenty to do. In that case do nothing. But somehow what I mean is that even if you have a lot to do then you must always create a sense of nothing. Nothingness. That's what Godot is all about Nothing-Something. Experience the paradox. You achieve Nothingness as the high state of consciousness in all spiritual practices, Zen, Kabbalah, Yoga. That's what it is all about. To be or not. Godot's opposite is not a tragedy it is the comedy "A Midsummer Night's Dream". In this comedy everyone is a very busy bee, being ever so creative. There is a big wedding and performance to prepare. There are love potions to prepare. Mischief to test Fate. There is much to do about nothing. There is nothing to be done. Don't just do nothing,... stand there!

Practically and creatively I work with nothingness often as a teacher and director. The actor regularly has to create from their own impulses. If they have no impulse then they must experience the state of no impulse. Be at one with that feeling. Do not control it, do not chase it out, do not correct it. Be bored, be angry, be tired, experience a pain. Put your hand where the pain is, then take your hand away, put it to the pain, take it away. Continue, repeat this action and it becomes a dance. You have now begun to create thru feeling, awareness, action, rhythm, change of sensation or changing your frame of mind. Thru the creative acceptance of yourself you go directly to a state of Nothingness. No ten day retreat. No fasting. No misunderstood philosophy. Directly thru and with your own self you can always achieve the high state of Zen Mind-No Mind, Nothingness. Soon you will spontaneously come out and do Something. You will begin to work in harmony with yourself and others. You will really create Theatre. Through your work practice you experience Timelessness and feel the need to take the Time to practice your Timing.

Note: Quantum Theatre: Slapstick to Shakespeare is composed of:
a Dot Chart of ten principles;
a Circle Chart of ten principles;
a list of Ten Principles based on the integers of 1 thru 10.

The Ten Principles are explained later, in chapter 42 in this book.

The practical introduction to Quantum Theatre: Slapstick to Shakespeare is the template of physical/creative exercises called The Four Articulations for Performance. That whole template is explained with step-by-step instructions in chapter 2 of *Clown Secret*.

- 35 -
SPEAKING OF NOTHING. THE SHAMAN

The one who speaks of Nothing is No-thing. Rapidly and recently the word, work, and world of the shaman is becoming quite common. What is a shaman? It is someone who sees inside and through what we normally call reality. The shaman can go into altered states of consciousness through elaborate rituals or directly by flicking a switch inside their mind and brain. The shaman can also assist others into altered states. It is also important that the journey is safe and that the return is assured. The Four Articulations for Performance is the practical base template that serves as a physical and creative introduction to Quantum Theatre: Slapstick to Shakespeare. The exercises in the template allow the actor to learn all they need artistically to turn the creative state on, and to make a safe journey back.

Shamanism is not a toy. It is a tool for healing. Healing means balancing Body, Mind and Spirit. It does not imply a miracle healing. Shamanism is quite natural and exists in all cultures. It is through understanding Nature's pathways that a shaman works. Particularly important is an understanding of how the Mind functions. This is more subtle than psychology. It is of course a great time when Shamanism is being revived but one must understand that there is an equal rise in the need to be cautionary about practices and practitioners. The indigenous people of many, perhaps all cultures still have the specific techniques of the shaman.

First and foremost the work of the Shaman is to assist in Healing by balancing the Body-Mind-Spirit of an individual or a group. Secondly this is done not by miracle nor by power but by applying knowledge of Nature. Third what is particularly important is to know Human Nature and the way the Mind functions. Fourth is to understand Nothingness and Emptiness as concepts which allow Healing to simply occur.

The fifth concept inside Shaman is what I call "Bag o' Bones". This is a concept for Healer and Healed to sense their own skeleton. As they allow their joints to relax and get in touch with their own knowledge of mortality and immortality.

Here the patient can simply relax on the bed or back or in a chair or sitting on the ground as the shaman guides them thru visualisation and relaxation. Allowing pain to release, illness to pass, confusion to stabilise. Become at one with the universe. At-one-ment. Atonement. The shaman is to assist at-one-ment to occur. Sound and silence are equally important.

The idea of experiencing the skeleton inside your own body is directly connected to the concept of Nothingness. This is also the process described in Patanjali's Yoga Sutras. As you practice a yoga posture, and asana, you must align your skeleton. Once the skeleton is in the desired position and shape you are to become Nothing. Experience your body as if you have always been just where you are at this moment. In Zen you then let the thoughts simply pass away. Let each thought die a natural death, effortlessly passing away. In the theatre though we must learn to know which thought or impulse to follow eventually learning to guide our self, our thoughts, our actions. In the theatre we must become our own shaman. Healer heal thyself. Actor inspire yourself.

Through practice, study, and clearing the mind we learn to understand inspiration. This was Stanislavsky's goal. His shaman was Leopold Sulerzhitsky. That shaman learned by living life to the fullest. Stanislavsky was trying to find a way to teach actors to invoke and to guide Inspiration.

This can only be done by teaching movement and acting technique and guiding the individual inspiration. That means giving the individual maximum space to explore their very own idea, their very own way. On a very practical level Quantum Theatre takes a unified approach to training Body-Voice-Acting-Creativity. To keep the actor grounded, centred and with a growing self confidence, training must also have a specific daily training in a single style of dance, mime, acrobatics or martial art. Many alternative schools which claim to teach different "styles" are usually off the mark when it comes to an individual discovering their own way. The shaman way cannot occur in a clear cut, organised way. It must have clear steps yet it must allow and encourage individual development, and at the same time in relation to the theatre you must have daily training in a formal movement technique...and this must occur over years. It is superficial to change movement styles every three, four or five weeks as many schools do. Often the more clear the set program is the more the actor is being programmed.

However there must be a base daily technique.

In Russia, when the Soviet's Moscow Circus School existed in full operation up until about 1990, the circus artist trained his or her body, impulses, drive, instinct. Through the process the potential of each artist was studied and guided. There was always a team of teachers. Naturally at some point a stronger relation will develop between an individual teacher and a Particular artist. This teacher then worked as a mentor (shaman) for the artist to reach their full human potential. This means using the performing arts as a valid life path. The next realisation step occurs when a direction and virtuoso act is visualised. Then a new team is created to achieve this act's potential. The team was: the mentor (shaman), musical director, director, master of the virtuoso skill, and masters of any related skills. That meant at least four teacher/directors involved in that process. It is a process of full empowerment.

As I have expressed briefly in other articles, the traditional circus knows everything about a world and journey into Self-Mastery through the arts that most theatre schools are guessing about. The traditional circus needs to grow and change too, but the truth is the traditional circus has always grown and changed.

The world of Western commedia, mime, mask, alternative theatre, movement theatre, circus theatre teaching is sometimes missing a knowledge of tradition, dance, history, acting, and Master Artists. Exceptions are the trainings/schools of Decroux, Marceau, Dimitri, Tomaszchevski. Generally the state traditional acting and theatre schools excel over the alternative schools.

The state schools often rely on teachers of: mask, mime, commedia, movement who have limited professional experience when compared to Mastery of Russian, Soviet nations, and Chinese experience in training actors. In the West the common exceptions are the training that a musical theatre performer must go through with the classic combined Actor-Singer-Dancer skills.

The shaman can speak directly to the point.

The freedom of the Western theatre takes us directly away from Mastery.

- 36 -
ALCHEMY

Alchemy is Mastery of the Elements. Alchemy in the theatre implies mastery of the key elements Body-Voice-Acting-Creativity. In another chapter called "Introduction to Quantum Theatre" I give the beginning formulas (blessings, ideas, concepts). I go into details in Chapter 39.

Alchemy in the Theatre means only Mastery over the elements involved in your production. It does not mean some quantitive, measurable thing. It means you have found the right blend, resolutions, and have overcome what was necessary and possible this time.

For example in one production of a Shakespeare play a theatre and director used approximately 300 lighting elements and approximately 150 lighting cues. This may be normal for a large musical but in a play perhaps one could say there was no balance nor proportion, at least not in that production. Perhaps if they had considered a simple fade-up and fade-out at the end of each act different thoughts would have arisen in the creative team about how to awaken the audience to the message and meaning of that play and their production.

So alchemy is very much about proportion and appropriate choices. There are no hard and fast rules, but one can say that excess is out. Whereas extravaganza may be just the right idea if it suits the occasion.

Here one must be aware of blanket statements such as: I liked it, I didn't like it, It was good, It was bad, It was interesting. You can say any of these things but the meaning is limited and quite relative.

There are infinite types of theatre for infinite types of audiences.

There are types of theatre which I have little interest in seeing or experiencing yet if it is well done in its own frame of reference, if the alchemy is right in proportion it will appeal to a wide range of viewers, including me. On these occasions I find myself saying, I don't like that type of theatre but this production was great and I loved it.

Alchemy in the theatre requires teamwork. Sometimes we say the chemistry was right. In the theatre the right chemistry is more about a dynamic interpretation rather than a safe, peaceful, conservative, altruistic harmony. Certainly the goal is a peaceful harmony but the path is a sparking dynamic of sometimes opposing forces.

When you understand the elements of Theatre Alchemy such as Time-Timing-Timelessness, Something From Nothing, Dot and Circle, Practical-Philosophical Balance, you can begin to discover your own Way Towards Alchemical Balance. You can turn basic elements into a Golden Experience.

In Alchemy of the Theatre a sparkly gold energy in the performance, audience, and backstage space is the goal.

Respect, Understanding, Joy are tools of thought to achieve this goal.

Alchemists understand that the state of mind is the key to mastering the elements. Alchemy implies understanding the elements; Fire, Water, Air, Earth, Ether or the Eastern; Fire, Water, Wood, Metal, Earth and their better Proportion in Ritual and in Season.

August Strindberg was the great absurd alchemist of the theatre. As he searched for the "real" alchemy he missed the fact that his direct artistic journey and expression was the embodiment of alchemy.

The search is not for outward form. The search is the inward journey and understanding.

As Stanislavsky searched, Sulerzhitsky already knew. The Shaman and Alchemist was standing right next to Stanislavsky as a mirror saying "you are already there, where you want to be."

- 37 -
HARRY HAYTHORNE, MBE (MEMBER OF THE BRITISH EMPIRE)

Seated at a desk in his busy office, dancer Harry Haythorne is hand-sewing a costume for his current production of Romeo and Juliet. Haythorne, Artistic Director of the Royal New Zealand Ballet Company since 1981, continued with the alterations as Ira Seidenstein asks about Harry's steps from vaudeville and eccentric dance to West End Musical Comedy, from Ballet Master and assistant to the choreographer Leonide Massine to guest of The Royal Ballet at Covent Garden.

Question from the interviewer, Ira: Harry, I would like to know your theory of how a story can be communicated to an audience, but first can you tell me something of your background?

Answer from Harry: I started dancing at the age of five in Adelaide, that was 1932. Jean Bedford taught me musical comedy dancing. Now it's called Jazz Ballet. From that I went to classical ballet and tap. Because of the popularity of Shirley Temple and Mickey Rooney, children were in demand on the stage. Austin Hall and I did a double act as miniature Fred Astaire's in Adelaide at the Regent Theatre. When I was 14 and still studying dance, World War II broke out. My mother ran a concert party that toured the army camps. Many of the acts later became professionals. Like the Amazing

Brittons (jugglers) and the Maxwells (acrobats). Harold Raymond asked me to join his traveling vaudeville show.

We toured country towns in South Australia and New South Wales in a large car with our luggage tied to the top. The profits from the show were given to the Brighton Children's Home for the deaf, dumb and blind. We were paid as professionals, it wasn't much but we were happy to do our part. People came to us from as far as 100 miles as our popularity grew. We played halls without stages or fly space or dressing rooms. Since I was the youngest and smallest I would climb up to the rafters and put eye screws in so we would have somewhere to hang our tabs and scenery. As soon as the show was over we would pack up and move 50 or 60 miles to the next town. We did this six days a week, occasionally we had a season of three days in a town like Broken Hill. There we played the Crystal Palace. That theatre was made of corrugated iron, it held the heat and the cold. During that three years of traveling with the show I finished my schooling by correspondence course.

The show would have famous guest comedians like Buster Nobel and Eddie Edwards. I learned a lot from them. It was a small troupe so I had to play in the sketches, sing, play the piano accordion and do anything and everything I was asked to do. That continued through most of the war. My parents thought I should be doing something more substantial. So I worked in the office of a cotton mill for a year. I was fired for always making the girls laugh. So it was back to show business until almost the end of the war when I was drafted into the Air Force. Later, I went to England to study dance to become a better teacher. I joined a metropolitan ballet company and also started to work in musical comedies in the West End. I danced in: Bells Are Ringing; Can Can; Listen To The Wind; Plain And Fancy; and, Pyjama Game in which I toured South Africa. I returned to Vaudeville in England where we did a repertory of five shows with headliners including; Bruce Forsythe, Jimmy Edwards and Jessie Matthews. I sang, danced and did sketches. I also did comedy numbers in a Victorian Music Hall. While dancing one night I hurt my back. But I had no choice and kept on working because in those days if you didn't work you got no pay. The first doctor said I would never dance again. Then my regular osteopath in London started to treat me. Eventually I returned to Australia and received chiropractic treatment. It was two or three years before I could dance again with out feeling pain. Now that I am older if I am tired or move badly the old injury erupts. (Harry still did a 45 minute ballet training every morning. He joked that. it has more to do with insomnia than discipline)

During my time in London I took advantage of the opportunity to study various forms of dance, dance history, the Kurt Jooss/Sigurd Leeder System, and Laban Notation. I was hired to notate the choreography by Hanya Holm in Where's Charley starring Norman Wisdom. They were impressed with my work, and jobs followed in Israel and Australia. Eric Edgley hired me to choreograph a show starring Winifred Atwell. George Balanchine was creating new ballets at La Scala in Milan and I was asked to go there and do the notations for them. In Italy I also auditioned as a dancer for Leonide Massine. My audition took place in one of the scenery bays. There was no music so we both hummed as I leaped out of packing crates and boxes. Massine offered me the jobs of Ballet Master and his assistant. He liked to have people of all nations.

I also worked with other ballet companies such as the Dutch National, in England the International Ballet, and the Scottish Ballet. With one of the groups I made a series for TV called Ballet For Beginners. Let's see, I was also in two films of Massine Ballets; Le Beau Danube and La Boutique Fantasque. He created a ballet on me called the Bal De Valour. As the lead dancer I played six different characters. It was at Covent Garden and was as guest of the Royal Ballet. As a result of my Covent Garden appearance I went to Paris to be one of the Ugly Sisters in Cinderella. It was a lavish production at the Theatre du Champs. We played the same ballet for eight months. This show introduced Galina Samsova to Europe (choreographed by Vaslav Orlikovsky).

After my fifth teaching visit to Israel I took a chance and returned to Australia and joined the Queensland Ballet where I created the dance program at the Brisbane College of Dance Education. In 1981 I became Artistic Director of the New Zealand Ballet.

Q from Ira: You use mime and gesture as punctuation points which communicate a story to an audience. Did you train in mime?

A from Harry: Initially that came from the comedians that I worked with. I had a natural ability for comic mime. Then I started professionally, with the comedians; as with any comedian you work with, there is just what gets the laugh. Where you have to be, how you have to be. I learned from them without actually saying to myself, 'Now I am learning this' - I absorbed it.

In all the choreography that I was impressed with, like Massine's, Gestures were extremely important. Even now I can remember how Massine would show the different ways a particular gesture gives different meanings. He made an extensive study not only of conventional mime, but of Neapolitan and Italian hand gestures. Walter Gore was another inspiration, for whom dance was indivisible from acting. He was initially an actor, and a great admirer of Massine.

At the time I was in Great Britain, there was a great interest in mime. There was a Dutch (Austrian born) woman named Cilli Wang who performed solo. It wasn't mime so much in gesture, but in use of costume. She would be an ostrich, and an owl and all sorts of things. Then Marcel Marceau visited London regularly with a big, big following.

I have always tried to find a way to make the story or theme of a ballet absolutely clear to an audience. There is a limit to what one can do with mime alone. Often people don't make the most of what is there. I don't believe people should have to read pages of program notes before they can understand what is going on. You can make a tremendous amount clear if you think about it, find ways of doing it.

From my point of view the most incredible was Max Wall. Although he wasn't a mime artist per se, he did acts in which not a word was said.

Q from Ira: How do you try to teach or bring the gesture out in choreography?

A from Harry: I've never really tried to teach it as a subject. It just happens when we produce a ballet. Some dancers are responsive to mime, some are not.

I did teach in Queensland, but three years was not long enough to develop a whole series of exercises. I would start people with naturalistic mime. Telling a story without words or stylisation, they would make up stories which could be told through gesture. Then they would incorporate the reality into the stylisation of classical ballet. I do feel that there is a whole world of gesture. Very often people don't search for the reason a particular gesture is chosen. If you search, you can make that gesture live again. It comes from the emotion.

Q from Ira: In classical ballet how are the gestures part of the choreography?

A from Harry: They are not usually thought of as such. It is like recitative as against aria in opera. The mime usually came as quite a separate thing. The gestures were still choreographed in that you didn't just do them when you felt like it. They were related to the music and had a certain shape.

There are some passages that are still known, but not always used. Act II in Swan Lake, Odet tells of the lake formed by the tears. The mime is often replaced with dance movement. Sometimes this is not an improvement.

I once saw Tamara Karsavina help with Giselle, to teach the mime passages. Once you had seen her do them they were no longer dead passages. She made them live, and made you see how you could make them live.

A lot depends on the conviction, the care, and the desire to do it. Some people don't want to, they just want to spin. In Russia, they certainly teach classical ballet mime.

Q from Ira: How do you select your programs for the Royal New Zealand Ballet?

A from Harry: What I look for in my programs here are a dance which has a story or drama, or heavy in the sense that the audience has become involved. Then something that is light, or comic.

A company has many needs. One is to keep its repertory alive, also to develop its dancers and a style. A company style, and in this case a New Zealand style. Because of the isolation of New Zealand I feel we also have a responsibility to mount the best of the classics. They have to be productions which have a viewpoint, which is true to the work and which doesn't do violence to the work in order to cut it down. If we don't do these works they don't get seen in New Zealand.

Back to mime, you have to make it possible for people to understand a work. We have a duty to show dances which are created outside the country, which are of interest to the development of our dancers. We have a strong need also to produce ballets created by New Zealanders.

We must create New Zealand artists in our particular field, that is choreographers. It is only from the work of choreographers that ballet can grow. You can't do it from theory or technique.

For a company to grow it is important for outside choreographers to come in, though this isn't always necessary from the audience point of view. The nature of ballet is such, that it is impossible to create in isolation.

Dancers must have the opportunity to be the first matrix or mould for a dance or ballet. It develops dancers. You think differently when a dance is created from you.

As a child I envisioned myself as a choreographer. However, that is something quite special. Although I have created dances. I am better at building upon someone else's ideas. So I see myself more as a producer/director who occasionally arranges a dance, rather than the choreographer who has created something right from the beginning. I don't think I'm at the age now where I am going to set the world on fire with my choreography.

A choreographer must have something in themselves that makes them see people and movement differently. They look at something the way we have never seen it before.

In ballet I missed the opportunity to speak. Although the dancers will tell you that I never stopped talking. I missed the singing. I felt very fulfilled in musicals. From the time of "Oklahoma" and choreographers such as Jerome Robbins, Agnes De Mille, Helen Tamiris, Michael Kidd, or Bob Fosse, the dancing that one had to do was quite interesting. It wasn't the old 'one-two-kick'. There was real choreographic interest.

Q from Ira: What was the difference between the world of musical comedy and ballet?

A from Harry: It wasn't so different for me. In my early days in Australia, you were in theatre. We called it being 'in the business'. That covered anything. When I moved to England, they didn't consider everything all together. I found I could move from one area to the other quite easily. I never considered myself a classical dancer, I was a comedy or character dancer. I still feel I am more a part of the 'theatre', than a specialist. If there is anything I have to offer my dancers, it is theatricality. It is our job to entertain, and move audiences, and to be true to whatever it is we are portraying.

It is not just steps. Some ballets are like that; but very often even if there is no story, there is an underlying theme, or an idea which we should be able to make clear.

- 38 -
BALANCE IN TRAINING AND PERFORMANCE

On an Equity panel some years ago a group of professionals sought to define a training that would yield a consistency of performances over a long arduous tour. We attempted, within the same concept, to also define a training which would produce multi-skilled actors. The only simple agreement was that we wanted an industry with actors who were consistent (i.e. reliable), multi-skilled, and versatile enough to perform in different styles.

I believe that to open one's potential to a long and fulfilling career it is a consistency of discipline which is required.

One asset of the Western performing arts tradition which is a study in consistency is ballet, which has been largely cast aside. Ballet, for better or for worse, contains secrets for new and progressive training. For one it is a living, growing, and unbroken tradition. In its history it has integrated science, folklore, folk-dance, imagination, and the most current technical toys. Today in Europe, USA, China, ballet is taught as a primary physical discipline for actors at the best schools. If you do not train the actors in a pure discipline such as ballet, it must be replaced with an equally scientific or detailed approach. Detailed to give flexibility, strength, and endurance to every sinew of the actor. This physical discipline could be mime, acrobatics, modern dance, certain martial arts, or even dynamic yoga. But it is the precision in the body which yields precision on stage.

The history of Western theatre is integrated with dance, from; Greek Drama, Commedia Dell'Arte, Shakespeare, to Musicals. Recently I spoke with Marcel Marceau about training. After twenty years of his school he has accepted that the pure technical base of his creativity is the technique of Etienne Decroux. That is his secret to share with students now. Most successful actors have some discipline as a secret. Usually it is a physical discipline such as dance, sport, or martial arts.

What students need is the right balance of discipline, freedom, and variety. Ideally the theatre practitioner is a student throughout their career.

A class needs to be disciplined, that is to go into the sinews of the actor. The actor needs detail of technique, awareness within, and freedom of expression.

Then they can begin to work.

I believe that actors also need to seek out their links with history and tradition. The teacher can do a lot to encourage this perspective by nurturing links with tradition.

Our Western tradition is now firmly linked to Stanislavsky. But it is rarely acknowledged that he was a product of his youthful obsessions of Circus, Vaudeville, and Puppetry. Under his direction the Moscow Art Theatre had a stage manager who gave a company yoga class every day for nine years. Three of Stanislavsky's disciples were allowed to branch into major projects with ethnic actors, circus performers, and trance acting.

So as we look for a brighter future of balancing training and performance I think we are overlooking our links with the past. It is important sometimes to go back to the sources which inspired great artists such as Stanislavsky, Grotowski, Brook. Often we look to the end of their journey rather than the stepping stones of their discoveries. Similarly it is important that future generations of actors are given more precise disciplines to base their craft and careers upon.

I find that if an actor is given detailed basic technique then they progress rapidly and naturally to a deeper understanding of how any discipline can be applied to Acting.

The study I have made during my career over forty+ years seems to lead me to re-discoveries of various techniques and in particular making "breakthroughs" in applying technique to performance. Once an actor makes a series of breakthroughs it is their own drive which must lead them to even further excellence.

My concern in training is not so much testing the actor but showing them very specific methods for opening a variety of doors. The practical foundation template is "The Four Articulations for Performance". Each exercise is explained with step-by-step instructions in Chapter 2 of the book *Clown Secret*.

Because it is specific physicality which can best lead to specific, repeatable, consistent performances. This goes hand in hand with an understanding of the text and character.

In learning a physical technique or skill we start with basics and specifics and move towards advanced and complex application and variation.

Once some specifics are in place the actor can begin to perform. At this point we can look at factors which influence the moment to moment choices. Here again physical action can reveal psychological choices the actor is using. We can reflect on whether these choices add to the audience communication or detract.

Before there can be a comfort with freedom, there must be an anchor in technique.

Now most importantly, this freedom must be practised, supported, nurtured. This must occur side by side with the learning of discipline and technique. The creative mind needs to be fed while the sibling technical mind is being fed.

In addition it is most important to realise that "learning" is a state of mind. More than anything, the actor, student, teacher, and director need to be in a learning frame of mind to make new discoveries and to create new applications.

When training we have to aspire to the pinnacle. When performing we must be prepared and aspire towards inspiration.

NOTE: Chapters 39, 40, 41, 42 provide details of the intellectual structure of Quantum Theatre: Slapstick to Shakespeare.

- 39 -
STRUCTURE - QUANTUM THEATRE: SLAPSTICK TO SHAKESPEARE

<u>WARNING</u>: This essay and its topic, Quantum Theatre: Slapstick to Shakespeare, are complicated.

<u>IMPORTANTLY</u>; Here is reference to symbols and metaphors drawn from 'mystical' traditions. Those symbols and metaphors <u>are not scientific truths</u>.

<u>NOTICE</u>: The symbols and metaphors provide imagery from several cultures which provide a way of analysis via one's imagination. Due to practical limits technically and financially for self publishing, the formatting technician suggested not to use any visuals including images or charts. Also ebooks download speed is slow when images appear, that means visuals can not be used. With internet search it is easy to look up any of the symbols or images mentioned. You may find that with a pen and paper it is useful to draw images described.

Introduction
Idea of the Dot and the Circle
System of 4 and 5
System of 5
System of 10, As Above So Below

Cross Reference System of Ten
Core Movement and Self-Discovery
Some Additional Notes

INTRODUCTION.

There are two primary images which give an overview of Quantum Theatre. The first is practical. Imagine a circle with an 'X' inside touching the edge of the circle. This divides the circle into four sections. That represents the four basics of acting and of theatre: Body, Voice, Acting, Creativity. The second image is philosophical. This is the Hebrew Tetragrammaton. Horizontally that image represents the universal and elemental concept of "Four".

One, as a metaphor, can represent Self. Two, can represent Opposition. Three, can represent Dynamic. Four, can represent a living harmony that includes Self, Opposition, Dynamic. Four elements represent the natural world. In the natural world Four can be seen as: a) mineral, vegetable, animal, human which are an interactive whole rather than completely seperate; and b) the ancient Western view of elements fire, water, air, earth.

The Hebrew Tetragrammaton, according to Kabbalah and Chassidus, is composed of four letters; yud, hei, vav, hei. One can say that is the four-letter name for God and God in this sense is not The Spaghetti Monster in the Sky. Rather, the four-letter name for God represents the Universe as an all-inclusive whole. A whole Universe, as quantum mechanics informs us, that has since The Big Bang's .0015 of a second explosion, has been a continuous expanding Universe. Some even consider that The Universe actually is comprised of multiple universes. Time will tell.

In terms of creation, Kabbalah and Chassidus offer that the Four is Four Worlds which are four logical sequential dynamics: 1st - initial inspiration; 2nd - broadening the concept; 3rd - emotional involvement in plans; 4th - building of a project. In clown or performance those four sequential dynamics could be; idea, improvisation, play, editing to choreograph a clown actor monologue or dance.

The 4-letter symbol itself represents the way the universe functions in its own ever changing harmony. That includes: Evolution; universe Expansion; and, earthly interaction of mineral, vegetable, animal, human; and, electron, proton, neutron, atom; as well the human mind and imagination. Vertically the Hebrew Tetragrammaton, coincidently, looks like a human figure.

The World of Theatre is a vast world that has a very practical and natural basis. QUANTUM THEATRE is a way to help the actors and theatres to conceive of a harmonic and natural working frame of mind. In a few minutes of reading you can get a clear overview and reflect on your own vision of theatre.

THE IDEA OF THE DOT AND THE CIRCLE.

The first two symbols: a circle with an 'X'; and, the Hebrew Tetragrammaton, each, represents 4 parts. In the Western cultures we actually have a fifth element called ether. In other cultures ether could be called prana, ki, chi. Ether would be the sub-atomic quality which creates the four elements which represent the natural world of matter. The circle divided into four quarters, the fifth part would be the CIRCLE and, also, the single unseen DOT where the two lines cross at mid-circle. The CIRCLE <u>contains</u> the whole and the DOT <u>creates</u> the whole. It is as if the four radial lines of the 'X', or four sections radiate from the DOT. In our own body (circle) this would be the navel (dot) or belly button where the umbilical cord (line) was severed. A similar symbolism occurs in nature when the sperm (dot and line) enters the ovum (circle). This is how all creativity operates. That is, two opposing forces merge and become one. This is already in the Taoist Yin/Yang symbol which quantum physicist Niels Bohr chose as the symbol within his own Coat of Arms. He created his Coat of Arms when he became a member of the Denmark's highest ranked honour called "The Order of the Elephant".

Quantum Theatre expands a DOT so that we imagine space inside of any idea or object. We then see a CIRCLE of possibilities and infinite points of discovery. The space itself represents: space to think; space to create; or, space to be with one's self. This base thought releases a potential of creativity and energy.

On the practical, logical, left brain view is: Body-Voice-Acting-Creativity. An expanded view would put a circle within each of the four sections of the original large circle. If each of those small sections were a circle, imagine another 'X' that divides each small circle into four sections. Now the body, voice, acting, creativity would each have four parts.

Body has four parts:	Strength	-	Endurance
	Flexibility	-	Awareness
Voice has four parts:	Volume	-	Pitch
	Clarity	-	Meaning
Acting has four parts:	Physicality	-	Text
	Method	-	Imagination
Creativity four parts:	Thought	-	Focus
	Adaptability	-	Application

The other symbol of 4 is borrowed from the Hebrew language and Kabbalah: Tetragrammaton is Greek for four/tetra gramma/letters, thus the symbol is referred to as 'the four-letters word for 'God' that is the Universe.

Around the four letters one can imagine an unseen CIRCLE and inside the letters one can imagine a DOT. The CIRCLE+DOT is the fifth element and is both in and around the other four. In the next section of this essay I will use this symbol in a practical way by shifting it from horizontal to vertical. Vertically and visually the letter yod is like a simple drawing of head and neck; the first hei is symbolic of the collar bone, shoulders arms; the vav is like the spine and central nervous system; the second hei is like the pelvis and legs. Thus the yod include the eyes and ocular nerve and brain; the first hei includes the expression of the hands and gestures; vav is the torso; the second hei includes the feet and gait (a character's way of walking).

THE SYSTEM OF 4 AND 5.
In the Chinese system of actor training there is also a system of 4 and 5 at the centre of their methodology.
Their system has 4 techniques and 5 principles.
The four techniques are: Singing
Speaking
Acting
Acrobatics

The five principles are: Eyes
Hands
Torso
Gait
Fa

Gait means the pace or way of walking, and, Fa means integration.

The Chinese system of training actors is one of the most highly evolved yet I would say it is also logical and common sense.

In the System of 4 here is how I would equate the Chinese system with Quantum Theatre:

Acrobatics	Body
Speaking	Voice
Acting	Acting
Singing	Creativity

In some way I would say that Singing is the last stage in creative acting. It is a logical progression and in some way Opera is the most highly evolved of the theatre arts because it can and often does involve any other art form or even style of theatre. Needless to say not every production lives up to Opera's potential. Musicals often equal qualities of Opera.

For decades I have used acrobatics as a key (and ki) to teaching acting and theatre. Acrobatics training though must be taught in cooperation with Ballet and Mime. That is the equal sided triangle on which to base the training of the actor's Body. The Body is the base on which to train not only actors, but also directors, teachers, and writers. Knowledge of the Body is where Knowledge of the Soul (one's creativity) is grounded.

THE SYSTEM OF 5

The Tetragrammaton has uses three Hebrew letters: yud, heh, vav; heh is used twice.
Yud - Heh - Vav - Heh

In the system of 5, symbolically, in relation to the Chinese system, I equate the:
Eyes with Yud
Torso with Heh
Hands with Vav
Gait with Heh
Fa with the vertical image of the Tetragrammaton

Again, Fa means integration. Integration is of all the body's parts including the eyes.

The Hebrew letter Yud looks a bit like a head and neck. On stage the Eyes are moved in relation to the head and neck. The letter Heh is like a line drawing of the collar bone and arms and relate with the actor's Hands and gestures. The Vav looks like a line and represents the spinal column and central nervous system i.e. the Torso and the actor's emotional expression. The Chinese Medicine views one's emotions as relating to our different organs encased mainly in the torso. The second Heh also looks like a line drawing of the pelvis and legs. Thus it is connected with the feet and Gait.

Together vertically the Hebrew letters look like a line drawing of the whole human body or Fa, integration.

An integrated Body means your fifth element, 'fa', the unseen CIRCLE - DOT, the equivalent of ether, prana, ki, chi; is flowing smoothly and we say the actor has presence or good energy.

The four-letters symbol is from the Hebrew and Jewish philosophy called Kabbalah. The Kabbalah is not science. Kabbalah is a system of Logic and Intuition which can express philosophically that the universe continuously evolves organically. Recently the logical and practical side of the Kabbalah as a mental image of creativity, has become recognised for its universal principles. Although Kabbalah is not a science, some people are able to envision it symbolically as similar to the latest developments in Quantum Mechanics and Quantum Physics.

As a metaphor, the logic of actor training can be to start with the EYES. Where the actor focuses, the audience will also focus. The actor, like the acrobat, mime and dancer must learn about the focus of the eyes, the weight of the head, the articulation of the neck and the power of thought as a priority.

The expressiveness of the HANDS and arms is infinite yet must be controlled at all times. A dancer or mime without expressive hands is a mechanical doll. When the hands, arms and shoulders are open so too is the healing and creative energy.

The TORSO is framed by the rib cage and at its core is not only the spine but also the central nervous system. Here is the flow of kundalini, the ida and pingala (male - female energies) which awaken our highest and fullest Self. Here in the torso are the important muscles of the abdomen and back plus the internal organs. The organs being the seat of the emotions which an actor must always work with harmoniously.

The GAIT is determined by the feet, legs, hips, and pelvis. Within the pelvis the spine begins so there is communication and integration between all four parts: gait, torso, hands, eyes.

The DOT is the navel where the hara is, from where the ki/chi flows. The CIRCLE is the aura, energy surrounding the Body.

As the actor trains and becomes sensitive and in control of energies and emotions one discipline can always keep them grounded and humble, acrobatics.

Acrobatics should not be a wild, risk taking affair. It should be logical, healing, fun, and a progressive challenge and regular discipline. All moves should be taught from standing rather than running. Logical mechanics and minimal effort should accomplish each task rather than force and momentum. Running, force, and momentum are appropriate only when logic and clear understanding have been mastered. Acrobatics is a great teacher of safety, space, and group awareness. Focus, concentration and logical progression is the only way to master movement and acting.

THE SYSTEM OF 10.

The System of 10 is formed by the inner and outer dimension in which The System of 5 (integration) operates in the theatre.

The System of 5 is integration. Integration of the mind in the body. The System of 5 incorporates the concept of the CIRCLE and DOT. This relates to 'fa', integration also as duality. Two other cultural ideas show integration as a duality: Macrocosm/Microcosm; and, As Above-So Below symbolised in a variety of cultures as a hexagram of two intersecting triangles. In Vedic culture from India the intersecting triangles is the Shatkona representing the union of both the male and feminine form. More specifically it is supposed to represent Purusha (the supreme being), and Prakriti (mother nature, or causal matter). The intersecting triangles are also referred to as The Star of David (Magen David) in Jewish culture. Both cultures have an understanding of a Primordial human being that is both male-and-female. Vedic also uses the intersecting triangles to represent the Primordial human interacting with the Universe. They name that Nara/Narayana and the Hebrew/Jewish/Kabbalah calls the Primordial figure Adam Kadmon or Adam h'Rishon. In the Taoist culture from China these same intersecting concepts are represented by the Yin/Yang symbol.

For the actor and any method of training acting or theatre, the inner and outer worlds must operate in harmony, as integration. That means we must work towards a harmony of process and result. We may never achieve a perfect harmony, since harmony is ever fluid, being both logic and intuition or Yin/Yang. That symbol helps us to conceive of the whole unseeable truth. Yin/Yang is usually considered a 'principle of two', however it is two halves (2), but each half (2) contains a dot of the other (another 2), and the whole, Fa, makes this also symbol of The Principle of 5 i.e. integration.

Returning to the Kabbalah and its inventive chart, The Tree of Life, I can best explain another important level to Quantum Theatre and to universal principles of theatre and an overview of its entirety. As a graphic, the Kabbalah's Tree of Life is visually composed of 10 dots called sephirot, 3 columns, 7 levels. For Quantum Theatre I'm primarily concerned with Quantum Theatre's 10 centres which each has an outer and inner expression as a chart. For example in the outer, one centre is Opera, but, in the inner that same centre represents Musicality.

Of the two charts, Outer is practical/logical, and, Inner is philosophical/intuitive.

The 10 centres are always interactive in theatre or Quantum Theatre. The symbol of 10 dots is pictured as a graphic just like the Kabbalah's The Tree of Life with the 10 centres laid out on the 3 columns at 7 levels.

Two charts. The first <u>describes</u> QUANTUM THEATRE and the second <u>explains</u> by giving the essence. The first is the CIRCLE and the second is the DOT.

THE CIRCLE CHART OF QUANTUM THEATRE

Your Vision

Ballet   Theatre

Opera   Circus

Commedia Dell 'Arte

Mime   Slapstick

Vaudeville

Clown

THE DOT CHART OF QUANTUM THEATRE

Spiritual or creative fulfilment thru the arts

Choreography   Dramatic intention and
                                     follow through

Musicality   Excitement and thrill

Direct communication with the audience

Physicality/body language   Rhythm

Creative freedom

Intuitive understanding

In each theatre production these 10 parts of The Circle Chart must be involved; and, interactive as the Dot Chart's inner meaning implies. That involvement and interaction is an ideal conceptual framework and metaphor for integrated and balanced theatre productions. One example below should clarify how the idea can be applied or understood practically.

Musicality on the Dot Chart represents Opera on the Circle Chart. If we created a mime play without music or words there must still be musicality in the space. The composition of rhythms and movement and sections must have a creative harmony even if there is discordant movement in silence. Likewise though there were no words used the drama element Theatre must still unfold and reveal the intended thoughts of the actors, characters, or artists as "dramatic intention and follow though".

Although no one should expect an actor to be a master of opera, a sensitivity to each of the 10 areas should evolve while training and must continue through a career and theatre artist's lifetime.

The Dot Chart's crown point, Your Vision, is an ever evolving study of Self which is bound to wax and wane through tempests and dreams.

I have seen a variety of performers active on stage in their eighties and nineties. They were full of energy and enthusiasm. I have seen actors in their twenties who were mentally, physically and spiritually lethargic (lazy). It is all a matter of where you put your thoughts.

CROSS REFERENCE SYSTEM OF TEN.

There is a Cross Reference system implied in the system of 10. For example if your vision is a Circus Theatre or a Theatre-Circus you must ensure that there is Rhythm through a whole show so when we look at Slapstick you may want no Slapstick and even no humour (God forbid!) but you must have Rhythm and surprise. Rhythm without surprise is monotony. Even Waiting For Godot has the threat of surprise. Of course in this case Samuel

Beckett is a master of rhythm in the theatre and this is thanks to his love and understanding of Slapstick, as he was an admirer of the clowns Laurel & Hardy.

In a traditional Circus there has to be a Dramatic logic told through a Regular variation of acts. So that by the end of the show the audience has had a catharsis through thrills, surprises, excitement and a concluding act and often a finale parade of the ensemble.

In the Circle Chart I would say my view of Commedia Dell'Arte is unconventional. I do not believe in most of the myths and training methods of Commedia Dell'Arte.

I believe that historically Commedia Dell'arte (CDA) died out of natural causes, those were: its relevance specific to its audience; theatre technology; and, social context. However, CDA transformed into more highly developed artistic expressions such as good plays (Theatre) with more satisfying logic, and, the evolving aesthetics of more contemporary societies. Those artistic changes were influenced by playwrights, such as; De Vega, Molière, Shakespeare. Goldoni, Goethe. CDA evolved to become Opera, Ballet, Circus. The rawest instinct of CDA also transformed to Vaudeville, Variety, Music Hall, Pantomime, Karno Troupes, Keystone Kops.

If we want to rebirth CDA, imagine the circle with an 'X' inside and four sections, and train the Body-Voice-Acting-Creativity. It is a poor method to try to force playful, talented, creative characters out of actors with masks who can neither Act, Speak, Sing, nor Acrobat. In other words a bit of logic would help. HERE IS WHERE FOR EXAMPLE THE SYSTEMS OF 4-5-10 CAN BE A TOOL FOR YOUR FA WORK. Musicals are an example of a transformed and modern Commedia dell'arte.

We know that CDA was comprised of family troupes. I suspect that Music, Song, and Dance were the primary base of the CDA, and some very fast speaking. The lessons of CDA even if mythical are still inspiring. The essence of CDA is still found throughout the world in many indigenous cultures, in puppet theatre, in dance dramas. When I look at CDA I have quite a broad view rather than the standard pursuit of the classic masked Italian characters which Carlo Mazzone-Clementi considered museum pieces. China has a form of Commedia which is an unbroken tradition in one southern province where there were, until recently, over 100 active troupes and nearly 10,000 actors who were all actors who can sing, speak and salto (do somersaults). I saw one of those troupes in 1994.

When I refer to Clown I mean it in the deepest sense. Profound humour which gives insight to our vision of life. Clown is an infinitely broad field. Its essence is pure inspiration yet IT IS TECHNIQUE, SKILL, AND TRADITION WHICH GIVES INSPIRATION ITS FULL POWER. In terms of clown training this means skills: dance, mime, music, acrobatics, poetry, voice, juggling, and magic all BUILT AROUND GAGS AND ROUTINES which allow the character to evolve naturally.

CORE MOVEMENT AND SELF DISCOVERY.

The final symbol imagine is a deconstructed yin/yang symbol: two dots, a line and a circle. From those elements you could create a theatre universe. Imagine a graphic mask with the 2 dots as 2 eyes, the circle as a nose, and from the centre of the yin/yang the 'S' line cut in half so one half turned up is the smile of a clown, or the turned downward half as a frown of the sad clown.

The Clown knows the Dot in between comedy and tragedy.

A great symbol of theatre is the Greek double mask of Comedy-Tragedy. It is a tragedy if a trilogy of classic Greek plays is not followed with a Satyr play. It is a farce that today's comedy does not seem to involve the fullness of tragedy. Shakespeare was a master of the comic-tragic balance. In Quantum Theatre: Slapstick to Shakespeare, Slapstick represents comedy, and, Shakespeare represents tragedy. Slapstick will have a dot of tragedy and Shakespeare will have a dot of comedy.

Quantum Theatre: Slapstick to Shakespeare is a method to open our minds, hearts, bodies and souls to create the many visions of theatre which we dream and which can be of real service. It is a way to improve community theatre and professional theatre. Two opposites which really are necessary to fulfil the other.

Teaching and directing theatre is hard and practical work. Yet theatre without philosophy is not at all practical and it is certainly not fulfilling.

On the practical side I start with "Core Mechanics" (explained with instructions in the book *Clown Secret*, chapter 2). Core Mechanics is a choreographic pattern of ten mechanical movements which takes ten minutes to do. This is a simple logical way to reveal all the basic mechanics inside activities such as, sport, dance, mime, acrobatics, martial arts, classical acting.

Then there is also a practical starting point for the actor's Self Discovery. In four parts each day the actor needs:

    A. Warm - up
    B. (Be) Creative
    C. Train. Then the actor is ready to be in a
    D. Class or Rehearsal

The Warm-up is a way for the actor to greet their Self in the studio. A different meeting each day.

The Warm-up, that I propose to use at least 2 days per week, is The Four Articulations for Performance. Within is included Core Mechanics. There are clear step-by-step instructions and explanations in chapter 2 of *Clown Secret*.

Creative means to begin moving creatively, intuitively, playfully. One day may be more playful than creative or more creative than intuitive. Each day evolves its own way.

Training should be logical, methodical, anatomical and focused on one thing an actor wishes to develop. Today is the day to start a handstand, a mime technique (create one), a pirouette (try it, then ask for help).

That is practical, simple, straight forward. Core Mechanics and Self Discovery.

Philosophically two dots represent masculine and feminine energies; Logic and Intuition. These operate every minute in the theatre! To understand them though you must integrate DOT and CIRCLE. Open up and understand. The wavy 'S' line from yin/yang can now be visualised with three dots: one at each end of the wave and the third dot in the middle of the wavy line. The three dots on the wavy line represents you or your Self as a trilogy:

Creativity / Sensuality / Spirituality.

They are the energies which drive us. You can steer them and direct them. In the theatre you can do this best and clearly by applying in your own way, your own understanding of the symbols and ideas introduced in this chapter.

That was a brief explanation of Quantum Theatre: Slapstick to Shakespeare.

However, the template "The Four Articulations for Performance" is the practical way. That template is provided with detailed instructions in chapter 2 of the book *Clown Secret*.

SOME ADDITIONAL NOTES.

This method was developed and used over twenty years. Then, since 1993, the method has become more structured and refined. The long research and late attempt for a specific form is due to my desire to experiment on myself as an actor, artist, and director in nearly all types of circumstances. As a performer I have worked in virtually every type of stage, theatre or performance environment including feature films and street theatre, ... three ring circus and cafe cabaret,...classic Shakespearean touring repertory and totally improvised theatre,...casino, opera, burlesque,...radio, mime, dance, plays and musicals.

An important feature is the Quantum Point, the point of Understanding that the Cross Reference Systems of 4-5-10, with the Circle and the Dot can be applied to assist the vision of any company, method, project, school or individual to achieve their goals without imposing an outside style.

In chapter 41 I will explain briefly the ten principles which start with The Principle of One meaning one's Self.

Naturally depending on the experience of individuals one is able to work quicker or more in depth. Regardless of levels of experience, "Quantum Theatre: Slapstick to Shakespeare" enhances Professional, Wholistic and Individual practice on every level.

At this moment in history we all face challenges not only in art but in life which are unique in the collapse of social planning. There is at the same time information being revealed quickly and clearly which can aid humanity which can assist in thinking holistically for individuals, communities and societies. Such ideas could be useful for theatres and theatre communities. Two sources of useful philosophical information are the Tao and the Kabbalah. There is also philosophical information being clearly revealed from Indigenous Peoples, as well as, Yoga as taught by B.K.S.Iyengar, Tibetan Yoga, and other practises which have a clear discipline and flexible rituals, as well as, clear moral and ethical principles.

If you wish to begin your own practice and study, begin today with even five minutes of Warm-up, Creative, Training then your own brief class of Body-Voice-Acting-Creativity.

Three books which I recommend: A.) *The Tao & The Tree of Life* by E.S.Yudelov, Llewellyn Publications, St. Paul, MN. 55164-0383 USA; B.)

B.K.S. Iyengar's book *The Yoga Sutras of Patanjali*; C) *Clown Secret* by Ira Seidenstein.

Those three books complement one another and it is advisable to find your own way to work creatively on your own physical practice which Chapter 2 of *Clown Secret* can help you with immediately.

Life is your own study and your own chance at Self-Realisation.

- 40 -
HEALING THE THEATRE FOR TOMORROW

Everyone in the theatre is already attempting to heal the theatre. As Western medicine is attempting to heal humanity, but, unfortunately Western medicine has given in to the gods of technology, drugs, administration costs, so too has the theatre.

To heal implies to reinstate balance. Balance of body, mind, spirit.

The first need to balance is between traditional theatre and alternative theatre. The traditional theatre schools need three central things to begin with:

1. Integrated classes of Quantum Theatre. That means two or three classes per week which integrate body-voice-acting-creativity. Often in most Acting schools there are acting classes which also integrate body and voice. That is very common. The creativity gets blocked though when the actor is forced to be 'truthful' or 'correct' to the character, style, or playwright before finding their own creative way of meeting with the material. Alternative schools integrate body and creativity but leave out voice and basic acting (truth, motivation, reasoning).
2. Developments of Skills. This requires at least two classes per week of a single skill over at least a period of two years. The need and

dreams of the actors though means they want variety. That can be achieved a few ways. For example there could be Basic Ballet for 60-75 minutes, a short pause 10 minutes then directly into an acrobatic class for 60 minutes, a brief pause then directly juggling for 20 minutes.

3. Creativity. Give the actors 2 hours a day and 4 weeks to create their own theatre project. Leave them alone, encourage them, perhaps have a work-in-progress showing once a week to encourage their discipline. Creativity can not be taught the way many alternative schools teach in 'styles'. For example 'clown' as a style. There can be 1000 types of clown shows so when you teach 'clown' as a style you will restrict not release. The actor in other words should decide what 'clown' means for themselves. One 4-weeks period half a day is for the student to create a show, not a play. Then later in the year give them 3 weeks to do their own version of a play. Let them cut text, add text, do it as a dance or as a mime, or in other languages, most important...let them go and encourage them. Again this is half a day, the other half of the day is for other classes.

Those three recommendations will drastically improve the learning and self-development of your actors. Naturally, you must encourage them. Encourage. Perhaps you must rediscover courage yourself.

For alternative schools.

1. Three classes a week in Quantum Theatre that is an integrated class of body-voice-acting-creativity. For the alternative schools here you perhaps need a classical actor to learn how to teach such a class. That is a classically trained actor who has performed in a variety of plays.
2. At least 2 classes a week with an actual, fully professional dancer, mime, or acrobat or gymnast over at least a two year period
3. Classes in Acting ... particularly Stanislavsky technique and concepts. 2 classes per week.

4. Classes in Voice at least 2 per week.
5. Creativity. Stop giving critique. Give encouragement, encouragement, encouragement. Positive, specific feedback. Ask them, the actors, to give their own self-critique. Listen. Ask the viewing actors what they saw or felt. Critique should be specific and focus on technique not on aesthetics. Encourage the direction the actor is going. They must work through things.
6. Early in their first year let them create their own theatre performances for full time schools leave them 2 hours per day for 3 or 4 weeks. For half time schools leave them 2 hours daily. See a showing each week as a work-in-progress. Encourage them. Help them to set goals. For example after each working day to have 1 to 3 minutes of new material so that after 5 days they can show 5-15 minutes and after four weeks there is 20-60 minutes of material which can then be edited, cut, shaped.
7. They need encouragement and assignments to read and study Theatre History, Literature, Spiritual Philosophy.
8. You must study along with them; Traditional Clowning, Circus, Theatre, Dance. For example in Clown you would learn the following classic routines; The Mirror, Boxing, Whip-cracker, Levitation, Musical Entree, Restaurant, Water gags or routines.

These suggestions are quite practical and will make a tremendous difference in giving your students confidence and in opening their minds.

For both the traditional and alternative schools there should be classes in Yoga and Tai Chi. You could begin with Iyengar style yoga that gives very clear anatomic alignments, corrections and adjustments if you have a qualified teacher. There could be the short training Tai Chi of Mantak Chia.

Theatre is a path of the soul and not a religion nor a cult. Each actor must define that path for themselves. Disciplines such as Yoga, Tao, Kabbalah which have related disciplines of Meditation, Study, Service, and Ethics, and Anatomy are needed. Oneness, compassion, personal discipline and humour should be the four corners in which actors can rest and realise their own truth and wisdom.

Folk dance and song adds to harmony and wisdom. A study of folk dance during three or four months in each school would add greatly to an understanding of theatre's communal, ritual, and seasonal natural origins.

For the three or four year traditional theatre schools I have listed three suggestions. For the one or two year alternative schools I have listed 8 suggestions. For alternative circus schools, acting, reading, voice, folk dance, and song are valuable to broaden the students' imaginations.

If you are thinking of creating a new three or four year program, read this book again and write to me if you wish - **iraseid@gmail.com**

For a one or two year course I'll give some structure for a full time course (7 hours a day).

A. For 8am to 9 have Quantum 5-Part Warmup: a) warm-up - 10 minutes of the actor's own physical exercises b) creativity - 10 minutes of the actors own free movement improvisation, c) training - 10 minutes of the actors own focused physical skill practice, d) visualisation - 15 minutes - see Mantak Chia's book *Six Healing Sounds*, voice - 15 minutes - three times in a standing position, sounding 'ah' in a single breath each time, as you roll down and up the spine; then with a partner one stands still and looks on the horizon, the other partner puts one hand on the vocalist's shoulder and with the other hand in a very soft fist gently bounce the fist along the partners spine using the soft heel of the hand. Do that for three breaths of 'ah' then change roles. Lastly with the first vocalist again standing straight and looking on the horizon the assistant again places one hand on the vocalist's shoulder and with the soft fist and soft heel of the hand very gently bounce the soft fist on the centre only of the breastbone/sternum. If the vocalist has any particular restrictions they must tell the assistant partner and they can make a way to adjust this practice. For example the assistant can have their hand open instead of a fist. The assist's hand or fist needs to stay only one centimetre away so the effect of the bounce is soothing.

B. 9:15am to 12pm Quantum Development Class. In the beginning this should be "The Four Articulations for Performance" (described in detail in chapter 2 of *Clown Secret*). After a week or two of learning this template there is a 45 minute warmup of all the preliminary exercises done in sequence. After 45 minutes some of the later creative exercises can be done in rotation of the days and weeks. And alternatively after the 45 minutes sequence any other acting or theatre training can be used for the remaining time.

C. 1pm to 2 - alternating days of either a mime class or a voice class

D. 2:15pm to 4 - any subject related to the current semester's topic, project, or play

E. 4:15pm to 530 - rehearsal

For a one year school of nine months you could have nine subjects or less. A nine project/subject suggested order:

1. Students create their own show
2. Mime. You do not have to be a mime. Let the actors mimic and interpret animals, archetypes, objects, machines, qualities, works of art, music, literature, give them improvisations and assignments then support and feedback. Some of the older mime books are excellent and filled with wonderful exercises. Books by Rose Bruford "Teaching Mime"; and, by Irene Mawer "The Art of Mime"; and Viola Spolin's "Improvisation for the Theatre".
3. Playwrights. You could read a play a week for 4 weeks. Each day you could read a part of the play together then create improvisations based on the themes, characters, situations. Choose a variety of four plays. A) Shakespeare, Strindberg, Pirandello, Beckett, or B) Moliere, Chekhov, Noh Theatre, African Saga, or C) African Heritage Playwright, Aboriginal Playwright, Noel Coward, Goethe.

4. Clown. There is the clown book by Mark Stoltzenberg which is excellent to begin with. Also your clowns can create a duet, a dance for two or three or four people, or create short acts and perform a collective show
5. Acting - monologues. Learn one monologue per week.
6. Acting - scenes, duets
7. Commedia - in four scenes: a song; a scripted science; a dance; a scenario with six short episodes of about 2 minutes each. The actors can improvise. Or take a comic scene from a scripted play.
8. Playwrights 2. Take a second group of four playwrights - one week for each
9. Students create a show

Second Year of study make a production of a comedy play; a tragedy play; a circus show; your own show.

Briefly each month study the body of work from a single playwright.

- 41 -
ORIGIN OF CREATION ....
ORIGIN OF IDEAS

There are parallels between theatre and yoga and tao and Kabbalah. They are reflective cultural tools with which to view or discuss creation and evolution of the human being. Theatre lacks the balanced practice that in yoga is named as the Sanskrit word sadhana. In the Kabbalah there is also complete sadhana though the asanas are replaced by what in yoga is called Bhakti or devotional work. There is a similarity to the Vedanta Yoga with song in Praise of God Consciousness, study of scriptures, work, family and service of a humanitarian nature. The aspects of concentration and devotion (Dharana and Dhyana) also have an adjusted form. Likewise the Tao is a complete (wholistic) system to assist in the creative evolution of the human being. This requires not only the 'right' seed (goals, information, wisdom), but, also 'correct' nurturing (earth, water, fire, air, ether). The elements by the way are not matters of material but are spiritual or philosophical concepts which help to define or express dynamics of life on Tellus (the Earth). On the deeper level this presupposes that the same dynamics occur universally as well as on the most material physical level. Again, Yoga, Tao, Kabbalah are in clear agreement.

In relation to theatre these systems also point out parallels to our own anatomic (an-atomic) creation. We require a seed (idea) and the seed must have a nurturing environment (circle) egg to even begin life. At the moment of conception the seed is engulfed by the egg. They merge. This is actually a nuclear, atomic reaction; a fusion, or an energy release, and will affect the balance of Gaia. This idea in a circle then requires a supporting environment of the womb and nourishment through the umbilical cord.

One of the moral dilemmas in the theatre is the creation, life and death not only of ideas but of communication, productions, careers and even whole theatres.

According to the Indian philosophy related to yoga called Samkhya, the universe has two principles: matter (prakrti) and spirit (parusa). Creation comes from matter and spirit interacting. Samkhya considers twenty-four stages of unfolding for creation. In The Book of Genesis (Bereishith) this is told in a parable of seven days. We can use our intelligent imagination and cross reference, as metaphors: 24 hours of a day; and, the seven essential chakras (energy centres along the spine).

This cycle of 24 hours, 7 days brings us into harmony with the cycles of the moon 28 days and the sun 365 days. The Jewish system of worship (self-knowledge) is based on these passages of time. Also, time passages of seasons and human development are accounted for in the cultural practices. It is a system which is anatomical, earthy, and universal with the goal to transcend time and space through our conscious use of the body. The same is true of the Tao and its philosophy of Earth, Humanity, Heaven. Tai Chi Chuan, the moving worship had the hands in an imitation of the moon and the sun revolving and rotating.

One reason Western theatre lacks some essential connection to peoples lives is that it no longer appears in natural cycles. The closest to a natural cycle is the traditional circus (circle) in a tent which relies on the warmth of Spring to begin, and, retreats when Autumn meets Winter.

How many theatre people long for a garden and a chance to live in harmony on the land? Our need to connect to the Earth and Heaven, with the Moon and Sun, with Humanity and all living matter is very deep. We need our tree roots and our conceptual Tree of Life.

The way to bring harmony into the theatre requires sadhana (practice). The strongest anchor and most difficult discipline is to balance the three Tan-Tien (Taoist energy centres in the body) of the Head-Heart-Stomach. The discipline to not harm any creature in neither action, through words, nor via thoughts.

Joy and humour are the important expressions of the Soul to heal itself and others. Joy in this case means the ability to share through the heart and humour means to en-joy without harm.

How does the creative impulse work in theatre? Sometimes I begin with a most simple anecdote or story. From this short (circle) the matter begins to split, multiply possibilities (dots), develop, incubate until rehearsal process finally begins and to have a life of its own.

An example, ever so simple, was a tale told by Lorenzo Aeilo. We were acting in "An Imaginary Life" and he told me of his father's journey to Australia as a new immigrant. The father was one of thousands seeking work and space away from war. Many started by working on the large sugar plantations in Queensland. The father brought one small suitcase with his belongings. Inside the case, and inside the clothes, was a piece of contraband, his most precious possession and the symbol of his hope. It was a branch of a fig tree from his home in Italy. Eventually this man owned land and a large farm so that when Lorenzo grew up there was a large orchard of fig trees whose origins were initially from that single branch.

From the seed image of this contraband branch of a fig tree, and the new immigrant hopes, I was able to have endless inspiration and energy to create a complex play about a new homeland. The play "A Play On Worlds" was created from a scenario I wrote inspired by Lorenzo Aeilo's story, with the text co-created with the actors.

Another show/play was based on a family story of another actor. This was "The Swedish Dybbuk". That actress I was directing in "The Dancer's Woman". She told of her great-grandmother who was a main activist for the Women's Suffragettes. The great-grandmother traveled through Sweden giving lectures and agitating for changes in education, labor, and voting rights for women.

That was a seed story. At the end of production it is irrelevant for the public to know the seed story. This is true even when the seed story appears in some way in the production.

In the cases of "A Play On Worlds" and "The Swedish Dybbuk" what developed were wild, rich, complex theatre experiences for the players and for the audiences.

Finally one more example was a show from several stories, "Harlequin Dreams". That show came about from many seeds and many angles. However, after the work was complete there was a single seed which was like a Black Hole in space. This seed seemed necessary to hold some kind of psychic tension through the whole piece. That story was told to me by a Cambodian-Australian cab driver. He told me how he lost his entire family, every relative due to war. That was not only mother, father, siblings but also cousins, aunts, uncles, everyone except him.

The seed story is important, but a seed story requires at least three elements to survive: soil, water, sun. For a short period I taught a "Three Energy Workshop" to explain or tell the story that a process of a living dynamic requires an interaction of at least three energies. Thus many indigenous cultures have a base idea of Earth, Human, Sky interacting to create life. In the workshop I provided examples of how Yoga, Tao, Kabbalah inter-relate conceptually rather than encouraging spiritual fundamentalism with one's preferred cultural practice.

In Yoga that is expressed in the philosophy of three Gunas or qualities. The three Gunas are: sattva; rajas; tamas. They are the qualities which are always interacting in all living matter according to Vedic literature.

Theatre is always an interaction and has much to learn from Yoga and its three keys of: practice (sadhana), concentration (dharana); and, devotion (dhyana). Yoga practice is much more than postures (asanas). Yoga or 'joining' has eight limbs: Yama (ethical precepts), Niyama (personal discipline), Asanas (postures), Pranayama (yogic breathing), Pratyahara (withdrawal), Dhahran (uninterrupted concentration), Dhyana (devotion via meditation), Samadhi (truth).

Sadhana (practice) has the first five aspects: Yama, Niyama, Asanas, Pranayama, Pratyahara. Samadhi (truth) does not follow automatically. It comes when it comes and goes when it goes.

It is only through Yama and Niyama that theatre can begin to heal itself and become a life giving environment rather than nihilistic.

A brief note in conclusion: One can go directly to Samadhi through meditating for the direct experience of transcendence. It is important however when one comes out of trance that one appreciates and enjoys the wonder of life itself. Confusion and difficulty are all part of it.

- 42 -
QUANTUM THEATRE - THREE SYSTEMS OF TEN

The world view of Quantum Theatre: Slapstick to Shakespeare is that any acting method can work, but most do not work for most actors. An acting method works, only when the learner has figured out certain principles consciously or usually unconsciously. So, Quantum Theatre sought out what were the underlying or 'universal' principles in acting and in the learning of acting. The vision is that if time, space and encouragement of some exploration were given to such universal principles, then more learners and actors would excel in their process and artistic expression, as well as in future work as teachers or directors. Quantum Theatre illuminates a type of practical-philosophical paradigm that can be used freely and interpretively according to one's aesthetic preference. Numbers are used to present a neutral set of principles and are explained logically.

The main example of how such principles work is the Principle of Four as the essential combination of elements yielding freedom and potentiality to any actor regardless of method or style. The Principle of Four implies that in order for an actor to be enlivened in their own actions and to enliven the performance space they need to embrace holistically, the four elements of body, voice, performance and creativity. Many actors, due to the way many directors work, are not much more than voices carrying text around the space. There is too frequently little relation between the body and the voice except for the obvious rudimentary practical nature of the voice coming from the body. It is the integration of body and voice that is part of the 'holy grail' of acting.

The Dot and the Circle is an idea put forth by Jeff Love (*Quantum Gods* 1976) to indicate potentiality in every moment. When one sees a dot, and concludes that it is only a 'dot', and not potentially more, an opportunity of potentiality is missed. When viewing the dot, with an expansion of consciousness, that allows the dot to 'expand' to become a circle comprised of many dots, and much potential space to move and develop, as well as diverse possibilities from each new dot. Here it is implied that such an idea and structure opens the actor's potential.

Quantum Theatre: Slapstick to Shakespeare is comprised of Three Systems of Ten.

The Three Systems of Ten are:

- The Outer System - Circle (chapter 39)
- The Inner System - Dot (chapter 39)
- The Practical System - Foundation of Ten Principles (listed below)

Principle of One - Self: all actions begin from one's self and return to one's self. This is associated with karma, responsibility for ones outer actions and inner intentions. This is expressed as; 'as you sow, so shall you reap'. In acting, performance, and PLA one is solely responsible for one's own experience. PLA is, professional learning for acting, and was central to my Doctorate thesis- "From the Liminal to the Visceral (2009).

Principle of Two - Feminine/Masculine principle or Yin/Yang. Every male and female embraces the Masculine and Feminine aspects of their personality within their being. This is also the dynamic of polarity, opposition in action, and juxtaposition artistically.

Principle of Three - this can be visualised and used in many ways. This the beginning of dynamic energy, interaction and flow. For example, in Quantum Theatre it is understood that people gravitate to acting and theatre for three essential reasons; Creativity, Social-Sensual, and Spirituality. For any individual one or the other of those reasons may be a proportion consciously, but, the other two though sub-conscious, become apparent soon after one embarks on the study of acting and theatre. It is understood in Quantum Theatre if these three aspects are more acknowledged and accounted for in PLA, then the learner will have a more satisfying and successful experience in their learning. Another example of the Principle of Three is: Time-Timing-Timelessness. Time is important in the theatre and PLA as there are practical limits in resources of space, properties, and personnel. Timing is the relative use of these resources depending on circumstances. Timelessness is the goal or desired experience of acting and theatre, i.e. to move beyond the normal perception of time's limitations.

Principle of Four - This is one of the key practical principles of Quantum Theatre. This would equate to cultural ideas such as the four elements, four seasons, four directions, and even to the Ancient Greek philosophy of the four humours. This basically shows that flow and complexity are a part of harmonious living and any part of living including education or acting. In acting the four elements that must interact within the embodied knowledge of the actor are: body, voice, performance, creativity. In Quantum Theatre the Principle of Four is the Acting Class or Base.

Principle of Five - is another key practical principle of Quantum Theatre. It equates to the five elements including ether; or, the Asian five elements of water, air, fire, wood, metal. In Quantum Theatre this is the Warmup or Foundation. One form of The Foundation is The Four Articulations for Performance (explained in detail in *Clown Secret* chapter 2). Four Articulations as a solo takes about 30 minutes. As a duet 45 minutes. As a group a minimum of one hour. Another form of The Foundation is one-hour and there are five parts: warmup (10 minutes), creativity (10 minutes), training (10 minutes), visualisation (15 minutes), voice (15 minutes). The

Foundation connects to The Principle of Three in the following ways: Time - the warmup starts on time and lasts one hour; Timing - perhaps it is not appropriate on some days to start exactly on time and perhaps the warmup needs to be much shorter; Timelessness, the second part of The Foundation, 'creativity', has an improvised nature and sometimes the group goes into a timeless way of working and rather than sticking to the structure's 10 minutes, it can go on for 30, 60, or 90 minutes for example.

The next three Principles each relate to a cultural philosophy and serve to remind that there are great bodies of knowledge from diverse cultures from which to draw guidance in one's artistic development. The three cultures are: Kabbalah (the metaphysical knowledge of the three Abrahamic faiths), Vedic (yoga), and Taoist (Tai Chi Chuan, Chi Kung, I Ching).

Principle of Six - this is a philosophical principle relating to 'as above so below'. It serves to remind the actor/learner/practitioner that to achieve their higher goals, attention to the detail and practice for the previous Principles can assist. 'As above' can be one's creativity, whereas 'so below' can be ones practical techniques.

Principle of Seven - this is philosophical/practical equating to the Seven Chakras (energy centres) proposed in Yoga. This implies that there are different energies that one can focus on when working as an artist. Note: The Tree of Life chart of Kabbalah has seven levels. Chakras, Tree of Life, Tan Tiens (of Taoism) each propose that the body has different energy centres, and within each culture's system those energy centres imply that one's objective is to live life with a balance between the centres.

Principle of Eight - this relates to the eight directions as in Taoist philosophy, and the eight seasons used by some Indigenous cultures.

Principle of Nine - in Taoist practices, the foot is seen to possess nine points - eight which are cushioned areas and a ninth point that absorbs energy from the earth. The articulation and expression of the foot are essential to all avant-garde training just as is for a dancer. "It is how lightly we tread on this earth, how we take a step at a time, or a quantum leap" Ellen Osborn.

Principle of Ten - is one's Vision of Acting and how one uses the other nine Principles in an integral sense.

- 43 -
COMMENTS - NEUROSCIENTIST JIM PICKLE

I first met Ira when he taught a short course at a performance school I was associated with. Later when I heard he ran short (3-week) courses at his ISAAC (International School for Acting And Clown) in Brisbane I leapt at the chance, and also attended some of his long course teaching in later years. Apart from occasional dance concerts at my dance school, I had absolutely no background in performing, being a complete amateur who had come to performing in later life. It was clear that this teaching was going deeper than any other teaching that I had had, and was just what I needed.

My background is that of a neuroscientist, working mainly in hearing. I am the author of "An Introduction to the Physiology of Hearing" (4 editions, latest 2013). I also have a more recent interest in contortion and its physiological basis, and in clowning.

The Mechanical Basis for Understanding the Body

Ira's classes always start with the exercises known as the Four Articulations for Performance. After initial exercises intended to warm up, focus and free the body (the Three Loosenings, including exercises such as Indian club-swings and leg swings), the class continues with Core Mechanics. The exercises in Core Mechanics are direct and straightforward (roll-down, undulations, etc). By aiming to make the core movements simple and mechanical without any aesthetic, i.e. without any expressive or cultural content, we aim to bypass the complexities known as *habitus* (Bourdieu). Habitus is not just your personality, but the embodiment of your personality, which is based on your family, your early schooling, your upbringing, your expectations, and your experiences later in life.

The directness and straightforwardness of the movements gives the student a clear foundation for building the more complex movements to be used in performance. As Ira said in conversation: "… to be engaged with the self, with the process – I use the physical to assist the person so we can look mechanically – I ask were your hands involved, were your fingers involved – that doesn't mean waving your arms and hands – but we can start to look mechanically, and the person starts to realise – Oh my God, I had no idea I was still on the same spot. Then we start to make headway, when they have that Oh my God experience. You can quote that."

The Seven Solos

In the next stage of the class, The Seven Solos, we progressively increase the complexity, using exercises that are chosen to challenge the different constraints (*habitus*) that we might bring to the classes. Each starts with a simple stereotyped pattern, which then evolves into a free improvisation that can become either simple and short, or long and very complex. The exercises have different initial sequences so that the freer elements each have different starting points. This allows us to generate novel movements and improvisations from any starting point, and frees us to make a range of different improvisations.

Ira again in conversation: "When I present an exercise, invariably, I present it with very simple and clear instructions. Now after the actor does the exercise, then I see that, and I may need to clarify some things and repeat them. For example one of the most simple exercises is the Three Walks, and after some time of doing that exercise, I realised that the word walk was putting people in the wrong direction, so now I change it to Shape, Pause, Rhythm. So what the artist is learning, is control of their body, and how their body moves in space. People realise that they're not engaged with their whole body – I explain when people engage, they need to engage with their arms, their hands, their knees, rather than thinking "I've got to go and do a walk". Its Shape, Pause (so you can feel the shape), and then you do Rhythm – the rhythm can be interpreted in a lot of different ways, so I won't define that…. Also, I'm introducing the idea of interpretation of instructions, so when I need to be explicit I am, and where I need to be ambiguous, I am."

In all these exercises, and throughout Ira's work, an awareness of one's own body is critical and fundamental, and everything is built up from there.

Mechanics and Creativity

Current ideas of creativity suggest that the different brain circuits have the capability of generating myriads of different ideas, movements, patterns, sensations, and emotions. In this way, our understanding of the world and of our capabilities is continually being explored, refined, and extended. A creative mind has an extra richness of these circuits, which are capable of being activated independently, so that different ideas, movements, and sensations can be explored to their utmost. Not only are ideas incorporated into these circuits, but links to the emotional structures of the brain, the "limbic brain" (part of the multiple layers of what was previously called the triune brain) are facilitated, enriched and deepened. However at some point the complex myriad processes have to be brought together, because the body is only capable of one or at most a few actions at any one time. The brain therefore also includes a "censor" that is able to select from the many different patterns to be chosen to be dominant at that time, which then becomes the guide action, whether that is primarily physical, or mental.

Again, the dominance of the censor varies between individuals. In some, the censor is so dominant, that the natural variety of mental processes is inhibited as soon as it is started. These individuals find it difficult to be creative; the basis of their creativity has been nipped off as soon as it has appeared. At the other extreme, the censor may be so underused that the different elements compete with each other, so that constructive and directed action is impossible. The creative ideal is to allow the individual circuits the freedom to explore, nourish, and develop their capabilities, but at the same time have their capabilities coordinated with their goals so that effective action and outcomes are ultimately possible. An example is the function of play in children – in play, the developing brain circuits are allowed the freedom to develop and explore their ideas, movements and emotions, with limited inhibitions in contrast to the generally more constrained goal-directed activities of adults. As adults, we draw on the great variety of neural circuits initially developed in play as children. Therefore creativity of all types needs the coordination of two opposing processes – firstly the free exploration and development of ideas, elements, movements, emotions and so on, and then the integration of the results of the exploration into coordinated action.

An extra-creative mind has an extra-richness of these circuits, which are not only capable of being activated independently, but has an extra-richness in the ability to coordinate them across very different realms, to create novel results unexplored by others.

Creative solos (and their further development in duos in the class) are therefore vehicles for play in movement, leading to further expansion of our repertoire and creativity. The opportunity and encouragement of improvisation without the operation of the censor (whether the censor is in ourselves, or a controlling teacher) leads to a nurturing of our own pre-existing creativity, allowing it to develop and flourish. This then leads to us building up a greater library of movements, fragments, emotions, and ideas, which can not only become more practiced, but can be drawn on instantaneously, and from whatever starting point we wish, when required during performance. To quote Helen Garner on writing: "you spot details you can't imagine any possible use for, note them down… and when the time comes, out they pop from the dark." This gives an emotional richness, and an expansion of range and vocabulary, so that emotionally-significant multiple threads can be called upon spontaneously, giving the feeling that (to quote Nick Cave discussing her music with Marianne Faithfull) "there is a lot going on under the surface."

Only when we truly and deeply have that encounter with ourselves, do we have the material to drawn on and have the true artistic experience within ourselves. And only when we do the creative activities for *ourselves*, do we fully explore the depths of own creativity. So the method deepens the composition of an artist's own integrity, with the result that whatever is done for the public has an integrity. And then we are able to make a gift of it to the audience, and invite the audience to share in what we have discovered (and if we are lucky, feel the warmth of the audience's response in return). But if we are missing that true artistic experience within ourselves, then there will be a shallowness and missing elements in our performance.

The Pause and Retriggering Creativity.

The Pause has a special role in Core Mechanics and in the Creative Solos. On the one hand, a pause by a performer allows the performer to communicate a supposed mental process to the audience. No pause means the movement was anticipated, and so it is read as part of a pre-planned sequence. A pause of about half or a third of a second (the simple reaction time) is read as a simple response to an event. A longer pause is a read as a reaction with thought.

For the performer, the pause has further multiple roles. It can be an occasion of stopping one sequence of movements and feelings, and give a time to scan and interrogate the body, interrogate the *habitus*, negotiate whether to continue the previous sequence, or change to something new. It is a time in which the automatic programming of our activity is on hold, and the creativity built up in the Creative Solos can manifest itself. It is one of the elements that help us to continually interrogate our own creative experience, and then share that with the public.

In the exercises, the pause is *anticipated*, so that it does not suddenly interrupt the stream of action, but is more fully incorporated into the sequence, and builds up the habit of anticipation. Anticipation is in fact an element of all the exercises, and constructive use of anticipation is essential in all movements as well as in pauses. We know from recording brain potentials that the brain starts preparing a movement at least half a second before the movement is made (and even before the individual knows that it is going to be made). The performer needs to develop the awareness of anticipation so that the artificial sequence of actions in a performance is perceived by the audience as a natural flow.

The exercises and the side-coaching from Ira have further guides to assist in re-examining and retriggering the creative process. One cue is to "add a detail" – this forces the performer to re-engage afresh with the idea. Or "do the opposite" – if a performer feels stuck, switching to the opposite idea can break a sequence that is no longer so productive, but, because of the focus on the opposite, rather than making a random change, is still continuing an engagement with the original idea.

The Primary Role of Movement.

In summary, in the Seidenstein Method, movement plays a critical role. We make a move, and interrogate the body. This generates or triggers feelings which we then respond to. The audience then perceives the movements, and responds emotionally to the feelings underlying them.

Because for the performer the primary focus is on the movements, they are made in a way that is natural, complex and varied. By becoming aware of our movements, we are be able to respond to and interpret them, and this in turn will then generate feelings. The feelings will then modify other movements, so we end up producing a rich complex of movements such as would be produced under the influence of real emotion. These are then perceived as such by the audience, generating a realistic and deep communication of emotion.

Jim Pickles.

- 44 -
COMMENTS - THEATRE PRACTITIONER NAREE SHIELDS

Unlocking the door to Creative Freedom:
Reflections on how the Seidenstein Method liberates creative voice
by Naree Shields August 2020

I have always been involved in creative pursuits. I grew up studying classical piano and dance then went on to study theatre at university. I have always thought that creative expression is about freedom and at the heart of what makes us human. In an ideal reality, a healthy human is free in their expression and connected to a vibrant community where creativity flows as the circuitry connecting its people. Considering the degree and level at which I have engaged with the performing arts, I have found it perplexing that my personal expression has been stifled and blocked: I have struggled in my personal life to voice my needs and often come away from a creative project feeling depleted and disconnected. My mentorship with Dr Ira Seidenstein has enabled me to understand the blocks getting in the way of my expression. The Seidenstein method has provided me with the tools to unlock the door to my Creative Freedom.

I first met Ira on April Fool's day in 2006. It was at a weekend workshop with the local woman's Circus in the Blue Mountains. At the time, my youngest child was still breastfeeding but I found the way to claim the time for myself and attend the workshop. It has been an ongoing challenge for me to keep finding the way to balance my need to create artistically and the reality of "normal family life", but I have always found the way... precariously. In that first workshop I had an extraordinary realisation that the source of my creativity is located within my anatomy. This realisation was visceral and I experienced it as a whole-body knowing. Not long after this workshop, I created a couple of performance pieces which I performed at the local Winter Magic festival with the Women's Circus. The ease with which these pieces came together was like a breath of fresh air.

The creative ideas came to me so freely and I was able to shape and craft the pieces seamlessly. This experience was significant as I had been stuck in "creative trepidation" for many years. It was as though the energies freed up in me because I was moving in a clarified way which enabled me to express my creativity freely. After the success of the Winter Magic performances I decided that I needed to Study "clown". Interestingly, it wasn't until a couple of years later that I discovered Ira was in fact a clown, and his methods supported the study of clowning. In 2010, I attended the first Quantum Clown Residency (QCR) in Brisbane. I made a pilgrimage to Brisbane each year for the next 8 years to attend the annual QCR. This "creativity retreat" was an opportunity for me to pause from the demands of my day-to-day life, and "play" without the pressure of having to produce professional outcomes or attend to the demands of family.

Each QCR was unique with a different focus; however, the principles were always the same:

Be aware of what you are doing inside your BODY. The Seidenstein method is grounded in the logic and biomechanics of the body. The first step to unlocking the potential of your creativity, is to be aware of what you are actually doing with your own body. (Not what you think you are doing but what you are actually doing.)

Over the past 14 years, I have communicated with Ira regularly. We have exchanged hundreds of emails communicating about vast ideas, from ridiculous & profane nonsense to meta-physical & sacred ideas. This communication has provided me with a space to share the many discoveries I have had in my work and has been a sounding board enabling me to deepen my understanding. It has also served as a springboard, empowering me to dive deeper and fly higher with the work I've been engaged with. Using the tools of The Seidenstein Method, I have come to know that the template of The Four Articulations is an indispensable tool for working creatively. Although I have had serious doubts about myself, I 100% trusted this process and I can guarantee that it works.

Over the past 14 years, I have shared creative space with very diverse people working in a variety of cultural settings. I have taught acting and theatre craft to young people; facilitated school projects geared at supporting students' creative voice and agency; delivered literacy and learning programs for kindergarten children; and mentored School teachers to deepen their pedagogy and capacity for creative teaching. I have also facilitated "Clowning Around" programs to enhance the lives of people living with "disabilities". I prefer to use the word "diverse abilities". Often the disabling factor is the limiting culture and belief systems of other people. In all of this work I have actively drawn upon the principles that the Seidenstein Methodology are based on.

The Seidenstein method is grounded in Universal principles. You are always balancing opposites and discovering the freedom that arises from restrictions. You actively balance both action and reflection. You train in a disciplined manner whilst always respecting your capacity on any given day. You train your body and mind with the choreography and the counts. You respect the form of your own body and the shape of the structure of 'the choreography'. But you also pause and come back to centre. It has taken me a long time to really understand that the pause is an essential aspect of the creative process. This is where you receive and celebrate the hard work. If you are going from one creative project to the next, without time and space to truly receive what you have done, then you can easily burn out and frazzle your nervous system. I had a nervous system burn out a few years ago. I worked incessantly and was compulsively driven. I didn't know how to respect the reality of all the demands for my energy from work and raising a family.

The pause is remarkable and an essential ingredient in the creative process. In the act of pausing & being aware of your breath, you become aware of your own senses. Seeing what your eyes perceive. Hearing what your ears receive. Feeling what is alive inside you. Why is it so hard to Pause? In my experience, I automatically skipped the pause because the act of pausing would mean feeling what was inside me, which was difficult. I grew up in a family culture that didn't tolerate challenging feelings. Suppression of these feelings was necessary in order to survive in the culture.

One of the greatest struggles I have encountered has been my battle with severe anxiety and shame. I wasn't aware that I was suffering from severe anxiety until about 2 years ago. In hindsight I understand that I have lived with this condition since childhood. A clinical diagnosis and the support of medication in conjunction with a skilled psychologist has been indispensable in the recovery of my health and wellbeing. For a number of years whilst performing, I started to have experiences where I became paralysed in the middle of my performance, due to some type of "trigger". The effect of the trigger caused a disconnect between my body and mind. The feelings of anxiety within me were crippling and affected my cognitive thinking and capacity. These humiliating experiences led me to search and uncover what was getting in the way of my expression. I wondered what was generating this shame inside me and interfering with my capacity to perform on stage and function in day-to-day life.

I pondered what would enable me to feel comfortable inside my own body? By doing the Path of Honour exercises and applying the principles connected to each of The Four Articulations, I have learnt how to transform the energies and feelings that live inside me. When you are stuck in a "shame-state", there is a type of paralysis that happens in your body and mind and you can feel completely disconnected inside yourself and to the world around you. When you are training in each of the exercises, you are constantly reminded that your feet are connected to the ground. In the foundational Core-mechanics you work through a series of logical mechanical movements, and scan your whole body whilst keeping your mind busy through counting. This simple yet powerful sequence of mechanical movements supports you to feel your body connected to the ground. There is strength in noticing what is going on inside you whilst being anchored to the ground and moving. This awareness is the first step in being able to move forward. Gradually as you start to move in any direction from your anchored place, you become more aware of what feelings are arising in you. The act of consciously moving the body enables the energy that has been trapped to release. This process happens gradually: With each slight shift, the fear lessens and your capacity to stand on your own two feet strengthens. As you do the creative exercises you learn to feel what it is like to move from a grounded place.

It has been profound to understand that my body can become a container that can transform all that scares me. Through being consciously aware of and directing what Is actually going on in my body, the forces of shame are released and transformed. In a sense, I can be my own Shaman when I inhabit my body. I remember reading about the idea of "actor as shaman" at University; however, it is another thing to viscerally understand something for myself.

The template of The Four Articulations gives you the tools to be effective and grounded in relation to your own creativity. The Four Articulations has been an indispensable tool for me because I have a tendency to jump from one idea to the next and get lost down rabbit holes. I have realised that creativity that is unfocussed, unstructured and undisciplined is precarious. When creativity is not grounded it can become a hindrance to wellbeing and sanity. It is good to be clear about all possibilities and then understand that creativity that is ennobling is always about choices, not compulsions. The Four Articulations have helped me understand the nature of things that inhibit my creative expression- and given me the tools to take positive steps that are in my best interest. When I lose my way I remember to come back to the basics: What is happening in my BODY, in SPACE, in TIME?

The creative exercises support you in harmonising your mind and body. You learn to become aware of the experience that you are having and then how to skilfully shape and express that idea. You also learn how to PAUSE and then make a creative choice. The structure and discipline supports creative freedom and your ability to take charge of your own energy.

A very important aspect of the training with Ira has been his belief that "You are already good". The training and mentoring is always in service of "how do we become 'gooder'?" A culture that is committed to healthy debate, healthy challenges within clear boundaries supports healthy creative practice and praxis. A compassionate belief system is very supportive for the growth and unfolding of artists and people in general.

One realisation I had recently whilst doing "The Six Directions" (a creativity exercise), was that the source of my creative power is located in the centre of my body. As I was moving through the six directions I realised for the first time, that "I" was the reference point for all the directions. I was the centre inside the action. All of the movement arose out of my centre. I finally understood what "move from your centre" actually meant. I had heard this expression a lot, yet I didn't understand viscerally what my centre felt like. Often in my own body I experienced a lot of discomfort and it was challenging to stay connected with that degree of discomfort. The effect of this was that I was connecting more with other people's thoughts and feelings and I believed they were more valid than my own thoughts and feelings. There is a lot that could be said about the cultural experiences that have shaped and informed this reality. That, however, is the subject for a book. For now, I'm committed in my work to providing spaces that support expression of different voices and encourage diversity to flourish.

This realisation about moving from my centre was a revelation and has changed my life. I am now working very successfully and enjoying the freedom of making decisive choices from a centred place. My main work at the moment is facilitating "Clowning around Programs" for people with diverse needs. I have been developing these programs over the past 10 years and since the start of the "Corona lockdown" I have discovered a whole new layer to the way I deliver my programs. The restriction has enabled greater creative freedom. The creative expression that I see arise from people who have very complex needs is awe inspiring. I come dressed in fabulous costumes that communicate to everybody that it's ok to be light hearted in this space. We sing, we dance, we play, we cry, we laugh. The other day we created a "fish ballet" because one woman wanted to do some twirls- I follow the ideas that come from my participants and I guide them on a fun, safe creative exploration. Always I hold in my heart & mind the question: what poss-ability can we create together in this moment?

I celebrate my wholesome work: it daringly allows poss-ability and gives voice to all the parts that express our human story. Wholeness is healing. It is an honour to provide a safe space for people to express themselves freely. My capacity to hold space for very diverse people and modes of expression has been cultivated and honed through my mentorship with Ira. The mentorship has supported me to be able to hear and receive my own creative voice and now I am able to skilfully offer that to other people.

- 45 -
COMMENTS - THEATRE MAKER THERESE COOK

What follows is an extraordinary statement from Therese Cook, and I'd like to mention a few ideas to serve as an introduction her essay. Therese mentions The Nothing Exercise, one of my most succinct creative solo exercises. I consider that much of my teaching and exercises can work holographically. That is, one exercise may contain the essence of the whole method. I emphasise Universal Principles in the exercises rather than the exercises themselves and therefore almost any of my exercises is a metaphor for one's own creativity. Therese will tell her story with that.

In my books, and as Therese mentions, I often refer to the threads of theatre lineages. Philosophically, I would say that a teacher should often reference their own teachers. The modern person needs to learn from the Indigenous cultures, to respect one's Elders. But, the Elder must respect past generations, the current generation and future generations. In my culture the word *rabbi* implies 'my teacher'. I have numerous modern Rabbis who I can go to in various ways. I source those Rabbis who maintain and reference our culture's Indigenous teachings which go back to our great teachers of centuries past and although there are an abundance, a few most prolific ones include: Maimonides; Issac Luria; the Baal Shem Tov; The

Vilna Goan. Yet, even their great teachings are firmly based upon their Elders the early Talmudic sages. The sages teachings in turn are firmly based on our wisdom tradition. That is my personal or one may say perhaps spiritual and cultural lineage.

Therese notes that in my teaching it is common for me to refer to my lineages of theatre, Clown, mime. In my professional life I replicate the Indigenous practice to acknowledge, that wisdom stems from our Elders. At the same time, every student is a gift to their teacher. Respect is a two-way street. You will soon see that Therese and her family, like many people in this world, went through a severe hardship. I hope you may also see that Therese is a gifted and earnest writer. Here is her essay.

"There were many things that you have taught me over the years that assisted me greatly in prison.
Who would have thought?
It was fragments of your teachings that (meant) I could create a framework to survive"

An excerpt from an email to Ira, March 6th, 2019, post prison release, I was still on extraordinarily strict bail conditions.

Ira Seidenstein has quietly influenced my life since June 2005.

A short introduction to community circus, run by circus trainers, Tahmour Bloomfield, Heidi Chappelow, Lazuli Kubenk and Alison Wheeler, in Katoomba, April, May 2005, gave me to a world, I fell in love with.

I wanted to learn more.
I wanted to understand what I needed to do, to learn, to create and to improve.

My trainers recommended I attend a clowning and movement workshop in Brisbane.
I attended.

Ira was teaching movement.

I was so new to the world of circus, performance, movement and, especially, workshops with working professionals and teaching professionals.
I became afraid, very afraid.
My hunger to learn had been replaced by my fear.
I did not understand, the seemingly, exotic language.
Everything was foreign to me.
I just did not understand.

I talked too much, anything to distract from my failings at absolutely everything.
I became the whiney student with any excuse, my favourite being, "it's just too hot up here in Brisbane".
Ira's reply, "Therese, it's only heat."

I knew I needed to learn.
I became a little, tiny bit less anxious, and learnt to live with the embarrassment from my constant failings.

Though I knew absolutely nothing, I recognised the value and wisdom of what Ira was teaching.

Back in Katoomba, I began to organise regular movement and clown workshops for Ira to teach.
Ira, generously, has been sharing his skills, teachings and his spirit with the Blue Mountains community since 2005.
Bringing Ira, to the Blue Mountains, to teach, has had a profound effect, not just on me, but other artists, within the community.

During Ira's workshops I tried so hard to hold onto to his words and teachings.
Little by little, I began an understanding of the specifics.
I became less rigid in my ways of understanding and was able to reconcile the seemingly opposing teachings.
I began to understand, the specifics, as part of the whole.

Ira demonstrated the importance of clarity of intention, discovered in stillness and time.
Ira taught me, the awareness and technique, to task, mechanically correct, shape and form.
Ira taught me that real, authentic, genuine physical discipline will assist me for the rest of my life.
Ira taught me discipline is the key: discipline, discipline, discipline.
With discipline comes freedom; art fuels further art, creativity fuels further creativity.

Ira is not a fundamentalist in regard to any of his teachings.
Ira honours the many "authentic" pathways, learnings and practices that clowns, teachers and artists have given.
He encourages engagement in any "real" physical discipline; "authentic" movement will feed other "authentic" movements.

Influenced, or perhaps, inspired, by Ira's teachings, I created a 40 hour weekly program of circus, performing and visual arts.
I wanted to bring other disciplines into practice, to connect other arts, to create a whole arts based practice.
This program operated, from The Shed, in Katoomba.
I was able to engage amazing local tutors and artists to teach circus, theatre, puppetry, singing, ceramics, aerial, ballet, drawing, painting and film making. It was important for me to create an arts based centre and culture, where diversity, creativity and artistry is celebrated and valued, and skills development is accessible for all abilities and ages.
We developed a quirky and wonderful performance ensemble, we performed and worked at many festivals, including the Sydney Festival.
In 2018, we were meant to be performing at festivals in Germany.

In addition to my work at The Shed, I taught theatre skills, at the Q Theatre, Penrith.
I incorporated many of Ira's teachings, my students particularly related well to The Nothing exercise, it was their favourite.

On February 5th, 2018, I was wrongfully arrested and incarcerated in maximum security prison.

I spent two hundred and six days, in maximum security prison.

Two of my daughters, who were wrongfully arrested, also, spent two hundred and six days in maximum security prison; we ended up in the same prison wing.

Other members of my family, wrongfully arrested, were in different prisons. The nature, of the charges, was absolutely horrific - abhorrent lies and false allegations had been crafted and created by relatives caught in a web, spun by an organisation that causes undue pressure - sometimes referred to as a cult.

The Department of Public Prosecutions dropped all charges on February 14th, 2020.

The trauma of being falsely accused and then falsely imprisoned brought me to a totally dishevelled state.

Human rights do not exist for prisoners within the N.S.W. prison system.

Prison is a dehumanising experience.

Prison is not a luxury destination.

Prison is not a holiday camp.

The treatment and threats from certain prison guards, induced in me, a constant state of fear.

A positive outcome of my training came early on when a guard shoved me forcibly and unexpectedly from behind.

Most women my age would have smashed to the ground – my training unconsciously and automatically allowed my body to catch itself and re balance.

The fourth cell I was locked into, had cell doors, I could see out of.

A woman in green, the prison uniform, was waving to me, from a cell opposite.

This woman intermittently waved and smiled at me.

I was too fearful to make any type of acknowledgment to her.

Hours later I noticed this woman exercising.
The movements were familiar.
It was my daughter, my beautiful and precious Yyani-Rose.
I did not recognise my daughter except through her movement.

It was the physical movement I recognised.
It was a whisper, an echo from the world I knew.
But I couldn't revive that world.
I didn't remember any patterns of movement.
It was as though my internal and external worlds had collapsed.
I had become frozen.

No expectations.
Spirit crushed.
Body threatened.
Breath collapsed.
Nothing.

The sixth cell I was caged in had access to the outside air.
My breath had freedom to escape.
At certain times there was the brief respite of the yard.
There was small sky, there was grass, there was dirt.

My feet carried me to walk.
Another echo, a murmur.
Create a discipline.
Count the steps.
Create a discipline.

I had to hold to the discipline of movement.
In my walking, I could not just, walk.
I needed to count each step so there was a discipline to the steps.
Thank you, Ira.
A framework - a clarity of intent.
To remember.

In my cell my feet began to remember.
A knowing I had to move.
Ballet rises.
Simple ballet rises.
A remembering.
Cross disciplines - thank you, Ira.

More and more ballet rises.
Slowly with breath.
Eight by eight by eight.
"Don't crush the eggshells beneath your heels"
Thank you, Mieke.

Remember……………
A twist, from warm up - only partially.
Engaged body
A fragment was all I could remember.
Hold tight to the discipline.
Thank you, Ira.
Repeat, repeat, repeat.
Look behind.
Constantly.
Find flexibility in the rigidity.

In prison you can not become attached to anyone or anything.
You can't.
You don't.
Prison is a constant flux.
Women trucked.
From.
To.
Unexpected bars and concrete.

Tomorrows are unknown lockdowns.
Never knowing how long.

Let out, locked up, let out, locked up………..
Never a constant.
No rhyme or reason.

I had nothing. I had nothing. I had nothing. I had nothing.

I had nothing.
Perhaps.
A fragmented and seemingly distant remembering.
A resistance.
I had everything inside me that I needed.
Perhaps.
To resist the system.
To survive.

Morning Muster: an exercise in intimidation, practiced by prison guards and officers.
Prisoners attend.
Roles are clear and defined.

Neutral face.
Neutral body.
Active, ready.
Eye line, correct eye line.
An extended pause.
Hostile house.
One line only, "yes".

A remembering.
Pause.
Shape.
"No dead fish for hands".
Thank you, Ira.

The pause.

The portal to another world.
Thank you, Ira.

A remembering.
I had the richness of The Nothing.
I had the tools to re imagine my current world.
Thank you, Ira.

How many times had I practised The Nothing?
How many times had I instructed students in regard to The Nothing?
Neutral movement, three neutral arm movements, to pause, to shape, to creation of story, a new world.

I lost the arm movements but remembered the discipline of neutral.

The Nothing gives tools to create, supports agency to create, from seemingly nothing, to creating a whole nuanced world in front of your self.
I could pause.
Stillness.
I could shape.
Seemingly so simple.
A pathway to re imagining my world.

Before I left prison, I measured the length and width of the prison cell.
I shared the prison cell with another prisoner.
I measured the cell in my foot lengths.
When I came home, I measured my foot for the prison cell dimensions.
The length of the cell was four metres and twenty five centimetres.
The width of the cell was two metres and twenty one centimetres.
It is not a lot of space for two people to live in: toilet, shower, eat, sleep, especially, when locked in, for days on end.

The Nothing gave form and permission to re imaginings.
The cell became my bedroom.
My top bunk became my reading loft.

My cell mate became my house mate.
The exposed toilet became the ensuite.
This was my home.
I decorated my new home.
Angry and ugly graffiti was covered.
Toothpaste becomes a cementing glue.
My cell walls became a gallery of received cards, postcards, artworks, verse and poetry.
A reflection of those who loved and cared for me.

For over three months, I was in a cell that no ray of sunshine could touch.
The Nothing gave me agency.
Clothes, towels, dried in the sun, caught the sun, held the sunshine for me to bring into the cell.
My re imaginings gave me light.

I clung to the discipline of movement.
In the cell every step was counted.
In the yard every length was stepped out and counted.
Lunges counted, forwards, backwards.
Downward dogs, cobras counted.
Side planks, planks, diagonal planks, timed with counted beats.
Chair step ups, one hundred, two hundred, three hundred, four hundred.
Always counting, a rhythm to make sense of.
I worked to create mechanically correct movement.
Discipline of body, discipline of mind and emotion.
Thank you, Ira.

Ramped: Official exercise carried out by prison guards and officers to invade and tear apart cells followed up by pat downs.

Pat Downs: Official exercise carried out by prison guards and officers. Prisoner's clothed bodies explored by guards and officers' hands, without prisoner permission.

Watching my two daughters having to spread eagle against prison walls, waiting for hands to traverse their bodies, without their permission. Helpless to protect, to intercede, to stop the violation.

Spread eagle against the prison wall.
Unknown hands on my body, moving over my body.
I had not given consent.
I was paused and shaped.
Still.

Could I create a new story?
Could I imagine a different narrative?
Could I find good intentions.
Could my still body resist and refuse to be dishonoured?

Massage.
Being massaged.............
I rated the intensity and duration of their hands.
Re imaginings.
Thank you, Ira.

Strip Searches: Regular prison de humanising procedure usually associated with seeing visitors in prison.

Strip searches are designed to de humanise, to humiliate and shame.
A transaction, the cost to see your loved ones.
Guards looking into your mouth, again and again, for however many times they deem appropriate.
Open, open, open again.
Arms up in the air.
Circle around and around, so breasts are seen, fully exposed, how many times around, depends on the guards.
I wished I could pirouette, make it something else, a dance.
Spread your legs, underpants to the knees, lift up one foot to balance on the other foot, repeat other side.

I didn't know how to turn that into a dance.
Perhaps a balance challenge?
How long could I stay on the one foot?
My training had taught me that bodies are strong, capable and flexible.
I, mostly, embraced that thought during strip searches.
Bodies are not to be humiliated but empowered to function in an anatomically and mechanically correct manner.
Respect and honour the body.
My body.
I could do that.
Thank you, Ira.
Hold the shape, move the form.

Summer inside maximum security prison, Western Sydney, is hot.
Regular days of temperatures 40 plus degrees celsius.
Cells were hot.
Rigid and uninviting plastic covered mattresses and pillows were even hotter.
How to sleep?
The yard was mainly unshaded.
How to keep moving in the crushing heat?
"Therese, it's only heat."
Ira's words from thirteen years ago, in Brisbane, came to me.
"Therese, it's only heat."
I moved, kept moving, used water to cool, kept moving.
I slept, kept sleeping, used water to cool, to keep sleeping.
"Therese, it's only heat."
External to internal. Heat is external, how you respond is internal. How you react to physical cues creates meaning and the story.

Deep horror and terror never entirely left me in prison, but it was mitigated by my circus, theatre and performance training and education.

Ira Seidenstein has quietly influenced my life since June 2005.

"Always my work is TOTALLY dependent on grace and grace as manifest in the heart and good intentions"
Ira Seidenstein

Therese Cook - Performer, Deviser, Teaching Artist - Blue Mountains, New South Wales

- 46 -
COMMENTS - CHOREOGRAPHER, DANCER OONA DOHERTY

From Ira: I first met Oona Doherty when I taught a three week intensive for the five members of Ponydance of Northern Ireland in 2009. The company was created by Leonie McDonagh. Oona was one of the original members. Later Oona worked four years with T.R.A.S.H. Dance Theatre of Tilburg, Holland. T.R.A.S.H. was an extreme physical theatre company. Its shows had characters of fervent passionate relationships combined with live classical musicians. Each show had original compositions. I saw Oona in a wild show of T.R.A.S.H. She arranged for me to meet the director and to co-create a show Swamp. By the time that project began Oona was away and starting to create her own projects. Finally, about 2018, I was able to see one of Oona's own pieces. That was a solo at the Irish Cultural Centre in Paris.

The piece, the performance, the acting, the movement were all sublime. I felt also that I was seeing the person who had taken my method/ideas to their furthest elastic extension. After her performance there were refreshments served. We chatted briefly then one by one audience members came up to congratulate her and for several in the arts who wanted more engagement Oona said "I'm just doing what he taught me" as she nodded or pointed to me.

The objective of my method and the Universal Principles that it reveals is for an artist or company to extend their own parameters and to use the method in their own unique ways. This is to enable the artist to explore and develop their individual aesthetics and personal artistic expression.

I do not try to turn out artists to become 'perfect red roses'. In the art and performance world there is room for many types of roses; and all types of flowers; as well as nutritious weeds.

Here is part of a recent review followed by some comments from Oona.

Excerpt from the New York Times Dance Critic Gia Kourlas. March 8, 2020

"This contemporary choreographer and performer from Belfast is astonishing — not merely raw, as she is often described, but exactingly articulate. She is in possession of a body with as much flexibility as her mind, as was revealed in her arresting exploration of the young men of her hometown. ... Ms. Doherty presented her take on masculinity like a living painting, morphing from a figure of swaggering confidence to one of feigning nonchalance. Rage became fear. Sounds gradually turned into words. All the while, Ms. Doherty's body turned into a wave as she rocked from side to side with her expressions both pained and preening.

In "Hope Hunt and the Ascension Into Lazarus," Ms. Doherty morphs into the hapless, posturing men of Belfast, before she transports her body to a place of vulnerability.

No movement or sound went astray; clearly, Ms. Doherty's work is choreographed within an inch of its life, but the material is so deeply embedded in her compact, pliable form that it also seems unpremeditated. It's also strangely natural when, say, her leg sweeps in an elegant rond de jambe before she collapses in a heap. Her balance is uncanny as physical tics — the sniffs and furrowed brow — take possession of her face.

There are dark moments here, but the work is not entirely about darkness. It says it all in the title: This is a hunt for hope. In the end, the dance transforms again when Ms. Doherty takes off her dark clothes to reveal an all-white ensemble for a final journey in which she transports her body to a place of vulnerability.

After a finger-pointing snarl, she leans back, and suddenly her face, perfectly still, glows as if she were made of wax. Braiding masculinity and femininity, her arms slowly swirl around her undulating torso. Her presence is beyond eerie: She is the most alone person you have ever seen, and you feel it in your bones.

Hope Hunt and the Ascension Into Lazarus."

The following is Oona's I.S.A.A.C. Associate statement:

"I have to say that Ira was the first teacher I had whose lessons and wisdom filtered into my life subliminally and subconsciously after the first meeting. It wasn't until 2010 in my work with Trash Dance Company that I fully became aware of the impact Ira had had; on not only on my performance technique/skills and drives. But also on my attitude as a human being and my work ethics. After this awakening I consciously strived to develop the metaphysical embodiment of characters in my work more clearly. I began teaching dance theatre in 2011 and was lucky to have another chance to dive-in and get lost with Ira in 2013. His commitment to the humble honesty the body can give. And the tools he provides artists in order to listen to that honesty. Cultivates imagination and therefore as an artist, creative possibilities. He is one of the leading forces and inspirations in my performance and choreographic work as well as my teaching.

I can only encourage any artist of any medium if you get the chance to play with the crazy clown, grab it like a bag of sweets! Unhierarchical sharing of potent wisdom like Ira's doesn't come around too often." Oona Doherty - www.oonadohertyweb.com

This is from Oona, November 22, 2002:

Training the performer to be lost. To start again as a beginner in the very moment. Destined to fail. is the only training worth working on day in day out.
we must practice the child.
the leap of faith into the unknown, eyes closed.
Ira knows how to do that. He built it for us. and he knows when your faking. good luck with the jump.
Oona

www.ingramcontent.com/pod-product-compliance
Ingram Content Group UK Ltd.
Pitfield, Milton Keynes, MK11 3LW, UK
UKHW021328180426
11947UKWH00017B/1502